PETER THE GREAT

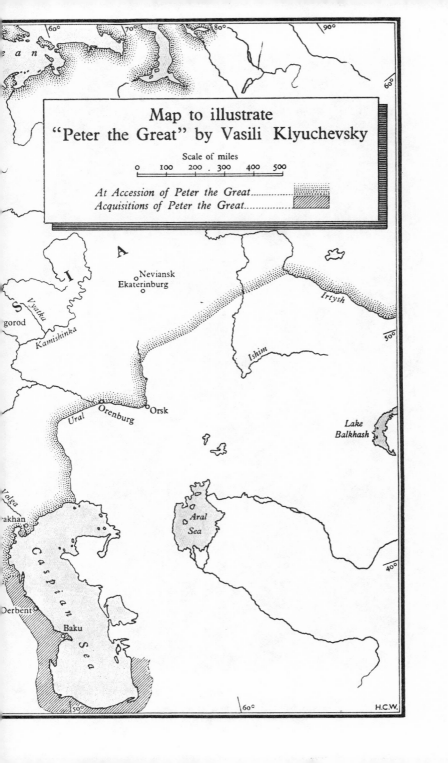

Map to illustrate
"Peter the Great" by Vasili Klyuchevsky

Scale of miles

0   100   200 . 300   400   500

At Accession of Peter the Great...............
Acquisitions of Peter the Great...............

PETER THE GREAT

From the portrait by Sir Godfrey Kneller
Reproduced by gracious permission of
Her Majesty the Queen

VASILI KLYUCHEVSKY

★

PETER
THE
GREAT

TRANSLATED BY

LILIANA ARCHIBALD

BEACON PRESS   BOSTON

First published as a Beacon paperback in 1984
by arrangement with St. Martin's Press
Beacon Press books are published under the auspices
of the Unitarian Universalist Association of
Congregations in North America,
25 Beacon Street, Boston, Massachusetts 02108
Published simultaneously in Canada by
Fitzhenry and Whiteside Limited, Toronto

Printed in the United States of America

(paperback) 9 8 7 6 5 4 3 2 1

Library of Congress Cataloging in Publication Data
Kliuchevskii, V. O. (Vasiliı Osipovich), 1841–1911.
  Peter the Great

    Translation of: Kurs russkoĭ istorii, v. 4.
    Includes index.
      1. Peter I, Emperor of Russia, 1672–1725.
2. Soviet Union—Kings and rulers—Biography.   3. Soviet
Union—History—Peter I, 1689–1725.   I. Title.
DK131.K5513   1984   947'.05'0924   [B]   84–45072
ISBN 0–8070–5647–2

FOREWORD

IT WAS NOT until I taught Russian History at the University of Otago, New Zealand, that I realised how little was known about the Russia of Peter the Great. Although there is a vast literature on Russia's relations with other countries in the eighteenth century, there is very little on the social, economic, and intellectual history of Russia. In spite of the fact that Klyuchevsky's *History of Russia* was first published nearly half a century ago, it remains the best, and certainly the most penetrating, large scale history of Russia. It is worth noticing that the Soviet state publishing house reprinted his work in 1937, and is now, in 1957, bringing out yet another edition. The edition of 1937 was the one used for this translation. Klyuchevsky took his History from the earliest times to the middle of the nineteenth century. The fourth volume, which is the subject of this translation, is concerned with the first quarter of the eighteenth century, and deals with the social and administrative changes which took place in the reign of Peter the Great. It also contains perhaps the most vivid portrait in existence of Peter the Great, both as a man and as a Tsar.

Most non-Russians are unfamiliar with the internal developments of Russia under Peter, and it is for this reason that this new translation was undertaken. An earlier translation by C. J. Hogarth does exist; it is, however, out of print, and is, in any case, both inaccurate and very difficult to read.

Vasili Klyuchevsky, the son of a village priest, was born in 1841 in the Province of Penza. In 1856 he entered an ecclesiastical seminary, but he was determined to attend a university, and in 1861, the year of the Emancipation of the Serfs, was enrolled in the University of Moscow. Here Klyuchevsky studied under Sergei Soloviev from whom he acquired '... his broad vision of history and the necessity of a mastery of sources and a sense of purpose in the historical process that did not permit an aimless flow of events.'[1]

Klyuchevsky won immediate attention with his early work, which was based on the accounts of the State of Muscovy written by foreign travellers. He was appointed to lecture on Russian history at the Alexandrian Military School and at the University of Moscow. Within a few years he had become widely known, and in 1879, when Soloviev became ill, Klyuchevsky was given the chair of History at the University of Moscow. As a lecturer, he was so popular and stimulating that his colleagues' lectures remained unattended if they happened to coincide with the course in Russian history. A description of Klyuchevsky by one of his former students[2] goes a long way to explain the enthusiasm aroused by his lectures which spread far beyond the narrow circle of specialists.

Attempts were made to persuade Klyuchevsky to publish his lectures in book form, but he was reluctant to do this because of the doubts he had about the definitive character of his work.[3] Finally, however, he agreed to prepare his lectures for publication, and in 1904 the first volume appeared, followed by a second in 1906, a third in 1908, and a fourth in 1910. The fifth volume was compiled from the notes of a former student, and appeared in 1921. Klyuchevsky died in 1911, so that the fifth volume was the only one that he was unable to revise himself.

[1] Anatole G. Mazour, *An Outline of Modern Russian Historiography*, D. Van Nostrand Company Inc., University of California Press, 1939, p. 45.

[2] Basil Maklakov, 'V. O. Klyuchevsky,' *Slavonic Review*, Vol. 13, 1934–5, pp. 320–9.

[3] V. O. Klyuchevsky, *Kharakteristiki i Vospominaniya*, Moscow, 1912, pp. 20–2.

There are some particular difficulties in translating from Russian into English: Russian names often look clumsy in English print. I have adopted a system of transliteration which, I hope, will not offend the English reader, and have, as far as possible, avoided phonetic signs. I hope that, as a result, the reader will find 'Dolgoruky', for example, no more strange than Gordon. Where possible an English word has been used in preference to a Russian technical word, i.e., the College of State Revenue, instead of the Kamer Kollegium. Unfortunately, certain words defy translation: nothing can be done with *zemski*, *dolia*, etc., and in these cases either the best English equivalent has been used, and the Russian word put into brackets after it, or, where no equivalent could be found, the Russian word has been left in the text, and an explanatory footnote added. As this work is intended for those who are unable to read Russian, I have confined my references to books and articles which have appeared in either English or in French, and are available in this country.

I should like to express my sincere thanks to Anthony Wagner, Richmond Herald, for the genealogical table. The responsibility for the information in the table is mine.

I should also like to acknowledge the help I received from the Librarian, the Head of Accessions, and the staff of the Otago University Library in obtaining books and dictionaries not readily available in New Zealand.

I am particularly grateful to J. G. A. Pocock, Research Fellow of St. John's College, Cambridge, for all his help.

But most of all I owe to my husband, Christopher Archibald, for his consistent patience and constructive criticism.

LILIANA ARCHIBALD

Otago University 1953
London 1957

TRANSLATOR'S NOTE

I am grateful to friends and reviewers for pointing out some errors which appeared in the first two printings. Any errors which still remain are, of course, my responsibility.

L.A.

London 1961

CONTENTS

LIST OF ILLUSTRATIONS

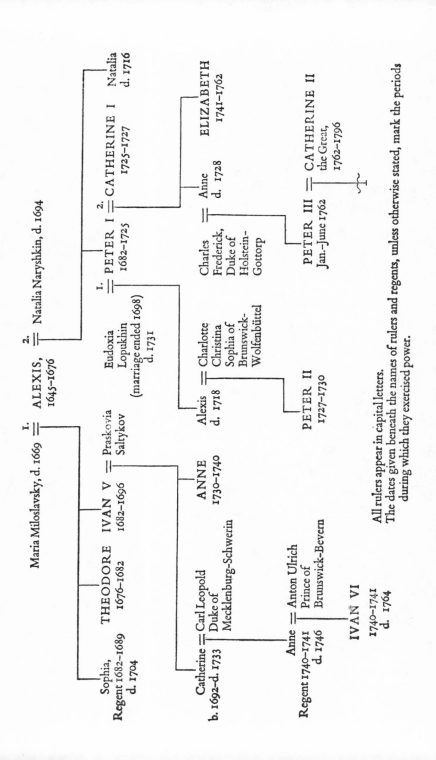

Maria Miloslavsky, d. 1669 ⟦1.⟧ ═ ALEXIS, 1645–1676 ═ ⟦2.⟧ Natalia Naryshkin, d. 1694

Sophia, Regent 1682–1689 d. 1704

THEODORE 1676–1682

IVAN V 1682–1696 ═ Praskovia Salrykov

⟦1.⟧ ═ PETER I 1682–1725 ═ ⟦2.⟧ CATHERINE I 1725–1727

Natalia d. 1716

Eudoxia Lopukhin (marriage ended 1698) d. 1731

Anne d. 1728

ELIZABETH 1741–1762

ANNE 1730–1740

Alexis d. 1718 ═ Charlotte Christina Sophia of Brunswick-Wolfenbüttel

Charles Frederick, Duke of Holstein-Gottorp ═

Catherine ═ Carl Leopold Duke of Mecklenburg-Schwerin b. 1692–d. 1733

PETER II 1727–1730

PETER III Jan.–June 1762 ═ CATHERINE II the Great, 1762–1796

Anne ═ Anton Ulrich Prince of Brunswick-Bevern Regent 1740–1741 d. 1746

IVAN VI 1740–1741 d. 1764

All rulers appear in capital letters.
The dates given beneath the names of rulers and regents, unless otherwise stated, mark the periods during which they exercised power.

Chapter One

★

TSAR ALEXIS was married twice, the first time to Maria Miloslavsky, by whom he had thirteen children, and the second time to Natalia Naryshkin.[1] Peter, who was born in the Kremlin[2] on May 30th, 1672, was the first child of this second marriage. Natalia Naryshkin, having been brought up by the Western-minded Matveev,[3] was herself a Westernising influence at Court, though even before her time foreign ideas had penetrated to the womens' quarters and nurseries of the Kremlin. Toys made abroad, most of them coming from Germany, were to be found in Peter's nursery, which contained among other things a sort of clavicord with green copper strings. It is perhaps significant that the two-year-old Peter was kept happy with musical-boxes, toy drummers, and large cymbals, which in themselves are highly suggestive, and show how partial Alexis' court was to the artifacts of the West. As Peter grew older his nursery began to look more and more like an arsenal, since it contained exact wooden models of the Moscow Battery, of horse-drawn artillery, and

[1] Natalia Naryshkin was the daughter of Cyril Naryshkin, a landowner in a remote part of Russia.

[2] An extremely interesting description of the architecture and art treasures of the Kremlin, as well as a discussion of its place in Russian history, can be found in Arthur Voyce, *The Moscow Kremlin*, University of California Press, 1954.

[3] Artemon Matveev was Tsar Alexis' close friend and adviser. Matveev was much influenced by Western European ideas, habits and customs. His wife was a Scotswoman, who entertained some of the more progressive Russians at her home, and Tsar Alexis often spent the evening with them.

I

of arquebuses, articles which reflected contemporary military preoccupations.

Tsar Alexis died when Peter was four years old, and Theodore, Maria Miloslavsky's son, succeeded to the throne. Because of Alexis' two marriages, his death saw the beginning of a struggle for power between two unscrupulous families whose hatred of each other was proverbial. The result was that, under Theodore, Natalia Naryshkin, and her relatives and supporters, found themselves in a very difficult situation: they were gradually pushed into the background, their supporters were dismissed from their positions, their most powerful adherent, Artemon Matveev, was banished to Pustozersk[1] near the river Pechora, and Natalia herself withdrew from active participation in politics.

It has often been said that Peter was brought up differently from his father and elder brothers. Yet early eighteenth-century sources show quite clearly that, at any rate up to the age of ten, Peter was brought up according to the traditional old-fashioned methods, perhaps more so than his brothers or even his father. The following story is told by a contemporary of Peter's called Krekshin who, though often unreliable and biased, spent thirty years indiscriminately collecting documents, verbal accounts, and anything else that was at all relevant to Peter's career.[2] As was customary in Russia, Peter's education began when he was five years old. Tsar Theodore, who was Peter's godfather as well as his elder half-brother, had frequently said to his step-mother Natalia 'Madam, it is high time our godson started his lessons'. So the Tsaritsa Natalia eventually asked Theodore to find a teacher who was gentle, peace-loving, and an authority on the Holy Bible. As

---

[1] Pustozersk, is near Archangel in North-Western Russia.
[2] Peter Krekshin, 1684–1763. His collection consisted of 45 folios, of which 27 were concerned with Peter.

if on purpose, the choice was delegated to a sanctimonious Old Believer, a boyar called Theodore Sokovnin,[1] who was famous for having given asylum to those who had dissented from the Nikonian innovations.[2] Tsar Alexis himself had punished two of Sokovnin's sisters, Theodosia Morozova and Princess Avdotia Urussova, for their stubborn insistance in clinging to the old beliefs and for their attachment to the Archpriest Avvakum,[3] by confining them to the Borovsk prison. A few years later a brother of Sokovnin's called Alexis was to be beheaded for taking part in a conspiracy of Old Believers directed against Peter. Anyway, Sokovnin suggested that the Tsar should appoint Nikita Zotov, a benevolent, virtuous, and easy-going clerk who worked in the Tax Collecting Department (Bolshoi Prihod). Zotov's introduction to his duties gives a very good idea of his capabilities as a teacher. Sokovnin, taking Zotov to be introduced to the Tsar, left him for a moment in an ante-room. After a little while a courtier came out of the Tsar's chambers, and asked 'Which of you is Nikita Zotov?' The future tutor was so overwhelmed that he was at first unable to move, and the courtier had to lead him by the hand. Zotov asked for a moment's grace in order to collect himself. Then, crossing

[1] Theodore Sokovnin was later accused of plotting against Peter and attempting to bring Sophia (Regent 1682-1689) back to power. This plot was responsible for delaying for a short time Peter's departure for Western Europe.

[2] The innovations introduced by the Patriarch Nikon (1652-8) were of a ritualising nature, and no question of dogma was involved. Cf. Florinsky, *Russia, A History and an Interpretation*, Macmillan, New York, 1953, Vol. I, pp. 286-95; D. S. Mirsky, *Russia, A Social History*, The Cresset Press, 1952, pp. 175-7; William Palmer, *The Patriarch and The Tsar: Services of the Patriarch Nikon to the Church and State of his country*, London, 1873-6, 5 vols.

[3] Avvakum was the leader of the dissenters. After Nikon's fall, Tsar Alexis tried to come to an understanding with the dissenters, but Avvakum refused to compromise and was exiled to Siberia. See *The Life of the Archpriest Avvakum by Himself*, translated by Jane Harrison and Hope Mirrlees, with a preface by D. S. Mirsky, Hogarth Press, 1924. Serge A. Zenkovsky, *The Old Believer Avvakum: His Writings*, Indiana Slavic Studies, I ,1956.

himself, he went in to meet the Tsar, who shook hands and
then started to examine him in the presence of the Patriarch, Simeon Polotsky,[1] who had been Theodore's tutor.
The Patriarch said that he was satisfied with the standard of
Zotov's reading and writing. Then Sokovnin took the newly
appointed teacher to meet the widowed Tsaritsa, who was
waiting for him with Peter at her side. 'You are a good man
well versed in the Holy Writ,' she said 'and I entrust you with
my only son.' Trembling with fear, Zotov burst into tears
and prostrating himself before her, cried, 'Little Mother, I am
not worthy to look after such a treasure.' The Tsaritsa then
took his hand and told him that he was to start teaching the
following morning. Both the Tsar and the Patriarch attended the first lesson. When the new books had been
sprinkled with Holy Water and prayers said, Zotov bowed
low to his pupil and began. It was during this first lesson that
Zotov received an honorarium; the Patriarch gave him one
hundred roubles (worth one thousand in the roubles of 1900),
the Tsar gave him a suite of apartments and raised him to the
rank of *dvorianin*,[2] and the Tsaritsa gave him two complete
outfits of clothes. As soon as the Tsar and Patriarch had left
the room, Zotov changed into his new clothes. According to
Krekshin, Peter began his lessons on March 12th, 1677, which
means that he was not quite five years old. Taking this story
into account, it is improbable that Zotov used any new
teaching methods, or that he taught his pupil Greek or Latin.
In the words of Kotoshikhin,[3] it was always the 'gentle,

[1] Simeon Polotsky was very much in favour of the Nikonian reforms. In 1666
he became head of a new theological school which laid special emphasis on
Latin.

[2] i.e. a nobleman.

[3] Gregory Kotoshikhin, a government official who was disillusioned about
the state of Alexian Muscovy, wrote a highly critical book about *Russia in the
reign of Alexis Mikhailovich* (O Rossii v tsarstvovanie Aleksiia Mikhailovicha),
3rd edition .St. Petersburg, 1884.

literate folk, who weren't likely to make nuisances of them-selves' who were chosen from the Departmental Clerks to teach the Tsarevitches. The story told above shows that Zotov was gentle and literate, but he did not quite fulfil the third condition as he was very fond of drinking. Many years later Peter appointed him 'Prince-Pope', President of the College of Drunkards. Historians often blame Zotov for having had a bad educational influence on Peter, but Zotov was not asked to educate him; he was asked only to teach him reading, writing, and grammar, and he did this no better and no worse than other tutors of Tsarevitches had done before him. Using the word-recognition system, Zotov taught Peter the alphabet, and went through the Prayer Book, the Psalter and even the Gospels, the Acts of the Apostles, and the Epistles. What is more, Peter had to learn all this by heart, as was the practice of the day. In later years Peter sang in the choir and was as proficient as any deacon, and it was said that he could recite the Gospels and the Acts from memory. Tsar Alexis and his elder sons were brought up in exactly the same way. But Zotov's lessons were not restricted to mastering the grammar. The pedagogue from the Taxation Department was influenced by the ocular method of teaching which had first been used by Alexis' tutor Morozov. The young Tsare-vitch was eager to learn, and in his free time liked either to listen to stories or to look through picture books. When Zotov mentioned this to Natalia, she told him to take from the Palace library the illuminated manuscripts dealing with history, and herself commissioned the master-engravers from the Ordnance Office to produce some new pictures. In this way she started a collection of interesting books illustrated in gold and many colours, some showing towns, buildings, ships, soldiers, and weapons, and others about people and events. Zotov put this collection, which had been created by the best available talent, in Peter's room so that, when the boy

B

became bored with the ordinary reading texts, the others could be brought out and their illustrations explained. According to Krekshin, Zotov told Peter a little bit about the past, about what had happened under Alexis, Ivan the Terrible, Dimitri Donskoi, Alexander Nevsky and even Vladimir. Though Peter subsequently never had enough time to study Russia's history, he never lost interest, and would talk a lot about compiling a history text-book, and stress the importance of history in the education of the people. Who knows, it is perhaps possible that all this was due to Peter's memory of his history lessons with Zotov. For this, at any rate, the ex-clerk deserves some credit.

On April 27th, 1682, just before Peter's tenth birthday, Tsar Theodore died, and Peter's elementary education came to an end, or to, be more precise, was interrupted. After Theodore's death, the following well-known sequence of turbulent events took place: Peter was proclaimed Tsar and the claims of his elder half-brother Ivan were ignored; the conspiracy of the Tsarevna Sophia and the Miloslavskys caused the terrible revolt of the Streltsy[1] in May; this led to the massacre of the boyars; as a result, Peter and Ivan were proclaimed joint-Tsars with Sophia as Regent; finally on July 5th there was a disorderly demonstration of Old Be-

---

[1] Singular *strelets*, a shooter. '. . . named because their chief weapons were muskets, although they were armed also with swords, pikes and battle axes. Some of them were mounted, but the majority were infantrymen.' George Lantzeff, *Siberia in the Seventeenth Century*, Berkeley, University of California Press, 1943, p. 66.

The Streltsy were formed in the reign of Ivan the Terrible. They were concentrated in Moscow and in a few other towns. They paid no taxes, and while not engaged in military duties were allowed to trade on their own account. In 1682 there were about 22 regiments of Streltsy in Moscow, each about one thousand strong.

'They were more addicted to armed outbursts than fitted for serious military operations. . . .' B. H. Sumner, *Peter the Great and the Emergence of Russia*, The English Universities Press, 1950, p. 13.

lievers in the Hall of Angels. Peter, who was an eye-witness of these bloody events, astonished everyone with his self-possession. Standing at his mother's side on the steps of the main entrance to the Kremlin, he did not move a muscle when Artemon Matveev and his supporters were stabbed to death by the Streltsy. But the horrors of May 1682 left their mark on Peter, so that one year later a foreign ambassador took him for a sixteen-year-old. Young as he was, Peter had understood what had happened and why. He realised that he had seen medieval Russia at her worst; the threat of hangman and torture chamber hung over the Kremlin; the maddened Streltsy ran through the Kremlin hunting out Naryshkins; the houses of noblemen and merchants were looted by the drunken, rioting soldiers, and the clergy did nothing but meekly obey the rebels' orders and give their blessing and sanction to the dual monarchy. Both the boyars and the courtiers went into hiding, and it was their serfs alone who tried to restore order. The Streltsy promised to free them, tore up their indenture deeds and titles of possession, which they scattered all over the Red Square,[1] and when this had no effect threatened to hand them over to the Office of Bonded Servitude (Kholopii Prikaz) for punishment. To all this the serfs replied 'Be careful lest you lose your heads. Why are you in revolt? Russia is too vast for you to master her'. Because there were so many boyars living in Moscow, their serfs outnumbered the Streltsy by two to one. The serfs were waiting for their masters to give them the order to quell the rising — but the order never came. And so, almost imperceptibly, Peter came to realise that the Streltsy, who were responsible for the maintenance of law and order, would have to be replaced. But with what? Peter's loathing of the Kremlin dates from this time, and he was

[1] For a description see Arthur Voyce, *The Moscow Kremlin,* University of California, 1954, pp. 93–5.

determined to abandon it, its antiques, its maze of apartments, and its population of priests, choristers, servants, attendants, and sisters, aunts and daughters of previous rulers.

The events of May 1682 finally forced the Tsaritsa Natalia to leave the Kremlin, and she took up residence at Preobrazhensky,[1] Alexis' favourite country seat. It was to become the Tsar's temporary residence, a post-house on the road to St. Petersburg. The Tsaritsa and her son lived here, taking no active part in the government of the country, and, in the words of Prince Boris Kurakin[2] they 'lived on what she was given by the Tsarevna Sophia'. In fact she was so poor that she had to borrow money secretly from the Patriarch of the Troïtsa Monastery[3] and the Metropolitan of Rostov. Forced to leave the Kremlin by the plots of his half-sister Sophia, the Regent, Peter grew up in full liberty at Preobrazhensky, a Tsar in name only. As a result he was left to his own devices far too young, and passed from the discipline of the schoolroom to the unrestricted freedom of the estate at Preobrazhensky. It is obvious that there was little to interest him in his mother's apartments where he saw only the sad-looking faces of ex-courtiers, and heard nothing but bitter speeches about the cruelty and injustice of Sophia,[4] her councillors, and humanity in general. Sheer boredom, therefore, forced him out into the Palace grounds, so that in 1683, with nobody's help, Peter invented an absorbing game which was to become an education in itself. Like all observant

[1] Preobrazhensky is on the River Yaüza, not far from Moscow.

[2] Prince Boris Kurakin married the sister of Peter's first wife, Eudoxia.

[3] The Troïtsa Monastery, near Moscow, was at this time one of the wealthiest monasteries in Russia. Eugene Schuyler, *Peter the Great*, London, 1884, Vol. II, p. 182, '. . . the Troïtsa . . . possessed 20,394 peasant houses. The Patriarch had as his own official property 8,842 peasant houses.'

[4] For an account of Sophia's regency see C. Bickford O'Brien, *Russia under Two Tsars 1682–1689, The Regency of Sophia Alekseevna*, University of California Press, 1952.

little boys, Peter began to play at what the grown-ups were talking and thinking about. Contemporary writers insist that his early interest in military matters was completely spontaneous. While it is true that this interest was in character, it is reasonable to suppose that it was the discussions of foreign armies, and Zotov's stories about Alexis' wars, that turned what had started as a game into something with a definite purpose. Besides, the vivid memories of the rising of 1682, coupled with a natural instinct for self-preservation and a desire to be revenged upon the Streltsy who were responsible for the illegal power that Sophia now enjoyed, made him realise how important it was to build up an army which could defend itself against the headstrong Streltsy.

Peter's early military pursuits can be traced systematically from court documents that have been preseved, and it is evident that as Peter grew older, and as new ideas and different weapons were tried out, his games became more and more complicated. The Ordnance Office at the Kremlin was kept busy finding and sending to Preobrazhensky Peter's requirements, which consisted mainly of weapons, while Peter sent back anything that had to be repaired, from a shattered arquebus to a cracked drum. Peter asked for a statue of the Saviour, a dining-room clock, a German carbine, gunpowder, regimental standards, halberds and pistols. The arsenal at the Kremlin was being gradually transferred to the rooms of the Palace at Preobrazhensky. At the same time Peter was leading a very active life, visiting the villages of Vorobiëvo and Kolomenskoe, calling at the Troïtsa and Savva Storozhevsky Monasteries, or poking about nearby estates and monastery settlements. On these expeditions he was always followed by his armoury, which was transported by horse and cart. The company he kept, his immediate friends, and the sort of games he played during these years are known. What is not known, though, is whether he ever looked at a book or continued his scholastic studies. In 1688 he asked the Ordnance Office to send him a Kalmuk saddle and a large globe; what he wanted a globe for just then is unknown, though it must have been used rather vigorously as not long after it was sent to the clockmaker's to be mended. Together with a performing monkey he is sent a book on fire-arms.

When everything he needed had come from the Kremlin's store-rooms, Peter collected together a group of youngsters of his own age. According to custom, as soon as a Tsarevitch reached the age of five a large number of gentlemen's sons was selected to enter his service as valets, butlers, equerries, and personal attendants, so that Peter had plenty of youngsters from whom to choose his companions. Previous Tsars had maintained grandiose establishments and large retinues. One of Tsar Alexis' favourite pastimes was falconry, and he had kept over three thousand hawks, falcons and other birds of prey who were trapped, reared and trained by more than two hundred hawkers and falconers. Over one hundred thousand doves and dovecots were kept to feed the birds of prey, and about six hundred bailiffs, grooms, ostlers, and saddlers were required to look after forty thousand[1] horses. Most of the Tsar's retinue were landed gentry who received salaries, wore livery, and were fed at the Tsar's expense. When Alexis died all these people were virtually unemployed, because Theodore's health prevented him from hunting, Ivan was too sickly, Imperial Princesses did not hunt as it was not considered proper, while Peter disliked falconry and hunting, and preferred either walking or riding. Peter decided that these idle courtiers and members of the household should be employed in a more serious capacity. He recruited the younger chamberlains and grooms, and added some of the falconers

[1] This seems so excessive that one suspects a misprint. 4,000 would be more plausible.

and hawkers. The ranks grew as courtiers volunteered, and even noblemen's serfs, until there were three hundred men in each of the two companies into which he divided them. These men were known as 'Poteshnie', the name given to Peter's 'regiment of boy-soldiers'. It would be wrong to suppose that they were soldiers in name only, for though the Tsar was as yet only playing, his companions actually served as soldiers, performed military duties, and were paid in the same way as those who were employed by the state. Eventually the name 'Poteshnie' became associated with a particular rank in the military hierarchy, as is illustrated by a sentence from a contemporary petition: 'I was given my rank because I was a "Poteshnie".' Recruitment to the companies was carried out in an official, departmental manner; in 1686 Cavalry Headquarters were ordered to send seven equerries to one of Peter's companies. Among the early recruits was Alexander Menshikov,[1] described by Prince Kurakin as 'by birth lower than a Pole', although, in fact he was the son of a court equerry. Later on young noblemen joined the companies, so that in 1687 Ivan Buturlin and the future Field-Marshal, Prince Michael Golitsyn, joined with a crowd of grooms, though because of his extreme youth Golitsyn served as a drummer-boy. Peter and his two companies kept Preobrazhensky in a state of turmoil; barracks, staff offices, and stables were built, and harness for the horse-drawn artillery brought from Cavalry Headquarters so that Peter could have it near at hand. Eventually all this became a permanent establishment with its own staff, budget, and treasury. Playing at soldiers was not enough; Peter wanted himself and his companions to be soldiers. Dark green

[1] Prince Alexander Menshikov (1672–1729). His origins are somewhat obscure. He became Peter's chief favourite, and held high civil and military offices. He was disgraced after Peter's death, and in 1727 was banished to Siberia. For a short biography see R. N. Bain, *The Pupils of Peter the Great*, Constable, 1897, pp. 42–4.

uniforms and arms were issued to everybody, and some of Peter's personal attendants who came from well-known families were appointed staff-officers, subalterns, or non-commissioned officers. Almost every day Peter subjected his men to strict military training on the estate, and himself went through the ranks, starting as drummer-boy. In order to teach his soldiers how to besiege and storm fortresses, he built an elaborate fort on the river Yaüza, called it Pressburg, and had it bombarded with mortars and other suitable weapons. A high degree of technical knowledge was required for many of Peter's military exercises, and he could never have achieved as much as he did with the knowledge he had at his immediate disposal. Near Preobrazhensky there had grown up a strange, self-contained colony, known as the German Suburb[1] of which the rulers of the Muscovite Empire were highly suspicious. Under Alexis it consisted mainly of foreign soldiers, amongst whom there were two generals, over a hundred colonels, and numerous other officers who had been hired to command Russian regiments on active service. It was to this colony that Peter turned when he had exhausted his own knowledge of military techniques. In 1684 a foreign specialist called Zommer showed Peter a mortar which eventually became one of his favourite weapons. Foreign officers were attracted to Preobrazhensky to serve. on the staff and help with the organisation. In the early 1690's, by which time the two companies had been transformed into two regular regiments taking their names from the villages

[1] In 1652 Tsar Alexis issued an ukaze ordering all foreigners to live on the outskirts of Moscow. The quarter they occupied was known as the 'German Suburb' because to the Russians all foreigners were 'Germans'. This suburb brought some of the upper class Russians into closer contact with Western European customs and habits, and some of the foreign expatriates who lived there had an important influence in Peter's life. See Francis Steuart, *Scottish Influences in Russian History from the end of the Sixteenth Century to the beginning of the Nineteenth Century*, Glasgow, J. MacLehose & Sons, 1913.

of Preobrazhensky and Semenovsky in which they were quartered, nearly all the colonels, majors, and captains were foreigners; only the sergeants were Russian. The Commander-in-Chief of both regiments, though, was a Russian called Avtamon Golovin, who was described by Peter's crony and brother-in-law Prince Kurakin as 'a stupid man, but one who knew his trade'.

As a result of Peter's interest in foreign-made novelties, his secondary education was quite unlike any previous Tsarevitch's usual course of study. Peter tells the following story:[1] just before leaving for France to take up his post as Russian Ambassador in 1687, Prince Jacob Dolgoruky happened to mention to Peter that he had owned an instrument 'by which distance and space could be measured without moving from the spot', only unfortunately it had been stolen. Peter asked the Prince to buy him a similar instrument in France. When Dolgoruky returned to Russia the following year, he brought Peter an astrolabe. Peter did not know how to work it, so he took it to a knowledgeable German 'doctor'[2] who admitted that he did not either, but promised Peter that he would find somebody who did. 'With great eagerness' Peter ordered him to do so, and not long afterwards the 'doctor' turned up with a Dutchman called Timmerman.[3] Under Timmerman's supervision, Peter began 'zealously and eagerly' to study arithmetic and geometry, the theory of ballistics and the art of fortification. Peter's copy-books, which are in his own hand-writing, have been preserved and are full of solutions and explanations of various problems. One of the most noticeable things about these copy-books is that they show how badly Peter had been taught grammar. He did not observe any grammatical rules,

[1] In his preface to the *Maritime Regulations*.   [2] Zacharias von der Hulst.
[3] Timmerman was a Dutch merchant who had settled in Moscow under Alexis.

his writing was poor, his letters badly formed, he did not know how to divide words, he spelled phonetically, and he even inserted a hard sign between two consonants.[1] It is also quite clear that he used mathematical terms indiscriminately. For 'additio' he writes either 'aditsoe' or 'voditsia'. Timmerman himself was not a very good mathematician; multiplication exercises in his writing are full of errors. But these notebooks do show how eagerly Peter learned mathematics and applied himself to the study of military subjects. Peter was quick to learn arithmetic and geometry, the theory of ballistics and the art of fortifications; he mastered the astrolabe, and learned to demolish fortresses and calculate the trajectory of cannon balls.

One day, as Peter and Timmerman were looking over a storehouse, which had been built by one of Peter's ancestors, Nikita Romanov,[2] in the village of Izmailovo, they came across a battered English boat.[3] This boat, according to Peter,[4] was the progenitor of the Russian fleet, since it was responsible for arousing in him the passion for sailing which led to the building of a flotilla first on the lake at Periaslav and later at Archangel. But Peter forgot to mention that the 'Father of the Russian Fleet' that he so praised had some obscure collaterals and that in 1687, more than a year before he discovered this particular boat, some 'small boats' had been sent from the Ordnance Office, which were probably his father's models dating from the building of the 'Orël'[5] on the

[1] In Russian this is an obvious howler.

[2] Nikita Ivanovich Romanov was a cousin of Tsar Michael Romanov who reigned 1613–45.

[3] 'It is believed that this boat had been sent from England by Queen Elizabeth, as a present to the Tsar Ivan the Terrible.' *History of the Russian Fleet during the reign of Peter the Great,* by a contemporary Englishman (1724), edited by Vice-Admiral C. A. B. Bridge, K.C.B., Navy Records Society, Vol. XV, p. xvii.

[4] In his preface to the *Maritime Regulations.*

[5] Built by Karsten Brant who had been brought from Holland in 1660 by Tsar Alexis.

river Oka; while Court documents mention that in 1686 pleasure boats were being built at Preobrazhensky. It is worth remembering that the Alexian administration had frequently agitated in favour of a Russian Fleet, so that Peter was not acting without precedent.

An enumeration of the salient features of Peter's childhood and youth makes it possible to follow his intellectual development. Until the age of ten he was taught his Church-Slavonic grammar in the traditional way, even though events during this period were not typical of the old Russia. Then at the age of ten, as a result of the terrifying and bloody events of May 1682, he was forced to leave the Kremlin, and was cut off from the typical old Russian environment. Moreover, the old way of life was inevitably associated with bitter memories. And so Peter was left alone to play with his martial toys and Zotov's picture books. The games that had started in the nursery were continued in the grounds and woods at Preobrazhensky where, surrounded by personal attendants and grooms, he had real people and real guns, not dolls and toys, to play with, and where there was no tutor or set of rules to keep him in check. This existence continued till he was seventeen. As a result he was completely cut off from the ideas, or rather the customs and traditions, of the Court which hitherto had been responsible for the outlook and methods of government of a Muscovite Tsar. Peter, however, had no way of replacing the old ideas with new ones. Zotov's teaching, prematurely interrupted, was continued later under somebody else's guidance and was pursued for totally different ends. Peter's elder brothers learned their Church-Slavonic grammar from a government clerk, and then went on to a more learned teacher who taught them to look beyond the usual Muscovite horizon, so that they somehow learned a little about political and moral ideas, about the people, government, and a ruler's obligations to his subjects.

Peter never had this type of teacher. Instead of Simeon Polotsky or Rtishchev[1] he had a Dutchman who knew something about mathematics and military affairs, but was no more erudite than Zotov. Zotov had been concerned with training Peter's memory; Timmerman's main interest lay in developing his co-ordination, dexterity, and sense of proportion. Neither appealed to his reasoning powers or to his emotions. It is not surprising, therefore, that Peter's tastes and ideas were somewhat one-sided. All his political thinking was dominated by the struggle with his half-sister and the Miloslavskys. His attitude to civic affairs was coloured by hatred of the clergy, the boyars, the Streltsy, and the Old Believers. He was more occupied with soldiers, guns, fortresses, and ships, than with people, political institutions, popular needs, or civic relations. For a long time Peter completely ignored the problems of society and human relations to which responsible people usually devote so much attention, so that before Peter could even realise that there could be any relationship between society and himself, he had stopped thinking about it.

Meanwhile the Tsarevna Sophia, with the help of her latest lover Theodore Shaklovity,[2] was organising a fresh outbreak by the Streltsy, which was to be directed against Peter and her step-mother. Aroused suddenly after midnight on August 12th, 1689, Peter fled in terror to the forest, and made his way to the Troïtsa Monastery, leaving behind him his mother and pregnant wife.[3] This was almost the only time that Peter was driven to such extremes and shows the horrors he expected Sophia to inflict on him. But the scheme failed, and the reign of the triumvirate, which was derided abroad

[1] Theodore Rtishchev was one of Tsar Alexis's advisers who held a high office at the Kremlin. He was one of the small group of men around Alexis who were eager to learn from Western Europe.

[2] Theodore Shaklovity was a Privy Councillor who was made commander of the Streltsy by Sophia in 1683.

[3] Peter had married Eudoxia Lopukhin on February 6th, 1689.

and wholeheartedly approved of at home (except by those at Preobrazhensky), came to an end. That 'shameful third person', as Peter called Sophia in a letter to his half-brother Ivan, was confined in a convent. Ivan remained Tsar and appeared at all ceremonial functions, while Peter went back to his soldiers, so that the power and authority had been transferred from Sophia to Natalia.

According to Prince Boris Kurakin, the Tsaritsa Natalia was 'not fit to rule as she was rather stupid'. The actual administration of the country was shared among her advisers, of whom the cleverest was that Prince Boris Golitsyn who had skilfully led the campaign against Sophia. He was well educated, clever, and spoke Latin, but unfortunately 'drank incessantly' and had been responsible for the destitution of Povolzhie,[1] which was administered by the Department of the Court of Kazan, over which Golitsyn had nearly unlimited authority. The other two advisers were Leo Naryshkin,[2] Natalia's brother, and Tikhon Streshnev,[3] who was related to the two Tsars through their maternal grandmother. Kurakin says that Leo Naryshkin was a fool, a drunkard, and a wastrel who 'did good for no other reason except that it appealed to his rather odd nature', and that Streshnev, as well as being a wastrel, was cruel, crafty, and 'a Court intriguer'. These people 'paid no attention to law or justice' and administered the country in a shocking manner. 'The time of wholesale corruption and state theft' had begun. They dominated the Council of Boyars to such an extent that 'the most powerful boyars became mere spectators, and never uttered'. The aristocratic Prince Boris Kurakin was highly indignant at the downfall and degradation of the cream of the

[1] A region of the Lower Volga.

[2] Leo Naryshkin was appointed Director of Foreign Affairs after Sophia's downfall.

[3] Tikhon Streshnev was appointed Minister for War and Minister for Internal Affairs.

nobility and the old princely families at the hands of 'such nobodies' as the Naryshkins and Streshnevs.

As a result of Peter's marriage more than thirty Lopukhins of both sexes suddenly arrived at Court, where they were treated with polite contempt. 'They were malicious, mean, slanderous and stupid.' The new governing set was well suited to every class of Muscovite society, since all behaved outrageously. An *okolnichy*[1] called Zheliabuzhky, who was a close observer of, and a participator in, Muscovite affairs, recorded in his diary a long list of boyars, courtiers, learned clerks, and ordinary scriveners who were tortured, beaten with rod and knout, who forfeited their salaries, had their property confiscated, and were even sentenced to death for such crimes as brawling at Court, 'uttering derogatory remarks' about their rulers, wife-beating, rape, forging documents, and even in one case, stealing government funds with the help of Streshnev's wife. Prince Lobanov-Rostovsky, who owned hundreds of peasant homesteads, attacked a convoy of Treasury chests as it was travelling on the road to Troïtsa, and was sentenced to be beaten with the knout; six years later, during manœuvres at Kozhukhovo,[2] he appeared as a captain in the Preobrazhensky Regiment! A conflict was taking place between the representatives of two sets of equally barbarous instincts and morals, rather than between the representatives of opposing ideas or tendencies.

This was the situation that Peter found when he appeared at Court after Sophia had been deposed. The impression made on him by these events did nothing to induce Peter to take an interest either in government or public affairs, with the result that he became more and more absorbed in his own pursuits. He became well acquainted with the German

---

[1] An *okolnichy* was a Courtier of the second class, attached to the person of the Tsar.

[2] A village on the River Moskva.

Suburb, and frequently invited the generals and officers who lived there to instruct his regiments in the building of fortifications and the use of artillery. These officers were also invited to take charge of manœuvres. Peter often rode out to the German Suburb to have dinner or supper with the veteran General Gordon[1] and other foreigners; and as Peter became better acquainted with the German Suburb, the ranks of the regiments swelled. Vagabonds and vagrants joined the butlers, personal attendants, grooms and gunners who were serving in the ranks. The ignorant, nearly illiterate, but alert and jovial bombardier 'Alesha' Menshikov, who could hardly spell his name, whose origins were obscure, and who was to become Peter's powerful favourite, served side by side with Franz Lefort,[2] a Genevese adventurer, who had travelled over half the world looking for fame and fortune before arriving in Moscow. Nearly as unknown as Menshikov, Lefort was fairly experienced, a cheerful babbler, full of life, and a staunch friend. He was an indefatigable ballroom cavalier, a good drinking companion, and an adept at organising banquets with plenty of drink, music, and dancing partners. Or as Prince Boris Kurakin, then one of Peter's attendants, put it, 'he was like a debauched Frenchman.' Sometimes these friends of Peter's were joined by the staid, punctilious old mercenary, General Patrick Gordon himself, who, as the Russian folk song has it, 'had fought in seven hosts, under seven kings.' While Peter accepted the foreigners in his regiments, he made sure that the important

[1] Patrick Gordon was born near Aberdeen in 1635. A Roman Catholic and a Royalist, he was educated abroad. He became a soldier of fortune, and served the German Emperor, the Swedes, and the Poles. He finally entered Russian service, and was sent on diplomatic missions by Tsar Alexis in 1665, and by Sophia in 1685. He took part in the Crimean campaign of 1687, when he was promoted to the rank of general. See *Passages from the Diary of General Patrick Gordon of Auchleuchries*, The Spalding Club, Aberdeen, 1859.

[2] Franz Lefort came to Russia in 1675, and became Peter's closest foreign friend. He married a connection of General Gordon's.

posts were held by Russians. Prince Theodore Romodanov-sky,[1] nicknamed Frederick, was the Commander-in-Chief of 'the 'King of Pressburg's' army. Romodanovsky was given extensive police powers, and was appointed Chief of the Pre-obrazhensky Military Inquisition and Minister in charge of Flogging and the Torture Chamber. He is said to have 're-sembled a monster, behaved like an evil-minded tyrant, and been drunk all day and every day', but he had a dog-like devotion to Peter. An old veteran, Ivan Buturlin, whom Peter called the 'King of Poland' or 'Tsar Semenovsky', and who was 'cruel, corrupt and a sot', was made Commander-in-Chief of another force, made up mostly from Streltsy. These two forces quarrelled, and even came to blows.

There was such a mixture of nationalities, dialects, and social classes that there were real difficulties of communica-tion. Two lines from a letter written by Lefort to Peter in 1696 will serve as an illustration of the difficulty. Although Lefort had then been in Russia for twenty years, the letter is written in Latin characters in a sort of pidgin Russian. 'Slavou Bogh sto ti prechol sdorova ou gorrod voronets. Daj boc ifso dobro sauersit i che Moscva sdorovou buit!'— 'Thank God you have reached Voronets safely. God be with you and bring you back to Moscow safely!' In his letters to Menshikov, Peter did the same sort of thing, only he wrote in German, using Russian letters! Peter wrote to the dignified Count Theodore Apraxin[2] in Latin characters, and called him 'Min

---

[1] Prince Theodore Romodanovsky was one of Peter's earliest companions. Feared and hated by most of his contemporaries, he was given enormous ad-ministrative powers by Peter. During the 1698 Streltsy rising, which was re-sponsible for Peter's early return to Russia from Europe, Romodanovsky took complete charge of affairs.

[2] Theodore Apraxin (1671–1728) was made governor of Archangel in 1693. He was a Russian admiral, and one of Peter's favourites. After 1700 he became a very influential member of the court. See R. N. Bain, *The Pupils of Peter the Great*, Constable, 1897, pp. 38–9.

Her Guverneur Archangel'. Titles were not used in the regiments, and Peter once severely rebuked Apraxin for being so formal and using titles in his letters. 'I do not approve of this,' wrote Peter, 'and since you once served in one of my regiments, you should have known this.'

Peter found the regiments much more attractive than his home, especially as his marriage to Eudoxia Lopukhin had been forced on him by the Naryshkins and Tikhon Streshnev. Stupid, quarrelsome, and superstitious, she was not a suitable wife for Peter. At the beginning they got on fairly well, but Peter's mother, who disliked Eudoxia, hastened the inevitable rupture. Peter arranged his life to suit himself, and was frequently absent from home for long periods. This caused their relationship to become colder, which in turn produced yet longer absences. Hence Peter began to live like a homeless, wandering student. He increased the number of military exercises, experimented with ingenious, home-made, but none the less dangerous fireworks, held reviews, and supervised building operations, military expeditions, manœuvres and engagements in which several were wounded and some were even killed. He experimented with new guns and, unaided by army carpenters, built a yacht on the River Yaüza. He borrowed books on ballistics from General Gordon and ordered others from abroad. He studied everything, looked at everything, tested everything, and questioned foreigners about military and European affairs. He ate and slept either in the German Suburb or in Sergeant Buzhenin's quarters at headquarters at Preobrazhensky, anywhere, in fact, so long as it was not at home where he only appeared when he wanted to dine with his mother.

Once, in 1691, Peter invited himself to General Gordon's house for dinner and the night. There were about eighty-five guests present, and after supper they bivouacked on the floor of the cellar. The next day they all moved on to Lefort's

c

house. Lefort, who had been appointed both a General and an Admiral, organised the banquet and the revelry. The company shut themselves up for three days in Lefort's villa, which Peter had built for him, and, in Prince Boris Kurakin's words, 'were drunk beyond description, so that many died of it.' Those who survived these carouses with 'Ivashka Khmelnitsky'[1] were ill for days; yet Peter would get up the following morning completely unaffected, and go to work as if nothing had happened.

Up to the age of twenty-four, Peter was constantly engaged in military affairs, going on expeditions to Alexandrovsk, Periaslav, and Archangel, and as time passed the 'game' lost its childish characteristics and became more serious. But even so, the nursery game had been taken seriously. As Peter grew older his attitude towards people and guns became more mature. His 'regiment of boy soldiers' was transformed into a regular corps under foreign officers; toy guns and gunners were replaced by real artillery and live people. It was unfair of General Gordon, who supervised the expeditions, to refer to them in his diary[2] as 'military ballets', since out of these apparently pointless and amusing exercises on land and on the lake at Periaslav, there grew the cadres of the regular army and the future fleet. Moreover the 'regiments of boy soldiers' had a certain educational value. Manœuvres lasting three weeks were carried out in 1694, below Kozhukhovo on the banks of Lake Moscow, and, according to Prince Boris Kurakin, who took part in them and who did not usually exaggerate, thirty thousand men were involved. The manœuvres were conducted according to a plan carefully

---

[1] The Russian equivalent of Bacchus.

[2] The diary, which is in six quarto volumes, has been preserved in Russia. It was translated into German by D. M. Posselt, and appeared in three volumes in 1849-52. Extracts from the diary were published by the Spalding Club, Aberdeen, under the title *Passages from the Diary of General Patrick Gordon of Auchleuchries*, Aberdeen, 1859.

worked out by General Gordon. A comprehensive record of plans and sketches of camps, battle formations, and supply lines, was kept. Prince Kurakin also said that, in general, these manœuvres provided useful training for the soldiers, and remarked that few contemporary European rulers could have bettered the manœuvres at Kozhukhovo, adding that, on this occasion, twenty-four people were killed and fifty wounded. Writing about this particular manœuvre in later years, Peter said that at the beginning he looked on it as merely a game, but as it turned out, it served as a preparation for the Azov campaigns of 1695 and 1696. These campaigns justified the manœuvres by putting their lessons into practice, since Azov was captured with the help of the artillerymen who had received their training during the manœuvres and of the fleet that had been built under Peter's personal supervision one winter on Lake Voronezh. That the fleet had been built at all was directly due to the knowledge and experience Peter had gained from the master craftsmen, with whom he worked on the wharves at Periaslav.

In 1697, when he was twenty-five years old, Peter at last saw Western Europe. His friends and acquaintances from the German Suburb had talked about it, and Lefort had constantly urged him to go. Thus the idea that he should tour abroad arose quite naturally. He was surrounded by Western European immigrants, had learned their crafts, spoke their languages, and in 1689 was signing letters to his mother 'Petrus'. He called the best galley in his Voronezh fleet 'Principium'. In order to set an example, and be able to teach others, Peter had served in the ranks of both his army and his tiny navy, thereby gaining much valuable experience.

Having sent scores of young Russians to study abroad it was natural that he should eventually follow suit. He did not travel like a leisured gentleman looking at works of art, but went as a workman in order to learn the useful crafts of which he was still ignorant; he went abroad to learn new techniques, not to admire Western European culture. Over the seal of letters which he wrote from abroad appear the words 'From one who would both learn and experience', and it was with this object that the tour was organised. Peter joined the touring Mission as plain Peter Mikhailov. Officially the Mission was to visit European courts to try to negotiate an anti-Turkish coalition,[1] to strengthen existing ties between Russia and the European powers, and, if possible, to form new ones. The Grand Ambassadors, Lefort, Golovin, and Secretary of Council Voznitsyn, were given secret instructions to look for capable naval captains and lieutenants 'who had reached their present rank through merit and not through influence', and for 'as many trained men as possible' to work the ships. Volunteers who went abroad were ordered to master the use of 'charts, maps, compasses and other naval instruments'; to learn to handle ships in peace and in action; and to familiarise themselves with ships' gear and instruments. They were to take every opportunity of being present at a naval action, and were to obtain certificate of proficiency from their instructors. Moreover, each volunteer was to bring back to Moscow two naval experts, whose expenses would be paid when their contract came to an end. Noblemen who sent their house-serfs abroad for naval training were to be paid one hundred roubles from the Treasury. In 1697 nineteen noblemen were sent to Venice with a letter of introduction, informing the Doge that the Tsar wished them to 'learn the new methods of warfare as practised in Europe at that time'. One of these noblemen was Prince Boris Kurakin, who mentions in his diary that they also took lessons in mathematics, learned something about astronomy, navigation, mechanics, and the attack and defence of fortifications, and went on cruises. This

[1] For details of the diplomatic background see B. H. Sumner, *Peter the Great and the Ottoman Empire,* Oxford, 1949, especially p. 19 and ff.

Grand Mission, travelling ostensibly for diplomatic reasons, was only one of many missions which were sent from Moscow to Europe in order to observe, learn new trades and crafts, and persuade skilled craftsmen to come to Russia. The first thing 'volunteer' Peter Mikhailov did abroad was to study gunnery. His instructor at Königsberg, a Prussian colonel,[1] gave Peter a testimonial saying that he was impressed with the speed at which Peter Mikhailov had learned, and that he was a careful, learned, skilled, and fearless mastergunner.

Peter's first appearance in European society was at a banquet, given by the Electors of Hanover and Brandenburg, in the Hanoverian town of Koppenburg. At the beginning Peter felt rather embarrassed, but soon pulled himself together, charmed his hosts, drank their health in the Muscovite fashion, confessed that he was not particularly fond of either music or hunting, and preferred sailing, building ships, and letting off fireworks, and then showed the assembled company his calloused hands. He joined in the dancing, during which the Muscovites mistook their German dancing partners' stays for ribs. Peter himself ruined the coiffure of a ten year old princess (the future mother of Frederick the Great) by lifting her by the ears to kiss her. Although the Muscovites were slightly bewildered by the rest of the entertainment, which was provided by two German society ladies, the banquet went off fairly well. But when it was over, the princesses did not hesitate to give their impressions: they said that he was attractive and witty, but extremely clumsy, and that his table manners were quite impossible. He was in every way a typical representative of his country, but they knew that without having to travel all the way from Hanover to Koppenburg!

It was natural that, with his particular interests, Peter was in a hurry to get to know the two European countries whose

[1] Colonel Von Sternfeld, chief engineer of the Prussian fortresses.

military, naval, and industrial techniques were the most advanced: Holland and England.[1] With a few companions, he travelled ahead of the Mission and worked for a week as an ordinary carpenter in a private dockyard in the little town of Saardam, which was a busy shipbuilding centre. By chance he met a blacksmith[2] whom he had known in Moscow, and from whom he rented a small room. Peter spent all his spare time looking over factories, sawmills, and spinning-mills, and visiting the families of Dutch carpenters who had gone to Moscow. But the red frieze jacket and white canvas trousers of a Dutch worker failed to preserve his incognito, and Peter soon found it impossible to move about Saardam without being stared at by inquisitive idlers who had come to gape at the carpenter-Tsar. On August 16th, 1697, Lefort and the rest of the Mission arrived at Amsterdam, where Peter joined them. On August 17th they all went to the theatre to see a comedy; and two days later they attended a municipal banquet and firework display held in their honour. On August 20th Peter travelled overnight to Saardam to collect his tools, returning immediately to Amsterdam where he joined the others at the wharves of the Dutch East India Company. Permission to work in Amsterdam had been obtained from the Burgomaster, Witzen, who had visited Moscow. The volunteers who had joined the Mission in order to study abroad were given jobs 'according to their capabilities', as Peter put it in a letter to Moscow. Eleven of them, including Peter and Menshikov, went to work as carpenters; the rest went to work as sail-makers, mast-builders, or seamen. Peter and his companions worked on a frigate which had been laid down for them, and after nine weeks it was

---

[1] For the English contribution to the development of the Russian navy see M. S. Anderson, 'Great Britain and the Growth of the Russian Navy in the Eighteenth Century,' *Mariner's Mirror,* Vol. 42, pp. 132–46.

[2] Gerrit Kist.

ready for launching. Peter worked every day, and spent his leisure hours visiting and examining the many things that interested him. Accompanied by Witzen, he went to Utrecht to meet William of Orange, King of England and Stadholder of Holland. Here Peter attended Professor Ruisch's lectures on anatomy, and was present during operations; when he saw the body of a child laid out in the anatomy room, he bent down to kiss it, because it looked so alive and smiling. At Leyden Peter visited the famous specialist, Dr. Boerhaave, and saw his Anatomical Theatre. He noticed that some members of his suite were squeamish about looking at corpses, so he made them tear out the corpses' muscles with their teeth. Always on the move, Peter spent his time looking at rarities and curiosities, visiting factories, mills, workshops, hospitals, educational institutions, and military and trading establishments. He looked over the observatory, visited or entertained some Dutchmen, and travelled everywhere to meet shipwrights.

After four months in Holland, Peter thought that he had 'learned everything a carpenter should know', and concluding that the Dutch had no original theories about naval architecture, left for England in 1698 to learn the new ideas that were being applied there. King William warmly welcomed him to England and gave him the new royal yacht[1] for a

---

[1] The *Transport Royal* which had just been constructed on a new plan, and which was armed with twenty brass cannon. Its subsequent fate is rather interesting. 'The *Transport Royal* was sent to Archangel under the command of Captain Ripley, and took a part of the collections of curiosities and military stores which Peter had collected in Holland. By the Tsar's orders, Franz Timmerman met it there, to take it to Vologda, and hence partly overland to Yaroslav. It was intended afterwards to convey it to the Sea of Azov, as soon as the canal between the Volga and the Don should be finished, but as the yacht drew nearly eight feet of water, Timmerman could not get it farther than Kholmogory, and it went back to Archangel, where it remained ever after.' Schuyler, *Peter the Great,* London, 1884, Vol. I, p. 376. The log of the *Transport Royal* has been preserved at the National Maritime Museum, Greenwich.

present. In London[1] Peter visited the Royal Society where he saw 'all sorts of wonderful things'. But he wanted to learn the theory of naval architecture, and become a specialist instead of remaining an ordinary carpenter, so he moved to Deptford and found quarters not far from the King's Wharf. From Deptford he made several trips to London, Oxford, and particularly to Woolwich; there he saw shells being made in the laboratory, and 'tried to cast a bomb himself'. He reviewed warships at Portsmouth, duly noting the number and calibre of the guns, and he witnessed a mock naval battle which had been specially arranged for him just off the Isle of Wight. He kept a Journal of all his activities. He went to the theatre, looked at churches, and gave an audience to some of the English Bishops which lasted for half-an-hour. He invited a giantess who was nine feet four inches tall to visit him. He was shown over the Royal Observatory, dined out, and often returned home 'quite merry'. He went more than once to the Tower of London, where he showed great interest in the Mint,[2] and the prison 'where honourable Englishmen were lodged'.

There is an interesting piece of information about Peter's one visit to Parliament, which must have been to the Upper House as he says that he saw the King on his throne, and the Peers on their benches. With the help of an interpreter Peter listened to the debate, and then said to his compatriots 'It is good to hear subjects speaking truthfully and openly to their King. This is what we must learn from the English'. From time to time the Journal states that 'we stayed at home and made merry', which generally means that they drank the clock round. The private house[3] near the King's Wharf,

[1] For details of Peter's stay in England see Ian Grey, *Peter the Great in England*, History Today, April, 1956, pp. 225–34.

[2] As Sumner says, there is no record of his having met the Warden of the Mint, Isaac Newton. See *Peter the Great and the Emergence of Russia*, English Universities Press Ltd., 1950, p. 37.

[3] Sayes Court, John Evelyn's house.

Deptford, in which Peter and his suite were lodged by King William's orders, had been especially redecorated for these eminent visitors. When the visitors left three months later, the owner of the house presented the Government a huge bill for damages. Even allowing for exaggeration in the statement of the damage, the bill makes a very bad impression. It was claimed that, as a result of the merrymaking, the floors and walls were liberally bespattered and smeared, the furniture smashed, and the curtains torn; that pictures were riddled and ruined because they had been used for target practice; and that the lawn had been utterly ruined, and looked as if a regiment of soldiers in iron shoes had drilled on it. A bill for three hundred and fifty pounds was presented to cover the damage.[1]

It is obvious that, when these students from Moscow came to Europe for educational purposes, they did not think it necessary to conform to European manners. They were so intent on learning their trades that they failed to realise that the foreigners with whom they had mixed in the German Suburb were outcasts, and not at all representative of Europe. Unaccustomed to a law-abiding, peaceful society, it is hardly surprising that, wherever the Mission went, it left traces of Muscovite habits and customs. No wonder then that thoughtful people began to have doubts about the Mission's being as enlightened and as representative of Russia as it

[1] Evelyn asked Sir Christopher Wren to estimate the extent of the damage. Wren's petition and report are printed in *Notes and Queries,* 2nd Series, No. 19, May 10th, 1856, pp. 365-7.

The Diary of John Evelyn, ed. by E. S. De Beer, O.U.P., 1955 Vol. V, p. 284, n. 1, contains a choice description of Peter's habits by a servant: 'There is a house full of people and right nasty. The Czar lies next your library, and dines in the parlour next your study. He dines at 10 o'clock and 6 at night, is very seldom at home a whole day, very often in the King's Yard, or by water, dressed in several dresses. The King is expected there this day, the best parlour is pretty clean for him to be entertained in. The King pays for all he has.'

professed.[1] This, at any rate, is the impression that Peter made
on Bishop Burnet, who remarked none too piously that he
had been astounded by his capabilities, his vices, and especially
his boorishness, and wondered that such a 'furious man had
been raised up to so absolute an authority over so great a part
of the world'.

In May 1698, before Peter had time to realise the sort of
reputation he was getting in Western Europe, he left hurriedly
for Vienna. He had engaged about nine hundred Dutchmen
for the Russian service, from a vice-admiral to a ship's cook,
and spent two and a half million roubles abroad. When he
heard that Sophia was conspiring against him, and that the
Streltsy were in rebellion once more,[2] he abandoned the idea
of an Italian tour, and in July left Vienna for Moscow.
It is easy to imagine the impressions with which Peter returned to Russia after fifteen months abroad. He had devoted his time to studying the technical side of Western
civilisation, and showed no interest at all in its other aspects.
He must have imagined that Europe was a large, noisy, collection of factories, foundries, mills, machinery, shipyards,
and wharves.

As soon as Peter reached Moscow he hastily began to investigate the causes of the latest Streltsy revolt, and for many
days was busy dealing with the old enemies whom Sophia
had stirred up to renewed activity. He was reminded of the
uprising of 1682, and of the terror that had been inspired in
him by the activities of Sophia, her friends the Shaklovitys,
and her relatives the Miloslavskys. It is hardly surprising
that Peter was beside himself with rage during the enquiry,
and it is said he himself beheaded some of the Streltsy in the

[1] For a more general discussion of English attitudes to Russia see M. S.
Anderson, 'English Views in the Age of Peter the Great', *American Slavic and
East European Review*, XIII, April 1954, pp. 200–14.
[2] Romodanovsky sent him this news by letter.

torture chamber. And then, before he had time to take command of the situation, he had to turn his attention to a much more urgent problem. Within two years of his return home the Northern War began. The mercurial and restless energy, which in his early youth had been spontaneous, he was now forced by circumstances to maintain without interruption almost to the end of his life. The anxieties, the early defeats, and the ultimate victory of the Northern War, were the biggest influences on his future activities, and fixed the direction and tempo of his reforms. He lived from day to day, trying to cope with fast-moving events and trying to deal with the most urgent requirements of state without having time to think things out or make a plan.

Peter's activities during the Northern War were in harmony both with his natural tastes and habits and with the impressions and knowledge he had gained abroad. He played the part neither of a traditional ruler nor of a typical Russian Supreme Commander. He did not issue orders from Court for his subordinates to act on, yet unlike Charles XII he did not personally lead his troops into battle. Poltava[1] and Hangö[2] are two glorious episodes in Russian military history, and in both of these Peter did participate. As a rule, however, leaving the front under the command of his generals and admirals, Peter took upon himself the less obvious technical work of the war. He generally remained behind the lines organising reserves, mustering recruits, drawing up operational plans, building ships and munition factories, accumulating ammunition, equipment, and supplies. He encouraged, scolded, nagged, quarrelled with all and sundry, hung defaulters, and travelled from one end of the country to another.

[1] 1709.
[2] 1714. Hangö was Russia's first naval victory. It was almost entirely a battle of galleys. See Roger C. Anderson, *Naval Wars in the Baltic during the Sailing Ship Epoch*, 1522–1850, London, 1910.

In other words, he was Commander-in-chief of Ordnance, Supplies, and Ships all at once. This tireless activity continued for nearly thirty years, and set its stamp on Peter's ideas, feelings, tastes, and habits. Though Peter was single-minded and narrow, he was at the same time ponderous and active, as cold, but as explosive, as one of his Petrozavodsk cannon.

Chapter Two

★

INTELLECTUALLY Peter the Great was one of those simple-minded people who can be read at a glance and are easily understood.

Physically Peter was a giant of just under seven feet, and at any gathering he towered a full head above everybody else. During the Easter service he had so much bending to do that he invariably suffered from back-ache. Not only was Peter a natural athlete, but habitual use of axe and hammer had developed his strength and manual dexterity to such an extent that he was able to twist a silver platter into a scroll; indeed so dexterous was he that if a piece of cloth was thrown into the air he could cut it in half with his knife before it landed. All the male descendants of the Patriarch Philaret,[1] father of the first Romanov,[2] had been feeble in body or mind. The first marriage of the Tsar Alexis had done nothing to remove this hereditary weakness from the line, but in his son by Natalia Naryshkin it vanished entirely. Peter took after his mother, and was also said to have resembled Theodore, one of Natalia's brothers. Nervous activity and mental agility were characteristics of the Naryshkin family. In later years it produced a number of wits, and under Catherine II a Naryshkin became a very successful court entertainer.

[1] Philaret had been elevated to the metropolitanate of Rostov by the First Pretender and was Patriarch of Moscow from 1619 to 1633.

[2] Michael, 1613–45.

According to a foreign envoy[1] who was presented to Peter and Ivan in 1683, Peter at eleven was a lively, handsome boy. Whereas Tsar Ivan looked at the floor, with the Crown of Monomachus[2] well down over his eyes, and sat like a lifeless statue on his silver throne beneath the ikons, Peter, who sat next to him on a twin throne wearing a duplicate crown made on the occasion of the joint Tsarship, looked eagerly and confidently about him, and found it difficult to keep still. But traces of a serious nervous disorder due either to the memories of the bloody scenes of 1682, or to his all too frequent debaucheries, or to a combination of both, ruined his health, so that in later years Peter made a different impression. Very soon, by the time he was twenty, he began to suffer from a nervous twitch of the head; and when he was lost in thought, or during moments of emotional stress, his round, handsome face became distorted with convulsions. This, together with a birthmark on his right cheek, and a habit of gesticulating with his arms as he walked, made everybody notice him. In 1697, some Dutchmen who were waiting in a barber's shop in Saardam, and who had been obligingly informed of these characteristics by some of their compatriots who had been in Moscow, easily recognised the carpenter who had just come in to be shaved as the Tsar of Muscovy. At times Peter's face and eyes took on such a savage aspect that nervous people were likely to become demoralised in his presence.

Two of the best known portraits of Peter are by Kneller[3]

[1] Engelbert Kämpfer, a German traveller, who was acting secretary for the Swedish Envoy, Fabricius.

[2] The Crown, with the Sceptre and Orb, were originally presents from the Byzantine Emperor, Constantine Monomachus, to the Grand Duke Vladimir of Kiev. They were not used after 1682 because Peter's successors were not merely Tsars, but Emperors. The Crown and pectoral cross of Monomachus were the visible symbols of the relations of the Muscovite Tsars to the Emperors of Constantinople.

[3] See the frontispiece to this volume.

and the Dutch painter Charles Moor. The first portrait, commissioned by William III in 1698, shows a Peter with long-
flowing locks, wide-open, round eyes, and a happy expression. Although his brushwork is rather insipid, Kneller has
captured something of the elusive, cheerful, almost laughing
expression which is reminiscent of a portrait of Peter's grandmother Streshnev. The other portrait was painted by Charles
Moor in 1717, when Peter went to Paris to try to bring the
Northern War to a speedy conclusion, and to try to arrange a
marriage between his eight-year-old daughter, Elizabeth, and
the seven-year-old King of France, Louis XV. Parisian observers described Peter as an imperious-looking sovereign
who, in spite of his fierce and savage looks, could be most
amiable to those who were likely to be of use to him. Peter
had such a sense of his own importance that he paid no attention whatsoever to the elementary rules of behaviour, and
behaved on the Seine as he behaved on the Neva. Leaving his
Paris hotel one day, he took possession of a carriage that did
not belong to him and calmly drove away. But Charles Moor
saw him in a different light. The moustache looks as if it has
been stuck on and is thicker than that of Kneller's portrait; the
set of the lips and especially the expression of the eyes, suggest
sickness, sadness, and weariness, so the general impression is
that of a tired man, overpowered by the sense of his own
greatness, who desires nothing more than to be allowed to
rest; there is no sign either of his youthful self-confidence or
of the mature satisfaction that comes from a job well done.
It is worth remembering that this portrait was painted when
Peter stopped at Spa, on his way back from Paris, in order to be
treated for the malady which eight years later was to be the
cause of his death.

Peter was never more than a guest in his own home. His
adolescence and youth had been spent either in travelling or
working out of doors. Had Peter at the age of fifty paused

to look over his past, he would have seen that he had been constantly moving about from one place to another. During his reign he had travelled the length and breadth of Russia, from Astrakhan to Derbent, from Archangel to Azov, and from the Neva to the Pruth. As a result of this perpetual mobility, Peter became so restless that he was constitutionally incapable of staying in one place for any length of time, and was always looking for a change of scenery and for new impressions. The haste with which he did everything was now normal. He had such a long stride and used to walk so quickly that his companions had to run to keep up with him. He could not sit still for long, and at banquets he would jump out of his chair and run into the next room in order to stretch his legs.

When he was young his restlessness added to his enjoyment of dancing. Peter was an ever-welcome guest at the parties of noblemen, merchants, or artisans; here he danced a great deal and, though the only dancing lessons he had were 'practices' during evenings spent at the Lefort establishment, he danced well. If Peter was not sleeping, travelling, feasting, or inspecting, he was busy making something. Whenever he could he used his hands, which were never free from callouses. When he was young and still inexperienced he could never be shown over a factory or workshop without trying his hand at whatever work was in progress. He found it impossible to remain a mere spectator, particularly if he saw something new going on. His hands instinctively sought for tools; he wanted to work at everything himself. He eventually became so skilled and dexterous that he was able to master new and unfamiliar techniques in a very short time. This attention to technique, which had developed from an intelligent curiosity, became a habit, and Peter felt that he had to master every new technique before he had even considered whether or not it was of any use to him, so that over the years his technical knowledge became most impressive. Even during his first foreign tour, the German princesses who had talked with him came to the conclusion that he was a master-craftsman in fourteen different trades. He felt quite at home in any factory.

After his death, it was found that nearly every place in which he had lived for any length of time was full of the model boats, chairs, crockery, and snuff-boxes he had made himself. It is surprising that Peter ever found enough leisure to make so many knick-knacks. He was so proud of his own skill and dexterity as a craftsman that he believed himself to be a good surgeon and dentist as well. Those of his companions who fell ill and needed a doctor were filled with terror lest the Tsar hear of their illness and appear with his instruments to offer his services. It is said that after his death a sack-full of teeth was found — a memorial to his dental practice!

But his favourite occupation was shipbuilding, and no affairs of state could detain him if there was an opportunity to work on the wharves. When he lived in St. Petersburg in later years, he would spend at least one or two hours every day at the Admiralty. He was such a competent marine architect that his contemporaries said that he was the best shipwright in Russia, since he not only could design a ship, but knew every detail of its construction. Peter took a particular pride in this ability and he stinted neither money nor effort in extending and improving Russia's shipbuilding industry. The Moscow-born landlubber had developed into a real sailor to whom the smell of the sea was as necessary as water is to a fish. Peter always said that sea-air and constant hard physical labour helped to keep him in good health in spite of his over-indulgent way of living. It was probably because of this that he had an insatiable sailor's appetite. According to his contemporaries, he was always hungry and whenever he went visiting he was ready to sit down to a meal, whether he had already dined or not. He used to get up at five in the morning

D

and lunch between eleven and twelve, after which he retired for a short sleep. Even when he was a guest at a banquet he would observe this rule, and return after his sleep ready to start the meal all over again.

Because political quarrels during his childhood and youth had kept him from the strait-laced functions of the Court, Peter surrounded himself with a motley group of unconventional youngsters, the consequence of which was that when he grew up he could not tolerate ceremonial functions. Moreover he led an essentially active life, and his happiest moments were those spent using an axe, a saw, or a lathe, or 'wielding a correctional cudgel'. During solemn ceremonies of state this otherwise masterful and self-willed monarch would become awkward and confused; when Peter had to dress up in all his ceremonial finery and stand by the throne in the presence of the Court to listen to a newly-accredited ambassador's wordy peroration, he would breathe heavily, grow red in the face, and perspire freely. In his private life Peter lived simply and frugally, and the monarch who was considered by the rest of Europe to be the most powerful and the richest in the world used to walk about in worn-out shoes and in stockings that had often been darned by his wife or daughters. When he was at home he would hold a reception as soon as he had got out of bed, dressed in a very old dressing gown made from nankeen and would then put on a plain, thick, serge kaftan which he seldom changed. He rarely wore a hat in summer, and used to go out either in a gig drawn by two miserable horses, or in such a shabby cabriolet that a foreign observer declared that a Muscovite tradesman would have thought twice about using it. On special occasions, when for instance he was invited to a wedding, Peter would borrow a coach from his foppish Procurator-General, Yaguzhinsky.[1]

[1] For a brief account of his character and career see R. N. Bain, *The Pupils of Peter the Great*, Constable, 1897, pp. 40–1, 45, 75.

To the end of his life, Peter retained the habits of previous generations, disliked large, lofty rooms, and during his travels abroad avoided living in sumptuous palaces. Bred on the vast plains of Russia, Peter found in Germany that the narrow river valleys surrounded by mountains oppressed him. It seems strange that a man who grew up out of doors and was used to large spaces could not live in a room which had a high ceiling. When he found himself in such a room he would have a low canvas ceiling put in. It is probable that the over-crowded surroundings of his early childhood were respon-sible for this particular trait. At Preobrazhensky, where he grew up, he lived in a small, old, wooden house, which, according to a foreigner, was not worth more than one hun-dred thalers. At St. Petersburg he built himself some small summer and winter residences with tiny rooms. The same foreigner remarked that 'the Tsar cannot stomach a large dwelling'.

When Peter left the Kremlin he left behind him all the primitive grandeur of court life to which previous Tsars of Muscovy had been accustomed. The only other European court which was comparable to his was that of the miserly King Frederick William I. Peter often used to compare him-self with Frederick William, and say that the one cared as little for luxury and extravagance as the other. At Peter's court there were no chamberlains, no seneschals, and no ex-pensive plate. The pre-Petrine court cost hundreds of thou-sands of roubles a year to maintain, while Peter's establish-ment cost only sixty thousand a year. Peter had ten or twelve personal attendants, young courtiers of obscure origin who were known as 'denshchiki'. Moreover Peter disliked fine liveries and expensive brocades. During the last years of his reign, he established for his second wife[1] a large and brilliant court which could compare with the splendour of any Ger-

[1] Catherine, whom Peter married in November 1707.

man prince's court. Though Peter himself could have dispensed with the glitter, he wanted his second wife to be surrounded by it, probably in order to try to make the courtiers
forget her humble origin.

Peter was equally free and easy in his relationship to people;
but his social manners were a mixture of the habits of a
powerful aristocrat of a previous generation and those of an
artisan. Whenever he went visiting he would sit down in the
first vacant seat; if he was hot he would take off his kaftan in
front of everybody. When he was invited to act as Marshal of
Ceremonies at a wedding he would fulfil his obligations
punctiliously and then, having put his Marshal's rod of office
away in a corner, would move towards the buffet, take a hot
roast of meat in his hands, and start eating. It was this habit
of dispensing with knives and forks at table that had so
shocked the princesses at Koppenburg. He had no manners
whatsoever and did not consider them necessary.

At the winter receptions at St. Petersburg which were attended by the fashionable society of the town, or at gatherings
held in the house of some dignitary, the Tsar had no hesitation
in sitting down to play chess with simple seamen, with whom
he would drink beer and smoke a long Dutch pipe; he would
quite ignore the ladies who were dancing in the same room.
Peter spent his evenings either visiting friends or entertaining
himself, and liked being surrounded by a gay crowd. At
these occasions he was merry, sociable, and talkative, and enjoyed listening to the unconstrained chatter that went on
around him as he walked up and down drinking Hungarian
wine. He did not like anything to break up these gatherings,
and would not tolerate malicious gossip, caustic remarks, or
brawling. An offender was 'sconced'; he had to swallow at a
draught either three beakers of wine or an 'eagle' (a large
ladleful) so that 'he would learn neither to lie nor to provoke'.
This sort of punishment was generally sufficient to stop any

tactless talk, though occasionally Peter's free and easy manner would encourage somebody to blurt out exactly what he was thinking. It so happened that Peter was very fond of a naval lieutenant called Mishukov, and thought so highly of him as a naval officer that he became the first Russian to be given command of a frigate. Once at a banquet at Cronstadt (this happened before the affair of the Tsarevitch Alexis),[1] Mishukov, who was sitting next to the Tsar, and was rather drunk, suddenly became thoughtful and then burst into tears. This surprised the Tsar who asked him what was the matter. Mishukov explained quite frankly, and loudly enough for everybody to hear. 'It's like this,' he said, 'this place, the new capital, the Baltic fleet, all the Russian sailors, and finally myself, Lieutenant Mishukov, Commander of a Frigate, all know how much we owe to your favour, and realise that this is all your work. When I thought about all this I realised that you are not getting any younger, and so I burst into tears.' And then Mishukov added, 'and who is there to take your place?'

'What do you mean?' Peter asked, 'I've got a Tsarevitch, an heir.'

'Oh, yes,' replied Mishukov, 'but he is an idiot and will undo all your work.'

Peter was rather pleased with the bitter honesty of the sailor's speech, but, since it was most inopportune and indiscreet of Mishukov to have mentioned this at a banquet, a reproof was clearly necessary. Peter laughed and hit him over the head. 'You are a fool,' he said, 'you cannot say these things in public.'

Peter was always honest and direct in his dealings with people, and expected them to be honest and frank with him

[1] There is no discussion of Alexis's conflict with his father in Klyuchevsky. For a brief account see Florinsky, *Russia*, Macmillan, New York, 1953, Vol. I, pp. 330-3.

and he disliked subterfuge of any kind. The following anecdote is told by Nepluev in his memoirs. On his return from studying in Venice, Nepluev was examined by the Tsar himself and appointed Superintendent of the St. Petersburg Docks, a post which brought him into almost daily contact with the Tsar. Nepluev was advised to be efficient, but, above all, always to tell the Tsar the truth. During his name-day celebrations, Nepluev got very drunk and the next morning overslept, so that he arrived at the Docks after the Tsar. At first the frightened Superintendent wanted to go home and pretend that he was ill, but on thinking it over decided that he would go and tell the truth.

'I am already here,' said Peter.

'It is my fault, your Majesty,' replied Nepluev, 'I stayed up too late last night, making merry.' Nepluev was shaking as Peter put his hand on his shoulder and said, 'Thank you for telling me the truth; God will forgive you; there is nobody who has not sinned. And now let us go and visit a woman in childbed.' So the Tsar and Nepluev went to visit the carpenter's wife who was expecting a baby. Peter gave the woman five 'grivni', kissed her, and told Nepluev to do the same. But Nepluev only gave the woman one 'grivni'. Peter laughed, and said 'Hey! I see that you do not like to give freely.'

'I have not got much to give, Sire,' replied Nepluev, 'I am a poor courtier, with a wife and children to support, and if it were not for the salary you pay me we would not be able to live.' As soon as Peter heard this he asked Nepluev how many serfs he owned and where his estate was. The carpenter brought out two glasses of vodka on a wooden tray for his guests; Peter drank his and ate a piece of carrot pie; Nepluev did not drink and refused the carrot pie. Peter said to him, 'Come on man, drink up, or you will offend our host.' Then breaking off a piece of pie, Peter added, 'Now eat up, this is not Italian, but good Russian food.' Peter was a kind man but a ruthless Tsar; and he drove himself as hard as others. As has been shown, the surroundings in which he grew up were hardly likely to encourage in him any care for people's feelings or circumstances. His natural intelligence, his age, and the position he occupied helped to hide these shortcomings, but even so they were sometimes still very much in evidence. When Peter's favourite, Alexander Menshikov, was young he received the full force of the Tsar's fist in his oblong face more than once. A characteristic incident occurred at a banquet at which a boring foreign artillery officer was boasting to Peter about his knowledge. Peter could not get a word in, and eventually lost patience. He spat in the officer's face, and then turned his back on him. Not unnaturally, behaviour of this sort made Peter a difficult man to deal with. But he became quite impossible when he had one of the attacks of nerves which usually ended with convulsions. As soon as his attendants saw the symptoms of such an attack they sent for Catherine, who made the Tsar lie down, put his head in her lap, and then gently stroked his forehead. Peter soon fell asleep, and as long as Catherine held his head in her hands everybody remained silent. After two hours Peter would wake up quite refreshed, and would behave as if nothing had happened. But not even the excuse of such attacks can justify the failure of this usually frank and outspoken monarch to take other people's feelings into consideration. This lack of consideration often spoiled the easy, unconstrained atmosphere that he enjoyed.

It is true that Peter liked to enjoy himself and make jokes, but it is also true that these jokes often went too far and were either very cruel or just vulgar. During summer feast-days Peter liked to entertain the aristocracy in a grove of oaks which he had planted himself in front of his Summer Palace. Here the guests sat on wooden benches at little wooden tables, while Peter entertained them like a good host, discussing politics with the officials and church matters with the clergy. Unfortunately Peter's cream choked the cat. He himself was used to drinking vodka neat, and expected his guests, including the ladies, to do the same. Sometimes guards appeared carrying buckets of corn brandy[1] which could be smelt all through the garden, and the sentries were ordered not to let any of the guests leave. It is hardly surprising that the guests were appalled, especially as the guard, all specially appointed, received orders that the guests were to be given corn brandy with which to drink the Tsar's health. Happy were they who managed to slip out of the garden! Only the church dignitaries did not try to avoid the beverage, and they sat at their tables, smelling of onions and radishes, getting progressively drunker. Indeed, visiting foreigners noticed that at these gatherings it was always the clergy who were the drunkest. A Protestant preacher was dumbfounded by this crude and public behaviour. A characteristic incident occurred at the wedding of the elderly widower, Prince U. U. Trubetskoi, to the twenty-year-old Princess Golovin in 1721. Glasses of jelly were served on a large tray at the wedding feast, and Peter, knowing that the bride's father was particularly fond of jelly, made him open his mouth and stuffed jelly after jelly into it; when Prince Golovin tried to close his mouth, Peter wrenched it open again with his own hands. Meanwhile at another table, the host's other daughter, the fashionable and wealthy Princess Cherkasky, was standing by her brother's chair. At a sign from the Empress, who was sitting at the same table, Princess Cherkasky began to tickle her well-brought up brother in the ribs; he reacted like a calf whose throat is being cut, while the high society of St. Petersburg laughed merrily.

Thus Peter's sense of humour turned his entertainments

[1] A rough drink used mainly by peasants.

into unpleasant affairs. Towards the end of the Northern War an important calendar of holidays was compiled, including celebrations of victories, to which, after 1721, the Peace of Nystadt was added. Above all, Peter enjoyed the launching of a new ship, when he behaved as if a new baby had been born. Eighteenth-century Europe drank heavily, and the Russian aristocracy were no different. Generally parsimonious, Peter would spend a large sum of money on alcohol to celebrate the launching of a new ship. Parties on board ship were attended by the capital's high society. These parties inevitably ended with General-Admiral Apraxin bursting into tears and moaning that he was an old, lonely, man, a waif with neither mother nor father, and with the Minister for War, the brilliant Prince Menshikov, dead drunk under a table, whereupon his frightened wife, Princess Dasha, and the other ladies, had to revive him with massage and cold water. But not all parties ended as simply as this. Sometimes Peter would lose his temper, and would withdraw extremely upset to the ladies' half of the ship. Whenever this happened he had guards posted at the gangways with instructions that nobody was to leave until he had returned. Until Catherine had succeeded in calming him, and he had had a nap, the guests remained in their places drinking and getting bored. The Peace of Nystadt was celebrated by a masquerade which lasted for seven days. Peter was beside himself with joy at the end of the war, and, forgetting his age and his ailments, sang songs and danced on the tables. This celebration took place in the Senate. In the middle of the banquet Peter got up, ordered the guests to await his return, and went to sleep on his yacht which was anchored on the Neva. The abundance of wine and the perpetual noise at these interminable festivities did not prevent the guests from getting bored and tired of staying indefinitely in one place in their compulsory fancy dresses. A refusal to wear fancy dress would have entailed a fifty rouble fine. For a whole week thousands of masked people walked, danced, drank, and bustled each other, so that when finally the enforced gaieties ended the participants were all equally relieved.

Though these official functions were oppressive and boorish, there were others which were worse and were openly indecent. It is difficult to know what caused such behaviour. Was it a search for vulgar relaxation after a hard day's work or was it merely lack of thought? Peter tried to give his debaucheries an official form in order to turn them into permanent institutions. In this way the 'Most Drunken Synod of Fools and Jesters' was created. Meetings were held under the presidency of a chief buffoon called the 'Prince-Pope', or the 'Noisiest, all-jesting Patriarch of all Moscow, Kokua and Yaüza'. There was a college of twelve cardinals, all tipplers and gluttons, who were attended by a large suite of bishops, archimandrites, and other dignitaries, whose coarse and obscene nicknames are too disgusting to print. Peter himself was a deacon of this Order, for which he drew up, with the same legislative skill that he expended on his laws, a Charter that minutely defined the method of electing and installing the 'Prince-Pope' and the ritual required for the consecration of the rest of this hierarchy of drunkards. The first commandment was that members were to get drunk every day, and might never go sober to bed. The Synod's most important tasks were to offer excessive libations to the glory of Bacchus, and to lay down a suitable procedure to ensure that 'Bacchus be worshipped with strong and honourable drinking and receive his just dues'. The Charter also prescribed the vestments to be worn, drew up a Psalter and Liturgy, and even created an 'All-jesting Mother Superior' with 'Lady Abbots'. It even went so far as to imitate the Catechism, and decreed that, just as a baptismal candidate was asked 'Do you believe?', so a candidate for this institution was to be asked 'Do you drink?' Those who lapsed into sobriety after initiation were to be debarred from all the inns of the Empire, and a heretic was to be banned from the society in perpetuity. In short, this was a most indecent parody of religious rites and ceremonial. The pious believed that its members' souls were damned eternally, and that those who resisted this apostasy would become martyrs. Over the Christmas holidays, about two hundred men would descend on Moscow or St. Petersburg in sleighs, and spend a night 'celebrating'. The procession was led by the mock Patriarch wearing his regalia and carrying his mitre, followed by a retinue who jigged along in their overcrowded sleighs, singing and whistling. Those residents who were honoured by a visit had to entertain the revellers at their own expense, and, as an eye-witness said, 'they drank an awful lot.' The first week of Lent was celebrated in a similar fashion, with a procession of penitents organised by the Prince-Pope and his Council for the edification of the faithful. The revellers, wearing their coats inside out, either rode on the backs of asses and bullocks, or sat in sleighs drawn by swine, goats, or bears. In 1699, at Shrovetide, after a particularly sumptuous Court banquet, the Tsar organised a service in honour of Bacchus. The Patriarch, Prince-Pope Nikita Zotov, the Tsar's old tutor, drank everyone's health, and then blessed the kneeling guests by making the sign of the cross over them with two long pipes, in the same way that a bishop would bless his congregation with a two- or three-branched candelabra. Finally, mitre in hand, Zotov began to dance. The only guest who could stand this ridiculous display no longer, and left, was a foreign ambassador. Generally most foreigners took the view that such behaviour served a political or even educational purpose, and that it was directed against the Church and its hierarchy, as well as against drunkenness. The Tsar wanted at one and the same time to ridicule an institution which he wished to discredit, and to divert his subjects while trying to make them contemptuous of bigotry and disgusted with debauchery. It is difficult to know how much truth there is in this view, particularly since it is more an attempt to justify than a genuine explanation.

Peter not only ridiculed the Church hierarchy and ceremonial, but also made a mockery of his own personal power by appointing Prince Theodore Romodanovsky King-Emperor, and calling him 'your Imperial Illustrious Majesty', while Peter called himself 'your bondsman and eternal slave Peter', or simply 'Petrushka Alexeev'. Surely his behaviour is the result of a peculiar sense of humour rather than of a particular personal bias. Alexis displayed the same type of humour, only with the difference that he himself did not like being made a figure of fun. Peter and his friends were more intent on playing the fool than in causing trouble. They made fun of everything, ignoring tradition, popular feeling, and their own self-respect, in the same way that children imitate the words, actions, and facial expressions of adults, without meaning either to criticise or to insult them. They did not mock at the Church as an institution, but merely showed their resentment of a class which contained so many worthless people. It is not surprising that no attention was paid either to the effect such orgies had on the people, or to the consequences, since Peter was always complaining that while his father had only one damned beard[1] to deal with, he had a thousand, though they were more likely to prove unpleasant than actually dangerous. Moreover, the accusation levelled against Adrian, the last Patriarch to hold office, that he did nothing but eat and drink without ever denouncing sin, could also be levelled against the rest of the ecclesiastical dignitaries. But, more serious than this, the people were already murmuring that the Tsar was Anti-Christ. The administrative classes, who were

[1] An allusion to the Patriarch Nikon.

seriously out of touch with public opinion, hoped that the use of the knout and the torture chamber would stamp out the anti-Christ legend. This barbarous usage though hard to justify, was, after all, in harmony with contemporary custom. It has always been a characteristically Russian habit to make fun of the Church and to give an anti-religious twist to any buffoonery. Equally familiar is the part played by Church ritual and the clergy in popular legend. The clergy had only themselves to blame for their debasement, because, while they expected the laity to adhere strictly to the precepts of the Church, they notably failed to do so themselves.

Peter shared the popular attitude to religion; he deplored the hypocrisy of the Russian clergy and the dissension within the Church. Yet, in spite of this, Peter was himself quite religious, knew the Liturgy by heart, and enjoyed singing in the choir. Nonetheless, in 1721, during the festivities celebrating the Peace of Nystadt, he organised a licentious travesty of the marriage service by making the Prince-Pope, old Buturlin, marry Zotov's widow in the Troïtsa Monastery. The ceremony was witnessed by rather merry and extremely noisy courtiers. What can there be political about a wooden receptacle for vodka which reminded the drunken brotherhood of the Holy Bible? This was no subtle political movement directed against the Church, although it emphasised what was common knowledge, that the authority of the Church was dwindling; it was simply the folly of a group of aristocratic revellers. Because of the monastic tendency of the times and the debasement of the White Clergy,[1] the priests substituted the government of the individual conscience for their proper concern with public morality.

Peter had yet another side to his character; he spent time and money generously in obtaining paintings and statues from Italy and Germany which formed the foundations for

[1] i.e., Secular Clergy.

the Hermitage Collection at St. Petersburg. The many pleasure palaces which he had built round his new capital indicate
his taste in architecture. At enormous cost he hired the best
European architects, like Leblond[1] ('my wizard' as Peter
called him) who was tempted to leave the French Court by
an immense fee. Leblond built the 'Mon Plaisir' pavilion at
Peterhof, which so excited visitors with its magnificent
carved cabinets, its view over the sea, and its shaded gardens.

Peter disliked the classical style, and liked his pictures to be
bright and cheerful, so that the pavilion at Peterhof was hung
with excellent Flemish landscapes and seascapes. Not even
manual labour made Peter indifferent to scenery, and he was
very partial to seascapes. He spent large fortunes in embel-
lishing his suburban residences with artificial terraces, cas-
cades, cunning fountains, and flower-beds. But even though
Peter's artistic taste was strongly developed, it was as one-
sided as his way of life. His habit of going to the heart of the
matter and concerning himself with technical details had
developed in him a keen eye and a strong feeling for perspective, form, and symmetry. He showed marked aptitude
for the plastic arts, and delighted in complicated building
plans; but here his artistic appreciation stopped. He himself
confessed that he did not like music, and found even dance
music unpleasant.

Occasionally serious discussions were held at the Drunken
Synod's uproarious meetings. Peter's discussions of policy
with his collaborators were held with greater frequency as
the war spread and his own reforms multiplied. These discussions are interesting not only for the ideas that were put
forward, and the opportunity they give us to get a closer look
at these men, and their motives and attitudes, but also because
they go a long way to mitigate the bad impression made by

[1] For Leblond's contributions to the architecture of Petersburg, see Christopher Marsden, *Palmyra of the North*, Faber & Faber, 1942, pp. 60-7.

the Drunken Synod on posterity. Through the smoke and above the clinking of tankards, political ideas were thrashed out; and this makes those statesmen look rather better. Once, in 1722, Peter was talking to a group of foreigners, and, under the influence of large quantities of Hungarian wine, told them about the difficulties he had met during the early part of his reign. Simultaneously, he said, he had had to create a regular army and navy, educate his idle, ignorant, subjects, and teach them to be courageous, loyal, and honest; all this had been incredibly difficult, but, thank God, it was all in the past and now he could take life more calmly. Peter went on to say that, like all rulers, he must nonetheless still strive to know his subjects better. It seems likely that Peter had had these ideas for a long time, and had given them a great deal of thought. Moreover it is likely that he himself started the legend about his creative activities. If contemporary evidence is to be trusted, this legend was crystallised in a cartoon which showed a sculptor working at the half-finished form of a human figure carved out of a rough block of marble. This signified that after the end of the war with Sweden, Peter and his collaborators realised that there was still a great deal to do, although as a result of all their efforts, a war had been won and many reforms enacted.

In his *History of Russia*, Tatishchev[1] records the following dinner-table conversation, which he probably heard from a witness, and which took place in 1717, when there was hope that the war with Sweden was in its last phase. At a banquet with some important officials, Peter suddenly began to talk about his father, his achievements in Poland, and the difficulties Alexis had had with the Patriarch Nikon. When Peter

[1] Vasili Tatishchev (1686–1750) has been called 'The Father of Modern Russian Historiography'. For a discussion of his attitude to history see *An Outline of Modern Russian Historiography*, Anatole G. Mazour, D. Van Nostrand Co. Inc., 1939. Tatishchev had also served under Peter in the campaigns of Narva, Poltava, and the Pruth.

had finished, Mussin-Pushkin began to praise Peter's achievements and belittle Alexis's achievements, saying that in reality
they were due to Morozov and other ministers, and that
everything had depended on the ministers. In fact, he said, the
Tsar was only as good as his ministers were. This speech irritated Peter, who replied 'Your disparagement of my father's
achievements, and your praise of mine are more than I can
listen to.' Peter then went over to Prince Jacob Dolgoruky,
who was never afraid of arguing with him in the Senate, and
said 'You criticise me more than anybody else, and plague me
with your arguments until I sometimes feel I could lose my
temper with you. But I know that you are sincerely devoted
to me and to the State, and that you always speak the truth,
for which I am deeply grateful. Now tell me how you estimate my father's achievements, and what you think of mine.
I know you will tell me the truth.' Dolgoruky replied 'Pray
be seated Sire, while I think for a moment.' Peter sat down
near him while Dolgoruky, as was his habit, stroked his long
moustache. After a time Dolgoruky replied as follows: 'It is
impossible to give a short answer to your question, since you
and your father were preoccupied with different matters. A
Tsar has three main duties to perform. The most important
of these is the administration of the country and the dispensa-
tion of justice. Your father had enough time to attend to this,
while you have had none, which is why your father accomplished more than you. It is possible that when you do give
some thought to this matter — and it is time you did — you
will do more than your father. A Tsar's second duty is the
organisation of the army. Here again your father is to be
praised, because he laid the foundations of a regular army,
thereby showing you the way. Unfortunately certain misguided men undid all his work, so that you had to start all
over again, and I must admit that you have done very well.
Even so, I still do not know which of you has done better;

we will only know that when the war is over. And finally we come to a Tsar's third duty which is building a fleet, making treaties, and determining our relationship with foreign countries. Here, and I hope you will agree with me, you have served the country well and have achieved more than your father. For this you deserve much praise. Somebody to-night said that a Tsar's work depends on his ministers. I disagree and think the opposite, since a wise monarch will choose wise counsellors and will know their worth. Therefore a wise monarch will not tolerate stupid counsellors because he will know their quality and be able to distinguish good advice from bad.' Peter, who had been listening patiently to Dolgoruky, embraced him and said, 'Faithful, honest friend, you have been true to me in little things, I will now give you something important to do.' Tatishchev finishes his story by adding that Menshikov and others were offended, and did everything in their power to discredit Dolgoruky in Peter's eyes, but were unable to do so.

Peter worked hard, both mentally and physically, all his life; he was always ready to adopt new ideas, was extremely observant, and became a highly skilled craftsman. But he had no time for complicated reasoning, and found it easier to grasp the details of a plan than to view it as a whole, so that he was better at devising ways and means of implementing it than at seeing its consequences. He was more a man of action than a thinker, which not unnaturally heavily influenced his way of life and his political programme. His early childhood was spent in the sort of company which was least likely to turn him into a responsible and politically minded individual. The court — full of nonentities — and the royal family of Alexis's day were rotten with enmity and petty intrigue. Court intrigues and palace revolutions were Peter's first introduction to politics. Driven from court by Sophia's malice, he was completely cut off from the political ideas of the courtiers.

E

This isolation was in itself no loss. The confused rubbish which served seventeenth century Russian courtiers for a political system consisted partly of custom and ceremony inherited from previous generations, and partly of those political lies and equivocations which prevented the first Tsars of the new dynasty from understanding their true position in the country. It was Peter's misfortune that he had no coherent political understanding, but only a vague, confused, notion that he had unlimited power and that somehow this was menaced. For a long time nothing was done to make good this deficiency. His early passion for manual labour and craftsmanship left him no time for meditation, and distracted his attention from those subjects which form the basis of a political education.

As a ruler, Peter knew neither moral nor political restraints, and lacked the most elementary political and social principles. His lack of judgement and his personal instability, combined with great talent and wide technical skill, astonished all foreigners who met Peter when he was twenty-five; their verdict was that nature had intended him to be a good carpenter, not a great sovereign. In spite of the facts, that Peter's early moral guidance had been bad, that he had ruined his health, that his manners and way of life were uncouth, and that he had been unbalanced by the terrible experiences of his childhood, he remained sensitive, receptive, and extremely energetic. These qualities went a long way to mitigate the faults which were due to his environment and way of life. As early as 1698 the English Bishop Burnet had remarked that Peter was doing his best to overcome his passion for wine. However little notice Peter took of the political and social customs of the West, he was sensible enough to realise that it was not the knout and the torture chamber which had given the Western peoples their character and power. The bitter experience of the first Azov campaign,

and the struggles around Narva and the Pruth, showed Peter
the extent to which he was politically unprepared. He realised
that, if he was to effect the improvement he wanted, he must
examine more seriously his ideas of state and people, of law
and duty, of monarchy and the duties of the monarch.
He sacrificed everything to his sense of duty, but never succeeded in changing his personal habits. While the events of
1682 cut him off from the political affectations of the Kremlin, he never managed to rid himself of the biggest fault of
Muscovite politics — their arbitrariness.

To the end of his life he never understood the logic of
history or the nature of the life of his people. Yet he can
hardly be blamed for this. Leibnitz, a clever politician and
one of Peter's correspondents, could not understand it either.
Leibnitz maintained that the more ignorant a country, the
easier it would be to educate it, and he persuaded Peter that
this applied to Russia. The introduction of all Peter's reforms
was accompanied by force; he thought that only force could
bind together a nation lacking in cohesion, and he believed
that with force he could completely transform the traditional
way of life of his people. His devotion to his people led him
to overstrain their resources and waste their lives recklessly.
He himself was honest and sincere, and did not spare himself;
he was also just and kind to others. But, owing to his
interests, he was better with inanimate objects than with
people, whom he treated as if they were merely tools. He
quickly found out who was useful, but could neither learn
not to overtax people nor put himself in another's place. In
this respect he differed greatly from his father. Peter knew
how to manage people, but either could not or would not
try to understand them. These characteristics affected his
relations with his own family. He may have had a vast
knowledge of his own country, but he hardly knew his own
family and home, where he was never more than a guest.

He never really lived with his first wife, and he grumbled about his second; he never came to terms with his son, Alexis, the Tsarevitch. Moreover Peter did nothing to preserve Alexis from the evil influences which were finally responsible for his destruction and endangered the very existence of the Romanov dynasty.

It is obvious, then, that Peter differed greatly from his predecessors, in spite of a certain family similarity. He was a great statesman who knew where the sources of Russia's wealth lay and understood her economic interests. His predecessors of both dynasties were also statesmen, but they were sedentary men who preferred to benefit from the work of others, while Peter was an active, self-taught master craftsman, an artisan-Tsar.

Chapter Three

★

WE MUST NOW face certain problems which arise at this stage in the history of Peter the Great. There is a tendency to think that Peter was born with his own private programme of reforms — all his own work! — which were the product of his own creative genius, and that the work of his immediate predecessors was only a preparation for reform which provided Peter with some intellectual stimulus but neither with the actual plans nor with the means to implement them. In reviewing the work of his predecessors I showed conclusively that the whole Petrine programme had been drawn up in outline by the statesmen of the seventeenth century. A distinction must be made between the problems with which Peter was confronted and the reforms and other means which he adopted for dealing with them. The problems arose from the needs of state and people, and seventeenth-century statesmen had recognised that they did. But the Petrine reforms were influenced by contemporary conditions, which had nothing in common with the conditions of the previous era. These conditions were partly the result of Peter's own actions, and partly the unexpected result of other factors. Peter's programme of reforms gained nothing from traditional opinions; it was the result of pressing needs of state which were evident to all.

War was the most important circumstance of his reign. Peter was rarely at peace; he was at war with somebody the whole time, now with his sister, now with Turkey, then with Sweden, even with Persia. Of the thirty-five years of his reign, beginning with autumn 1689 when the regency of Sophia came to an end, only one year, 1724, was completely peaceful; in all the rest it is possible to find only thirteen months of peace. Moreover Peter's wars with his principal enemies, Turkey and Sweden, were wars of coalition or alliance, and in this they differed from the wars of his predecessors. In order to understand the significance of this it is necessary to look at seventeenth-century Muscovy.

To secure the safety of the country Peter had to solve two inherited problems. First, since at least half the Russian people lived outside the political boundaries of his state, he had to find a way of uniting them. Second, he had to modify those of the existing frontiers, particularly in the south and in the west, which were especially vulnerable to attack. Before Peter, little headway had been made with these problems. The territorial problem had led to a clash in pre-Petrine days between Muscovy and its two enemies, Sweden, from whom it was necessary to wrest the eastern shores of the Baltic Sea, and the Crimean Tartars, that is to say, Turkey. Similarly, the problem of unification had resulted in a series of desperate wars with yet a third enemy and near neighbour, Poland. Well before Peter, the Muscovite administration had realised that it was impossible to solve both problems at the same time. Tsar Alexis's government had seen that a war on three fronts, against Poland, Sweden, and Turkey simultaneously, was out of the question. Hence the statesmen of the seventeenth century had to discriminate between their enemies, and make peace, or at least maintain friendly relations, with one or other of them, if they were to achieve anything against the third. Because it was necessary to make a choice there was a sudden break in the continuity of Muscovy's foreign policy under Alexis. The new policy was primarily aimed at Russia's closest western neighbours, the Poles, whom the

Russians had been fighting for centuries. In 1667 the Truce of Andrusovo[1] brought a long interruption to the fighting. A weak Poland was no longer considered dangerous; she could be left in peace for a while, and it was even possible to maintain friendly relations with her (as Ordin-Nashchokin[2] had foretold). In 1686 the Treaty of Moscow converted the truce into a 'permanent peace', and the two countries even joined together in an offensive alliance, both joining the Austro-Venetian 'Holy League' against the Turks. Thus even before Peter, the plan of political and national unification of all Russia had been abandoned for an indefinite period. If friendly relations with Poland were to be maintained, it was impossible to think about adding South-West Russia to Greater Russia.

At the beginning of his reign Peter accepted the international position he had inherited. He also concentrated all his strength in the south, that is to say, he gave priority to the protection and alteration of the southern frontiers. To do this, it was necessary to secure and fortify the coast lines of the Black Sea and the Sea of Azov. It was on the Sea of Azov that the first Russian fleet appeared, and it was here that ports and dockyards were built. Later, though, the Western European situation changed. Since the Thirty Years' War Sweden had been dominant in Central and Northern Europe. Those countries adjoining the Baltic Sea, Denmark, Poland, and Muscovy, found the situation oppressive. Sweden had in-

[1] The Truce of Andrusovo (1667) was to run for thirteen and a half years. Its terms provided for the partition of the Ukraine, Russia retaining that part which was on the left bank of the Dnieper, as well as Kiev, which, however, was to be evacuated after two years (a provision which was not fulfilled). See M. Hrushevsky, *A History of Ukraine*, New Haven, 1941.

[2] Ordin-Nashchokin was another of Tsar Alexis's intimate friends who was eager to learn from Western Europe. For a time he had been Minister for Foreign Affairs, and was responsible for the conclusion of the Truce of Andrusovo. R. N. Bain calls him Russia's first diplomatist and statesman in the modern sense of the term. See R. N. Bain, *The Pupils of Peter the Great*, Constable, 1897, p. 23.

curred Denmark's enmity by protecting her implacable enemy, the Duke of Schleswig-Holstein, and had taken Livonia and Esthonia — a large territory — away from Poland in the seventeenth century. Both these countries resented being despoiled by Sweden, and sought a third ally in Muscovy, which, by the peace of Kardis in 1661, had had to relinquish Ingria and Karelia. Hence Peter turned his attention from the Black Sea and the Sea of Azov to the Baltic, where he concentrated his forces in readiness for war. The new capital was in consequence built at St. Petersburg instead of at Azov or Taganrog. In these circumstances the decision to rectify the southern frontiers was reversed in favour of expansion in the north-west, where Peter realised the aims of his ancestors. He did not extend the scope of their foreign policy, but, on the contrary, curtailed it, thereby limiting his own work. It was because of the wars of coalition against Sweden and Turkey that Muscovy first became a European power and became involved in the affairs of Western Europe.

At that time there were three aggressive powers in Europe: France in the West, Sweden in the North, and Turkey in the South. The rest of Europe had formed a series of alliances against these three. England, Holland, Spain, Austria, and the German Empire were allied against France. Turkey's enemies were Austria, Venice, and Poland. Sweden was opposed by Poland, Denmark, and Prussia (then the Electorate of Brandenburg). Since no attempt was made to fuse the different coalitions, the result was a further complication of the European situation. By the Treaty of Moscow of 1686, Muscovy joined Poland in the alliance against Turkey. The interests of the allies were divided; thus Austria, expecting to be heavily committed in the War of the Spanish Succession, lost no time in disembarrassing herself in the south-west by signing the advantageous Treaty of Karlowitz in 1699. Meanwhile, in order to safeguard the Austrian frontier from the

Turkish Tartars, she did everything possible to persuade Peter to continue the war alone. Peter's friend Augustus II, the new King of Poland, was finding his throne most uncomfortable. While Ukraintsev,[1] the Muscovite ambassador, was at Constantinople in 1700 trying to negotiate for peace, the Polish ambassador was trying to obstruct him, and promising to dethrone the Tsar's friend, the King of Poland.

The alliance came to an end in 1699 with the Treaty of Karlowitz, whose terms were advantageous to the Venetians and the Austrians. The Venetians took the Morea away from Turkey. The Austrians acquired Transylvania, Turkish Hungary, and Slavonia, thereby closing the Turks' mouth, as Voznitsyn, the Muscovite ambassador, put it. The Poles were given a devastated Podolia, and Muscovy acquired Azov and the small new towns which had lately sprung up round the coast. Peter found himself in an awkward situation. His work at Voronezh had been completely destroyed; the fleet which had cost so much in money and effort, and which had been intended for the Black Sea, was left to rot in the ports of Azov. He had been unable to acquire Kertch, and was not firmly established in the Crimea. The canal which was to have linked the Volga with the Don, and which had been started by thousands of workmen, was abandoned; the newly awakened aspirations of the Balkan Christians were ignored; the security of Southern Russia, which was menaced by the Turks, was neglected. Peter had suddenly to change fronts, and move from the south to the Baltic, where a coalition against Sweden had been formed. The latest combination of events in Europe threw him, like a skittle in a game of bowls, from the mouth of the Don to Narva and the Neva, where absolutely nothing had been organised. Peter, who had spent

[1] For details of Russian diplomatic representation at Constantinople, see B. H. Sumner, *Peter the Great and the Ottoman Empire*, Blackwell, Oxford, 1949, pp. 59–75.

so many years in training to be a Black Sea sailor, who had gained a great deal of experience at Periaslav, on the White Sea, in Holland, and in England, had now to fight a protracted land war in order to open the way to a strange sea.

Seldom even in Russia has the outbreak of war been so unexpected; seldom has there been less planning and preparation. Who were Peter's allies at the outbreak of the Northern War? First of all there was Augustus II, King of Poland, though not in his capacity as King of Poland. Augustus was an Elector of the German Empire, a Saxon adventurer who somehow managed to occupy the throne of Poland (where nearly half the country wanted to get rid of him). Then there was Denmark, which had been unable to muster enough soldiers to protect her capital from 15,000 Swedes arriving unexpectedly by sea. A few days after their descent, Denmark shamefully withdrew from the coalition and made peace at Travendal. The guiding spirit behind the alliance had been Patkul,[1] a Livonian adventurer who intended to make Peter, the only serious participant in this comic opera coalition, the dupe of a vulgar farce, and who was to receive the swamps of Ingria and Karelia as a reward for future victories.

At the beginning the war limped along after a fashion. The immediate aims were decided, but no plans were made to implement them. Five months before the outbreak of war Peter had managed to buy some cannon from the Swedes which he intended to use on them at the beginning of the war. His army moved on Narva. It consisted of thirty-five thousand men, most of them conscripts commanded by bad officers and foreign generals who inspired no confidence. There were no strategic highways, and it was impossible to transport enough food and ammunition along roads already sodden from the autumn rains. A fortress was bombarded,

[1] His plan for the formation of an alliance against Sweden is discussed in E. Schuyler, *Peter the Great,* London, 1884, Vol. I, pp. 442–50.

but the artillery was worthless and, anyhow, the bombard-
ment had to be called off because of the shortage of powder.
An eye-witness remarked that the besiegers circled the fortress
like cats around a plate of hot gruel, but took no steps to prevent Charles XII from advancing. Under cover of a violent
November snowstorm Charles stealthily approached the
Russian camp where, with a brigade of eight thousand
Swedes, he dispersed the whole Russian infantry. But the
extent of the Swedish victory was in doubt. The Swedes
were frightened lest the Russian cavalry, made up of noblemen and Sheremetiev's Cossacks, attack their rear; but, as
Charles remarked, they were kind enough to turn tail and
swim across the River Narva where thousands of horses
drowned. The victor was so afraid of the conquered that he
made special provision to help them in their flight across the
river: during the night he hurriedly had a new bridge built to
replace the old one which had collapsed under the weight of
those who had already fled.

Peter had left the camp on the eve of the battle so as not to
embarrass the commander-in-chief, a foreigner.[1] In truth, the
commander-in-chief was not at all embarrassed; he was the
first to give himself up to the enemy, and took with him
several other foreign officers who had been frightened by
their infuriated Russian troops. A medallion was subsequently circulated through Europe which depicted Peter in flight
from Narva, throwing his épée away, his hat falling off his
head, and wiping his tears away with a handkerchief. The
inscription on the medallion was a quotation from the
Scriptures: 'He went out and wept bitterly.' Those Russian
soldiers who remained alive after the battle, and who had not
been starved or frozen to death during their flight, reached
Novgorod, according to a contemporary, 'completely de-

[1] Charles Eugene, Duke de Croy, Prince of the Holy Roman Empire. See E.
Schuyler, *Peter the Great*, London, 1884, Vol. I, pp. 481, 482 and 485.

spoiled by the Swedes,' with neither cannon, tents, nor baggage. Twenty-four years later, Peter, then a great emperor, had the humility to confess, in his programme for the third celebration of the Peace of Nystadt, that Russia had entered the war blindly, without any realisation either of her own unpreparedness or of the strength of her enemy. Nearly a third of the siege-train, all the artillery, and one hundred and sixty senior officers, including ten generals, were captured. The eighteen-year-old Swedish king was delighted at the ease with which he had recovered Narva,[1] dispersed the Russian army, and captured its generals.

Eight months later, by another unexpected manœuvre, Charles recovered Riga, and completely routed the Russian and Saxon armies on the west bank of the Dvina who were intending to besiege the town. Either from stubbornness or from irresponsibility, Peter did not lose courage, but immediately began to build up an army by new recruitments; he confiscated one quarter of all church and monastery bells, and turned them into cannon. It is true that Charles XII came to Peter's help by chasing Augustus II through the towns and forests of Poland; moreover Charles only left weak Swedish detachments to guard the Russian frontier.

For the next seven years there were only intermittent clashes. Taking advantage of this welcome lull, Peter reformed his shattered army, and, by minor skirmishes, sieges, and assaults on small frontier posts, prepared his troops for more important action. Everything was sacrificed to this end; no attention was paid to the condition of the people. Peter played recklessly, staked everything he had, and promised to subsidise his ally, Augustus, without knowing where the money was to come from. The situation was complicated

[1] The Swedish victory at Narva caused alarm in the rest of Europe. Sweden once again seemed invincible, and it looked as if Charles had regained the dominant position in the Baltic enjoyed by Gustavus.

yet further by internal risings which were closely related to the war. In the summer of 1705 there was a rising in Astrakhan, a distant echo of the Streltsy's revolt, which diverted a large force from the main theatre of war. Hardly had this rising been quelled before Charles, who had been lying low at Warsaw, suddenly appeared near Grodno in January 1706. By a rapid forced march during which three thousand men out of twenty-four thousand dropped out and were frozen to death, Charles cut in half Peter's main force of more than thirty-five thousand men. This movement was even more unexpected than Charles' Narva campaign of 1700, but Peter was able to move up twelve thousand regular soldiers from Minsk, and many cossacks who were wintering to the southeast of Grodno, at Slonim, Mir, and Nesvige.

The Russians had still not recovered from the effects of 1700. Peter was exceedingly worried and 'suffered the torments of Hell'. He had the frontier from Smolensk to Pskov hurriedly fortified. He ordered the Hetman Mazepa[1] himself to come from Volynia with his Cossacks, and though Peter's army was now three times as large as Charles's he could think of nothing but how to save the army at Grodno. He drew up an excellent and detailed plan for retreat, and ordered his soldiers to 'take very little with them, and if necessary to leave everything behind'. During the March thaw the Swedes were unable to cross the Niemen and follow the Russian army, who had jettisoned over a hundred cannon and their caissons in the river. 'With great difficulty and hardship' the Russians skirted Brest, crossed Volynia, and arrived safely at Kiev by by-passing the impenetrable Polessia to the south-west. By 1708 Charles, who had already disposed of Augustus, found himself against Peter alone. Charles marched his well-organised army of forty-four thousand men from Grodno

[1] The part played by Mazepa in this episode is discussed in Florinsky, *Russia,* Macmillan, New York, 1953, Vol. I, pp. 339–42.

directly towards Moscow; another army thirty thousand strong was ready to come to his support from Lithuania and Finland.

Simultaneously with this movement, a revolt of the Bashkirs[1] involved all of Kazan, Ufa, and the region beyond the Volga. This was followed by a rising on the Don led by Bulavin, the result of arresting and prosecuting military deserters who had fled as far as Tambov and Azov. These revolts embarrassed Peter, who was forced to divide his forces and keep an eye on his rear as well as on his enemy in the West; they made him realise how much hatred he had aroused. Though ill and 'weak as a babe from all the medicine', as he himself confessed, he took a variety of measures against the rebels. He wanted to abandon his army in the West and leave for the Don. On the one hand he promised to pardon the rebels, and on the other he ordered the rebels to be broken on the wheel and stake 'in order to free himself from similar incidents during the course of the war'.

Once more Charles remained faithful to his habit of coming to Peter's help when he was in difficulties: they were enemies in love with one another. In July 1708 Charles crossed the marshes of Lithuania and occupied Mogilev. He had wasted the whole of 1707, and now had neither ammunition nor supplies. Peter, therefore, had to prevent Charles from joining with General Löwenhaupt who was bringing him desperately needed munitions and supplies from Livonia.[2] Had Charles been able to join General Löwenhaupt he would have been invincible. But Charles, who had been moving towards Smolensk, suddenly turned south towards the Ukraine, which had plenty of wheat, and where he was awaited by the traitor Mazepa. Abandoned by Charles,

[1] See R. Portal, 'Les Bachkirs et le gouvernement russe au XVIIIᵉ siècle, *Revue des Etudes Slaves*, 1946.

[2] Löwenhaupt expected to meet Charles at Mogilev. When Charles decided to turn south, however, he sent Löwenhaupt new orders to meet him about one hundred and fifty miles south of Mogilev, at Starodub.

Löwenhaupt was defeated by Peter with fourteen thousand Russian troops on September 28th at Lesnaya on the River Sozh. Löwenhaupt lost two-thirds of his force of sixteen thousand men and all the supplies Charles was awaiting.[1]

The Swedes' faith in their own invincibility was shattered. The victory at Poltava[2] was made possible by the battle of Lesnaya. In later years Peter admitted that Lesnaya was the mother of the battle at Poltava nine months later. I do not intend to judge the strategic merits of Charles's sudden detour from Mogilev to Poltava in the south-east. Contemporaries say that the Ukraine attracted Charles because of its immense food supplies, its lack of fortresses, its proximity to the Crimea and Poland, and because he hoped that he would find reinforcements among the Cossacks, and with their help be able to take Moscow more easily without having to fight his way through Peter's troops at Smolensk. Did Charles have a presentiment, a century in advance, of the fate that was to overtake Napoleon? It is hard to say, but, however it came about, Poltava relieved Peter of a nine-year burden of anxieties. The Russian army which he had created utterly routed the Swedish army, or, rather, the thirty thousand hungry, ragged, and demoralised Swedes, who had been brought into the heart of the Ukraine by their headstrong twenty-seven-year-old prince. Peter celebrated his victory at Poltava in a magnanimous manner, feasted the captured Swedish generals, drank their health, and called them his

[1] It would be wrong to suppose that the Russians captured most of the supplies. The Swedes burned most of their stores, and sunk the guns and powder in the marshes around Propovsk. For a discussion of Charles's campaign in Russia, see W. G. F. Jackson, *Seven Roads to Moscow*, Eyre & Spottiswoode, 1957, pp. 34–57.

[2] For a description of the battle of Poltava, see W. G. F. Jackson, *Seven Roads to Moscow*, Eyre & Spottiswood, 1957, pp. 49–55; General J. F. C. Fuller, *The Decisive Battles of the Western World*, Eyre & Spottiswood, 1954, Vol. II, pp. 161–86.

teachers. In his excitement he completely forgot to give chase to the remnants of the Swedish army. He was delighted with a rolling panegyric, delivered in the guise of a sermon by Theofan Prokopovich,[1] rector of the College of Theology, in the Cathedral of St. Sophia at Kiev.

But the victory of June 27th did not bring peace any closer. On the contrary, it complicated Peter's position yet further, and indirectly prolonged the war. Both Lesnaya and Poltava showed that Peter was in a stronger position alone than when he had allies. Yet as a result of Poltava Peter resurrected the coalition that Charles had destroyed. Moreover his plans grew more ambitious. In 1701, after Narva, Peter and Augustus had signed a new treaty in anticipation of victory, whereby Peter was to acquire Ingria and Karelia, but was to renounce his claim on Livonia and Esthonia in favour of Augustus and Poland. In 1707, when Charles, who had beaten Augustus, was ready to march on Moscow, Peter was prepared to content himself with a solitary port on the Baltic Sea. Now after Poltava, Peter sent Sheremetiev to besiege Riga, and Menshikov to Poland to reinstate his dear ally on the throne he had lost through his own folly. In 1710 Peter overran the whole Baltic littoral from the western bank of the Dvina to Viborg. The Treaty of Thorn, signed in October 1709 between Peter and Augustus, provided that Livonia should become the hereditary property of Augustus as Elector of Saxony.

[1] Theofan Prokopovich (1681–1736) was probably one of the best educated Russians of his day. He was a poet, a dramatist, and above all, a publicist. He became the leading ideological spokesman of Petrine Russia. He was also an ambitious, ruthless and intriguing politician. See J. Serech, 'On Teofan Prokopovic as Writer and Preacher in his Kiev Period,' *Harvard Slavic Studies*, Vol. II, See also, H. F. Graham, 'Theopan Prokopovich and the Ecclesiastical Ordinances,' *Church History*, Vol. 25, June 1956, pp. 127–35. For an account of the ideas held by men opposing Prokopovich see J. Serech, 'Stefan Yavorsky and the Conflict of Ideologies in the Age of Peter I,' *Slavic and East European Review*, Vol. 30, No. 74, December 1951, pp. 40–62.

Once more Peter began to disperse his forces. His attention was given first to one thing and then to another. Moreover his military success now attracted the attention of French diplomacy which involved both Charles and Peter in a new Turkish war. Paying too much attention to the pleas of the Christian subjects of the Turks, and to the baseless promises of the hospodars of Moldavia and Wallachia, and full of the self-confidence gained at Poltava, Peter, in the summer of 1711, crossed the burning steppe without enough men[1] and with little knowledge of the military situation. This time he set out, not to defend Little Russia from Turkish invasion, but to destroy the Turkish Empire. On the banks of the Pruth Peter learned another lesson. Surrounded by a Turkish army five times as large as his own, he just escaped capture. In a treaty with the Vizier,[2] he agreed to surrender all his strongholds on the Sea of Azov, thereby sacrificing the efforts of sixteen years at Voronezh, on the Don, and at Azov. Peter consoled his government and himself with the hope that his set-back in the south would strengthen his position on the northern front, which was unquestionably the more important. Just as he regretted nothing and nobody, he spared nothing and nobody. This defeat retarded by half a century the settlement of the Black Sea question; the Empress Anne's absurd war against Turkey,[3] although it was victorious, settled nothing.

Peter's efforts were now concentrated on the Baltic. He assiduously helped his allies to chase the Swedes from Germany. The Swedish fleet, hitherto mistress of the Baltic, was

[1] The army consisted of about 40,000 men.

[2] July 12th, 1711. Peter also agreed not to interfere with Poland and the Cossacks, and more important, he had to allow Charles XII free passage through Poland. See B. H. Sumner, *Peter the Great and the Ottoman Empire*, Blackwell, 1949, pp. 37–44.

[3] For a short description of the Russo-Turkish War of 1735–9, see Florinsky, *Russia*, Macmillan, New York, 1953, Vol. I, pp. 462–5.

F

defeated by Peter's enlarged Baltic fleet at Hangö in 1714. In two years Peter, without any foreign support, conquered the whole of Finland. Unfortunately, as it turned out, he was joined by two new allies, Brandenburg and Hanover, whose Elector became King of England, and Peter discovered a new game, that of meddling in German affairs. He sent his nieces to obscure parts of Germany, where one married the Duke of Courland and the other the Duke of Mecklenburg. The result was that Peter became entangled in a network of petty court quarrels and dynastic intrigues typical of feudal Germany. Moreover this Muscovite meddling was irritating, and caused a certain amount of alarm. For no good reason Peter interfered in a quarrel between his nephew by marriage and the Mecklenburg nobility. The latter, through various intermediaries serving at the courts of Hanover and Denmark, were responsible for the rupture between Peter and his allies, who now became openly insulting. Peter's interference in Germany completely changed the direction of his foreign policy. It turned friends into enemies but failed to turn enemies into friends.

Russian policy began to vacillate again. Peter barely escaped entanglement in the scheme of a Holsteiner called Goertz,[1] in the service of the King of Sweden, who wanted to bring about a reconciliation between Russia and Sweden so that they might combine together to eject the Elector of Hanover from the English throne and re-establish the Stuarts. As soon as this fantastic scheme collapsed Peter went to France to try to arrange a match between his daughter, Elizabeth, and the young King, Louis XV, and by matrimony and diplomacy convert an old enemy into an ally. Thus Peter's true interest after Poltava, which was to dictate terms of peace to Sweden after delivering a decisive blow on the

[1] For a detailed discussion of this scheme see E. Schuyler, *Peter the Great*, London, 1884, Vol. II, pp. 296–8, 507–12.

Baltic, was neglected for the sake of Saxon, Danish, and Mecklenburg trifles which prolonged for another twelve years a ruinous war that had already lasted nine.

In the end Peter achieved nothing. He had to make peace with Charles XII, and promise to help Sweden to recover those German possessions for whose loss Peter had been primarily responsible, and he had to drive his friend Augustus, whom he had so long and so generously upheld, from the Polish throne. But fate was to mock at Peter once again. After the death of Charles in 1718, near the Norwegian fortress of Frederikshald, the Swedes made peace with Peter's allies, though not with Peter, who was left without a single supporter. Once more, as at Poltava, Peter struck decisively by twice invading Sweden, in 1719 and 1720. In 1721 the Peace of Nystadt brought this twenty-one-year-old war to a belated end. Peter dubbed it his 'threefold school' where generally the pupils study for seven years, but he had been slow to learn and had had to study everything three times, clinging to his allies and fearing solitude. It was his enemies the Swedes who opened his eyes, and showed him that the Northern War had been fought exclusively by the Russian forces and not by their allies.

Though the victory at Poltava led to no improvement in Russia's wretched foreign policy, it had a profound influence on internal affairs. Kurbatov, the Inspector-General of Municipal affairs, who could almost be called the Minister of Towns and Finance, wrote Peter a letter in the form of a canticle, with the refrain 'Rejoice ye', congratulating him on his victory, and reminding the Tsar that his army 'had been polished like gold in a furnace', and that it was now the turn of the civil administration; that the successful outcome of the war had led to the absolute ruin of the people, and that it was imperative to alleviate the burden of retroactive taxation which was causing 'such vociferous popular protestations'.

Poltava effectively changed the direction of Peter's internal policy. Until Poltava everything had been done from hand to mouth. The government's most important and terrible weapon was Peter's pen. His immense correspondence with those who were responsible for the execution of current affairs covered every aspect of government. These letters took the place of laws; their recipients became departments of state. Because of military requirements, the administration was turned into a military headquarters. Reforming activities were directed for material benefit. On January 22nd, 1702, Peter wrote a letter to Major-General Bruce[1] of the Artillery, ordering him to find an honest man capable of building oak gun-carriages, who was not wasteful, who used the largest trees, and who split them lengthwise and not transversely 'in order to save wood'. Bruce replied that since the carriages were not for field artillery, oak need not be used, and fir would do just as well, providing that it was well painted.

Before Poltava there were only two legislative acts of an organisational character: an ukaze of January 30th, 1699, dealing with the restoration of local government institutions, and an ukaze of December 18th, 1708, dealing with the division of the country into Provinces. Although Peter had not received the sort of political education that would make him pay attention to the 'vociferous popular protestations' caused by the retroactive collection of taxes, the subject was forced on his attention by other, less humanitarian, considerations. Though he was as obtuse as ever about the wishes of his own people, he had become far more sensitive to his position in international affairs. The victories of Lesnaya and Poltava had shown that he had achieved his main purpose of

---

[1] General Bruce, a Russianised Scot, was one of Peter's best military and naval organisers. He was a director of the schools of Navigation, Artillery, and Military Engineering. Of great service to Russian diplomacy, he was sent in 1718 to the Aland Congress as one of the two Russian Plenipotentiaries.

creating a regular army and a Baltic fleet, both of which had to be maintained at the existing level — and if possible increased. The victory at Poltava involved Peter in European politics, and this meant new expenses. The West began to fear him. Muscovy's new position as an international power had the effect of turning old friends into enemies. Her new military and diplomatic prestige was dearly paid for.

The sources of public revenue were drying up, arrears in taxation were not coming in, and Kurbatov made it plain that more efficient collection would merely exhaust the taxpayers. Five months after the battle of Poltava, Peter ordered that taxes were only to be collected for the two previous years (1707 and 1708). In 1710 a balance sheet was drawn up for the years 1705 to 1710. It was found that annual receipts covered only four-fifths of total expenditure, of which two-thirds was spent on the army and navy. Because of the inability of contemporary financiers to find funds through what are now called credit operations, the deficit had to be made up by asking the taxpayers to pay supplementary taxes.[1] It became more and more obvious that the state was living beyond its income. For this reason attention was diverted from military to internal affairs, and to the search for new sources of revenue for the Treasury. It was only possible to get more revenue if the working conditions of the people and the general economy of the country were improved; because of the lack of time during the wars, these had been completely neglected.

This change in policy is mentioned in a collection of materials for a history of the Northern War which was edited by Peter himself, and which is known by the title of *A History of*

---

[1] For a detailed study of Russian financial policy in the first quarter of the eighteenth century, see P. Miliukov, Ch. Seignobos, L. Eisenmann, *Histoire de Russie,* Paris, 1932, Vol. I. This volume contains a useful summary of P. Miliukov's findings which were first published in Russian in 1892.

the Swedish War. Here it is noted that, after the celebration of the victory of Poltava, Peter gave his attention to the 'administration of civil affairs'. Even the incomplete digest of Russian legislation which is known as the 'Complete Collection of the Laws of the Russian Empire of 1830' bears witness to this renewed legislative activity. For the period 1700 (a date which Peter considered to mark the beginning of a new era) to 1709, the Complete Collection contains five hundred acts; for the next ten years, to the end of 1719, there are 1,238; and nearly as many again were issued between 1720 and Peter's death on January 28th, 1725. Among them is a long list of important laws, regulations, statutes, instructions, and international treaties. It is evident that legislative activity increased with the progress of the war. Before Poltava, Peter dealt with each new demand, whether created by the war or by administrative shortcomings and abuses, by a hurried letter or ukaze which indicated the *ad hoc* measures to be taken; and in this way he dealt with affairs in all departments of government. Later on, when Peter had more leisure and greater administrative experience, these temporary measures, with suitable modifications, were turned into laws or regulations, and into completely new institutions. All the fundamental Petrine laws stem from the second half of the reign, the epoch after Poltava. The war turned Peter, the builder of navies and the organiser of armies, into a versatile administrator, and turned temporary into permanent legislation.

It is now possible to explain the connection between the war and the reforms. Superficially it would seem that Peter's reforming activities have neither a plan nor continuity. Growing gradually, they eventually covered every part of state organisation, and affected the most varied aspects of the nation's life. But nothing was changed suddenly, at one time, and completely; every reform was accomplished piecemeal, intermittently, depending on the exigencies and requirements of the moment. It is easy to see the tendencies of any given group of reforms, but it is difficult to guess why they were dealt with in their particular order. The aims are clear but the plan is not. In order to find an explanation it is necessary to study the process of reform in its proper setting, that is to say in the context of the war and its varied results.

The war indicated the sequence of reforms to be undertaken, and dictated its own tempo to them, and even the procedure to be adopted. Reforming measures did follow the order imposed by the necessities of war. First of all the country's military forces had to be reformed; then followed two series of measures, one establishing the regular army and navy, one providing for their maintenance. Both measures changed the order of, and relationship between, the social classes, and made people work harder and produce more, thereby increasing the state's revenue. The military, social, and economic innovations imposed so much urgent work on the administration, and raised so many strange, complicated, problems, that the existing machinery of state was incapable of dealing with them. Side by side with these innovations, and sometimes even preceding them, the whole governmental machinery was being partially rebuilt; on this depended the success of the other reforms. In order for the new administrative departments to work smoothly and efficiently, it was essential to have trained executive officers with the necessary knowledge and qualifications; it was also imperative to have a society ready to uphold the reforms and to understand their nature and significance. It was for these reasons that Peter became more and more concerned with the dissemination of scientific knowledge and the foundation of general, professional, and technical educational establishments. This is the general plan of the reforms, or rather their order, determined not by any well-thought-out plan of Peter's, but by events and the force of circumstance. The war was the principal cause of Peter's reforming activity; initially a military reform, it became ultimately a financial reform.

Peter began by a reform of the country's defensive system which led to a reform of the national economy; the rest of the measures followed inevitably, either from the initial steps, or because they were necessary to achieve Peter's main purpose. Peter himself linked his reforming programme to the war he had just waged. During the last years of his life, while collecting material on the Swedish war, he gave some thought to the content of his history, and left some notes on the subject. In 1722 he made a note 'to mention in my history everything that was accomplished during this war; what the military and civilian dispositions were, and what regulations were issued dealing with them; the state of the Church, the construction of forts, harbours, ships, galleys, manufacturing establishments of all kinds, the buildings at St. Petersburg, at Kotlin and elsewhere'. A month and a half before his death he made a note 'to mention in my history at what time and why we began to make articles for war and other similar things, as for example the musket when there was an embargo on it, and so on'.

It is possible to deduce that this history was to contain a discussion of everything connected with the war, not only the measures taken to organise military affairs, but also civil and ecclesiastical affairs, as well as a study of industrial and commercial development. This is the plan that is going to be followed here. It is as follows: (1) the military reform; (2) measures taken in order to maintain a regular army and navy, with special reference to changes in the position of the nobility effected to increase their efficiency; (3) preparatory measures aiming at increasing the quantity and improving the quality of the taxpayers' work with the object of increasing the revenue; (4) financial innovations; and finally (5) the general measures taken to ensure the successful execution of the military and economic reforms, with particular reference to the administrative reform and the establishment of educational institutions. It is important to stress once more that this plan does not mean that the reforms were effected in this order, each being completed before the next was begun. Reorganisation was carried out simultaneously in different departments, by fits and starts and fragmentarily, so that it is only by the end of Peter's reign that reconstruction had assumed the form which has been outlined above.

Military reform comes first in the order of Petrine reforms: it demanded the greatest effort, and imposed the heaviest burden on both Peter and the nation as a whole. This reform holds an important place in the history of Russia. It is not merely a question of the nation's defence; the reform profoundly affected the organisation of society and influenced future events.

According to the lists of 1681, the largest part of the Muscovite army (89,000 out of 164,000 men, not counting the Cossacks of Malorossia) had already been organised in formations of foreign pattern. It is improbable that this system was carried further. The army of 112,000 men which Prince Vasili Golitsyn commanded during the second Crimean campaign in 1689 contained the same sixty-three regiments, organised in the foreign style, that were mentioned in the lists of 1681. Since these sixty-three regiments only contained eighty thousand men, the complement of the individual regiments must have been less than it was in 1681. The mounted militia of the nobility, organised in the Russian manner, contained only eight thousand men, which was one-tenth of their cavalry counterpart in Western armies, while, according to the lists of 1681, it was only five or six times as small. This is why the number of men sent on the first Azov campaign is so completely unexpected. Among the thirty thousand men, including Peter, who at that time was only a bombardier in a company of the Preobrazhensky regiment, there were only fourteen thousand men organised in foreign formations, while a large militia force of one hundred and twenty thousand men, who had been sent to create a diversion in the Crimea, was entirely composed of irregular soldiers organised in the Russian manner who, in the words of Kotoshikhin, knew nothing about 'military organisation'. Where had this mass of irregulars come from, and where had the sixty thousand regular soldiers disappeared to, who, with the exception of the fourteen thousand men who went with Peter to Azov, had taken part in the Crimean campaign of 1689? The reply to this question was given by Prince Jacob Dolgoruky at that banquet in 1717 we have already mentioned. Dolgoruky knew all about the state of the Muscovite army during the reigns of Theodore and Sophia, and had been Prince Vasili Golitsyn's close companion during the second Crimean campaign. During the banquet Dolgoruky told Peter that his father, Alexis, had shown him how to organise a regular army 'but that, later on, certain misguided statesmen had undone all his work', so that Peter had had to begin almost from the beginning again to put the army on a better footing. Prince Dolgoruky could not have been referring to either Theodore or Sophia: on the eve of Sophia's downfall, during the second Crimean campaign, the troops of foreign formation were in good condition.

The nobility, however, had actively supported Peter's mother in her struggle against Sophia and the Streltsy. After Sophia's overthrow the Naryshkins, Streshnevs, and Lopukhins came into their own, and allied themselves with the new Tsaritsa, who was very stupid and not at all concerned with the well-being of the army. It is evident that it must have been these people who changed the organisation of the army of the nobility from the foreign system, which was fairly complicated, to the relatively simple Russian system. Recruiting was also completely disorganised. In peace-time the regiments were disbanded, and both noblemen and soldiers were sent home, to be recalled only in time of need. This was the mobilisation of those on leave or the reservists who were experienced men and had already seen service. By the time Peter was recruiting an army for the war against Sweden, these reserves had vanished. The foreign formations were reinforced in two ways: either 'volunteers were called for', or they were recruited from the estates of the nobility in proportion to the number of homesteads on the estate. Peter ordered freed serfs, and peasants who were fit to serve, to be inscribed as soldiers, and even allowed serfs to join the army without their masters' consent. Thanks to this recruiting system, the conscript units, so hurriedly organised and trained by Germans, were nothing more than conglomerations of worthless soldiers, recruited from the rabble (this is what they were called by Korb,[1] the Secretary to the Austrian Legation, who was in Moscow from 1698 to 1699). Weber, the Resident of Brunswick, who lived in Russia from 1714 to 1719, called them 'a sorry multitude'. Peter's first army in the Northern War was recruited in this way. Twenty-nine new regiments, each of one thousand volunteers and conscripts, were attached to four veteran regiments, two of the Guards and two of the line. Narva revealed their military qualities!

It was the war itself that eventually turned this mass of volunteers and conscripts into a real force. During the interminable struggle the newly formed regiments, after years of campaigning turned themselves into a real army. There was an incredible wastage of manpower after Narva: the regiments recruited with such haste perished in battle and were further depleted by famine, disease, mass desertions, and

---

[1] Korb's diary was first published in Vienna in 1700. It was, however, offensive to Peter, and at his request many copies were destroyed, and, as far as is known, only about twelve survive.

forced marches over enormous distances from the Neva to Poltava, from Azov and Astrakhan to Riga, Kalisz and Wismar. At the same time the extension of the theatre of military operations called for yet further reinforcements. In order to fill the ranks and increase the army's complement, levies of volunteers and conscripts followed one after the other, and were carried out through all classes of society: sons of boyars, tradesmen, courtiers, sons of members of the Streltsy, and even unbenificed sons of the clergy were recruited. In 1703 nearly thirty thousand men were recruited in this way. The army gradually became an army of all classes; it was completely inexperienced, and the rawest of raw material was constantly being added in the field. Such a haphazard system called for another method of recruitment, a method which would result in regular and well-trained reserves. Therefore the fortuitous and disorderly recruitment of both volunteers and conscripts was replaced by periodic general levies; but, even so, the old mistakes were sometimes repeated. Bachelor recruits aged fifteen to twenty, and, later on, married men aged twenty to thirty, were concentrated at 'muster points' in the nearest town, in companies of five hundred to one thousand men. They were put in billets; lance-corporals and corporals were selected from among them; and officers who had been retired through wounds or illness were put in charge, with orders to 'train them unceasingly in military exercises according to military precepts'. From these 'muster-points' and training centres the recruits were sent where they were most urgently required, to fill 'vacant places', to supplement existing regiments, or to form new ones. Peter himself explained the part his military nursery was to play: 'When fresh drafts are asked for, let there always be some available to fill the gaps.' The soldiers were known at the time as the 'immortals'; an ukaze ordained that if a soldier died at his training centre, or was killed or deserted, he had immediately to be replaced by another conscript from the same district, 'in order that the complement be maintained and everybody always be ready to serve his sovereign.'

The general levy was first effected in 1705, and was repeated every year until 1709, always in the ratio of one recruit to twenty tax-paying homesteads, which meant that at least thirty thousand men were recruited at a time. These five levies were supposed to raise a total of one hundred and sixty-eight thousand men, but the levies were never complete and the exact number is not known. It has been reckoned that from the beginning of the war against Sweden to the first general levy, volunteers and conscripts formed an army of one hundred and fifty thousand men. Adding up, it follows that, during the first ten years of the war, three hundred thousand men out of a population of fourteen million were absorbed into the army. The second army, the army of Poltava, was formed in this way; this was a regular army which, towards the end of 1708, and due to the first three levies in 1701 of forty thousand men numbered one hundred and thirteen thousand.

During the following years this army was maintained and reinforced by the same methods. Weber, who has already been mentioned, and who made a careful study of Russian military organisation, wrote in his curious memoirs on the reformed Russia (*Das Veränderte Russland*) that in general twenty thousand recruits were to be enrolled each year. In reality, though, there were sometimes less and sometimes more; by conscripting one man to fifty, seventy-five or eighty homesteads, the totals came to nearly ten thousand, fourteen thousand, or twenty-three thousand men without counting the sailors, and in 1724, when the war was over, nearly thirty-five thousand men were needed to maintain the complement of line regiments, garrisons, artillery regiments, and the navy. Conscription was necessary not only to increase the complement, but also to replace losses by

desertion, sickness, and the high mortality rate in those regiments where lack of supplies and the reforms had resulted in
mass slaughter. In 1718 those who had avoided conscription
numbered forty-five thousand, and deserters numbered
twenty thousand. Weber remarks that, because of faulty
organisation, more recruits died from hunger and cold than
in battle. Towards the end of Peter's reign, the regular army,
both infantry and cavalry, contained beween one hundred
and ninety-six thousand and two hundred and twelve thousand men. There were also one hundred and ten thousand
cossacks and other irregulars, excluding formations of
non-Russians.

Furthermore a new force was created hitherto unknown
in Russia: a navy. With the beginning of the Northern War
the Azov squadron was abandoned, and the battle of the
Pruth lost Russia the Sea of Azov. Peter therefore concentrated on building a Baltic fleet. As early as 1701 he was
dreaming of eighty men-of-war; and crews were hurriedly
gathered together. Prince Kurakin says that in 1702 'young
men were invited to become sailors and nearly three thousand
men were chosen'. The six frigates launched at the Ledeino-
polsk Wharves in 1703 composed the first Russian fleet ever
to appear on the Baltic Sea. Towards the end of Peter's reign,
the fleet consisted of forty-eight ships of the line, and nearly
eight hundred galleys and other small vessels, served by
twenty-eight thousand men.

A complicated administration was created to organise,
reinforce, maintain, and clothe the regular army and navy.
There was a Military college, a Naval college, an Artillery
Office under a General of Ordnance, a Commissariat under a
Director General of Supplies, and a Main Supply office under
a General of War Supplies who was in charge of recruits, and
whose duty it was to post them to regiments, pay them, and
supply them with arms, uniforms, and horses. To this must

be added a General Staff with its generals, which according to the lists of 1712, was composed of two Field Marshals, Prince Menshikov and Count Sheremetiev, and thirty-one other generals, of whom fourteen were foreigners. The troops were issued with standard uniforms, and illustrated works on Russian military history show Peter's Guards dressed in dark green tunics cut in the German style, with low three-cornered hats; they were armed with muskets and bayonets.

The reorganisation of the regular military force was based on the following technical changes. Peace-time regiments, 'the elected', as they were called, were transformed into permanent regiments, of which there were far more of infantry than of cavalry. The maintenance of the armed forces became the direct responsibility of the Crown. These changes, especially the last, considerably increased the costs of maintaining the army and navy. The budget of the General Staff alone, which had not existed prior to Peter, had grown in 1712 to 111,000 roubles (900,000 in the roubles of 1900). In the budget of 1680 the army was only allotted ten million roubles (in the roubles of 1900). During the whole of Peter's reign the land forces were continually increasing, and were costing more and more; by 1725 the cost of upkeep had increased five times and passed the five million rouble mark (Petrine money), while the navy cost one and a half million roubles. The two together add up to something like fifty-two to fifty-eight million roubles, or not less than two-thirds of the total budget of the day.

Chapter Four

★

IT IS NOW necessary to see what measures were taken in order to maintain the organisation of a regular army and navy. We have shown how Peter recruited his military forces by extending the obligation of furnishing recruits to classes of society hitherto exempt from military service — serfs, urban and rural taxpayers, vagabonds, and clerics; thus members of all classes found themselves serving in the army. Let us now see what measures were taken to recruit and increase the efficiency of those intended for command, who were of course members of the ruling nobility.

Peter's military reform would have remained an isolated incident in Russian military history had it not left a distinct and deep impression on the social and intellectual composition of all Russian society, and even influenced future political developments. The military reform itself made necessary other innovations, first to maintain the reorganised and expensive military forces, and then to ensure their permanency. The new recruiting methods, by spreading military obligations to classes hitherto exempt, and thus affecting all social classes, gave the new army a more varied composition, and completely altered existing social relationships. From the time that noblemens' serfs and servants joined the new army as ordinary recruits instead of only as menials or valets, the position of the nobility, which had been preponderant in the old army, was completely changed.

This change did not result entirely from the military reform; the course of events since the sixteenth century had already prepared the way. The *oprichnina*[1] was the first overt appearance of the nobility in a political role. The *oprichnina* was essentially a police force directed against the *zemshchina*[2] in general and the boyars in particular. During the Time of Troubles[3] the *oprichniks* had upheld their own nominee, Boris Godunov, and were responsible for the overthrow of Tsar Vasili Shuisky, the boyars' candidate. In a decree of June 30th, 1611, drawn up in a camp near Moscow, the *oprichniks* declared that they were not representatives of the country, but were the country; by so doing they completely ignored the existence of other classes. They carefully protected their own interests and, as pretended defenders of the Greek Orthodox religion and the land of the Mother of God, declared themselves the rulers of the country. The institution of serfdom (Krepostnoye pravo) was responsible for this particular fantasy, since it had estranged the nobility from the rest of society and had made it less patriotic. Yet at the same time it had provided this class with a common interest, and

[1] It is impossible to translate this word. Florinsky, *Russia,* Macmillan, New York, 1953, p. 1480, defines it as an 'entailed domain'. It was created by Ivan IV. To administer this domain, which was exempt from the jurisdiction of the general administration, a special household was created, and its members were called *oprichniks.* See D. Mirsky, *Russia,* The Cresset Press, 1931, p. 150, and Florinsky, *Russia,* Macmillan, New York, 1953, Vol. I, pp. 199–202.

[2] The *zemshchina* was the rest of the country. See D. Mirsky, *Russia,* The Cresset Press, 1951, p. 150, and Florinsky, *Russia,* Macmillan, New York, 1953 Vol. I, pp. 199–202.

[3] The 'Time of Troubles' is the name given to the period 1591–1613. The Tsarevich Dimitri, son of Ivan IV, was murdered in 1591. From 1601–3 there was a famine in Russia, which was followed by the struggle between those who supported the claims of the False Dimitri to the throne, and the followers of Boris Godunov. The Civil War was complicated yet further by the interventions of Poland and Sweden, and only came to an end in 1613 with the election of Michael Romanov to the throne. See Florinsky, *Russia,* Macmillan, New York, 1953, Vol. I, pp. 209–43.

G

had thus created a more or less unified nobility out of a heterogeneous mass of men of service.

With the abolition of *mestnichestvo*[1] the remaining boyars were engulfed by this class. By making a mockery of the old aristocracy of boyars, Peter and his low-born companions had managed to lessen its prestige in the eyes of the people. Contemporaries duly noted the date of this old nobility's death as a ruling class. In 1687 Sophia's current favourite, a peasant called Shaklovity, who was Secretary of the Council, told the Streltsy that the boyars were like a withered, fallen tree. Prince Boris Kurakin pointed to Natalia's regency (1689–94) as the period 'of the abasement of the most important families, while the name of the prince in particular had become hated and humiliated', and 'representatives of the lesser nobility' like the Naryshkins and the Streshnevs filled the most important offices of state. An attempt in 1730 by the aristocrats of the Supreme Council[2] to improve their social position was already a cry from the tomb. The boyars had been engulfed by the new nobility, whose numbers had been increased by the addition of those who owned 'heritable property'. This class of men, who were liable for state service, was known in Petrine legislation either by the Russian name of *Dvoryanstvo*[3] or by the Polish name of *Shlyakhetstvo*. It was

---

[1] *Mestnichestvo*, according to Klyuchevsky, established a hereditary relationship in the relative positions of the various families with reference to the offices held by their members in the government service. What mattered, therefore, was not the office itself, but the respective positions of the various officeholders. It was, in short, a system of precedence. It was abolished in 1682.

[2] This is a reference to the 'Conditions' which the Supreme Council tried to impose on Anne, Duchess of Courland, when they offered her the throne. For an interesting and very detailed account of this episode see *La Cour de la Russie 1725–1783, Extraits des Dépêches des Ambassadeurs Anglais et Français*, Berlin, 1858, pp. 7–89.

[3] For a study of the Russian nobility under Peter, see *The European Nobility in the Eighteenth Century*, edited by A. Goodwin, A. & C. Black, 1953, pp. 172–177.

quite without cultural background or influence. Above all a
military class, its members believed that it was their duty to
defend their country against its enemies; they were concerned
neither with educating the masses nor with developing and
spreading ideas of a practical nature. Yet history made this
particular class, more than any other, responsible for the execution of the reforms; though it is true that Peter found suitable men in other classes, even among the serfs. The nobility
did not have a more developed intellectual or moral sense
than the rest of the population, and the majority of them
were no less hostile to the heretic West. On the other hand
their military profession produced neither martial spirit nor
technical skill. Russian and foreign observers described the
military value of this class in the most contemptuous language. In his report on Military Conduct made to the boyar
Golovin[1] in 1701, the peasant Pososhkov[2] complained
bitterly of the cowardice, pusillanimity, ignorance, and
complete incapacity of the military class. 'A great number of
people are called to serve and if they are examined closely
the only result is a feeling of shame. The infantry are armed
with bad muskets and do not know how to use them. They
fight with their side-arms, with lances and halberds and even
these are blunt; for every one foreigner killed there are three,
four and even more Russians killed. As for the cavalry, we are

[1] Prince Golovin was a prominent military leader and diplomat.

[2] Unfortunately Pososhkov's writings have never been translated into English,
and very little has been written about this remarkable man. A short and superficial biography can be found in E. Schuyler, *Peter the Great*, London, 1884,
Vol. II, pp. 486–8. Pososhkov was mainly interested in the economic development of his country, and his writings show that he was concerned with the
development of technical and commercial knowledge. See *Continuity and Change
in Russian and Soviet Thought*, edited by Ernest J. Simmons, Harvard University Press, 1955, pp. 15–16. For a discussion of Pososhkov's economic beliefs, see
C. Bickford O'Brien, 'Ivan Pososhkov: Russian Critic of Mercantilist Principles,' *The American Slavic and East European Review*, December, 1955, pp.
503–11.

ashamed to look at them ourselves, let alone show them to the foreigner: sickly, ancient horses, blunt sabres, puny, badly dressed men who do not know how to wield their weapons. There are some noblemen who do not know how to charge an arquebus, let alone hit their target. They care nothing about killing the enemy, but think only how to return to their homes. They pray that God send them a light wound so as not to suffer much, for which they will receive a reward from their sovereign. In battle they hide in thickets; whole companies take cover in a forest or a valley and I have even heard noblemen say "Pray God we may serve our sovereign without drawing out swords from their scabbards".'

There was a class of higher nobility, which, because of its position in society and in the state, had acquired habits and ideas which could be turned to useful account. This class consisted of families of men of service, who, ever since the establishment of a princely court at Moscow, had been settling there. Their settlement took place in the appanage period of Russian history, when men of service from other Russian principalities, from abroad, from the Tartar hordes, from Germany, and especially from Lithuania, flocked to Moscow. After the unification of Muscovite Russia the size of this nobility was increased by newcomers from the provincial nobility who had distinguished themselves by their merit, exemplary service, and competence. In time a complicated hierarchy which depended on the nature of their court functions, was formed within this class. First of all there were the *stol'niki* who served food and drink at the Tsar's ceremonial banquets; then there were the *stryapchie* who carried the Tsar's sceptre, head-dress, and mantle in processions or at church (in war time they looked after the Tsar's armour and sword); finally there were the *zhil'tsi* who took turns in groups to sleep at court. On this ladder of rank, below the *stol'niki* and *stryapchie* but over the *zhil'tsi*, came the 'Muscovite noblemen', the highest rank a *zhilets* could attain. The *stol'niki* and *stryapchie* came from the ranks of the 'Muscovite noblemen'. A *stol'nik* or *stryapchie* not of boyar rank who, after twenty to thirty years of service in his own grade, was no longer able to fulfil the obligations which were attached to his court duties spent the rest of his life as a 'Muscovite nobleman'. This title was not connected in any way with special court duties. A 'Muscovite nobleman' was a functionary of particular merit, who might be sent, as Kotoshshikhin puts it, 'on sundry affairs': as a provincial governor, on an embassy, as a commander of a contingent of provincial noblemen. The wars of Tsar Alexis in particular attracted the provincial nobility to the capital. Muscovite rank was the reward for wounds, loss of blood, or for having been a prisoner; it was also given to those whose fathers or other relatives had died in battle or on campaign. That the metropolitan nobility flourished in time of bloodshed has never been seen so clearly as under Alexis. The defeat at Konotop in 1659, where the flower of the Tsar's cavalry perished, and the surrender of Sheremetiev with the whole army at Chudnov, were sufficient to swell the Muscovite ranks with hundreds of new *stol'niki*, *stryapchie*, and courtiers. This influx turned the metropolitan nobility of all ranks into a large corps; according to the lists of 1681 there were 6,385, and in 1700 11,533 were sent on the Narva campaign.

Before the epoch of general conscription, the metropolitan nobility who owned large *pomesties*[1] and *votchinas*[2] used to

[1] A *'pomestie'* estate was an estate held in service tenure. The enjoyment of estates of this type was conditional on the tenant and his heirs performing military service and other duties. Lands on conditional service tenure began to be granted on an extensive scale by Ivan III, and under Ivan IV this form of tenure was even further extended. See James Mavor, *An Economic History of Russia*, J. M. Dent & Sons Ltd., 2nd edition, 1925, Vol. I, pp. 34–41, 107–8; Florinsky, *Russia*, Macmillan, New York, 1953, Vol. I, pp. 102, 176–7.

[2] A *'votchina'* estate was an hereditary estate originally unencumbered by service obligations.

take with them on campaign armed serfs, or had themselves replaced by recruits who were taken from the estates in tens of thousands. Attached to the court through service, the Muscovite nobility lived in Moscow itself or on nearby estates. In the period 1678–1701 three thousand out of sixteen thousand homes in Moscow belonged to the Muscovite nobility and the members of the Duma. The Muscovite nobility fulfilled the most varied functions. The court was the court of the Tsar, so that in Petrine legislation they were called *tsaredvortsy* (the courtiers of the Tsar) to distinguish them from 'the *shlyakhetstvo* of all other ranks', that is to say the urban nobility and sons of boyars. In peace time the metropolitan nobility made up the Tsar's retinue, did duty at court and furnished the personnel for the central and regional administration. In war time the metropolitan nobility became the Tsar's personal regiment, the first corps of the army; its members also served on the staffs of other units, and were put in command of battalions of the provincial nobility. In other words the metropolitan nobility were an administrative class, a general staff, and corps of guards. As a reward for this onerous and expensive service, the metropolitan nobility received comparatively larger salaries and greater rewards in land than the provincial nobility. The metropolitan nobility filled the executive posts in the administration and enjoyed personal financial security. They became familiar with public affairs, became accustomed to occupying situations of authority, and developed *savoir-faire* in their social relationships. The metropolitan nobility considered that state service was their particular vocation and their only social function. They resided permanently in the capital and rarely took advantage of periods of short leave to visit their estates, which were spread all over Russia. They grew accustomed to considering themselves the highest class in society, and to dealing with important affairs of state. They were well-placed to know about the government's international relations, and knew, better than any other class, those countries with whom Russia had dealings. Their situation made them more eager and able to spread Western influence than any of the other social classes. This influence was to be beneficial, but only the governing class could undertake the necessary task of winning over those who remained hostile.

When, in the seventeenth century, Western innovations were first introduced into Russia, and capable men were needed to implement them, the government used the metropolitan nobility as the most suitable instrument, and chose officers from this class to command the regiments of foreign organisation side by side with foreign officers. More supple and subservient than their contemporaries, the metropolitan nobility produced the first defenders of Western influence, among whom were Prince Khvorostinin, Ordin-Nashchokin and Rtishchev. It is understandable, therefore, that under Peter this class was to become the main executor of the reforms. In organising a regular army Peter gradually turned the metropolitan nobility into regiments of the Guard. Officers from either the Preobrazhensky or Semenovsky Regiments were sent on many missions connected with the reforms. A *stol'nik* turned into a Guards' officer might be sent to Holland to study navigation, or to Astrakhan to study saltmining, or be made Procurator-General of the Holy Synod.

There was also a class of provincial noblemen with hereditary titles to perform service, called in the Code[1] 'the children of boyars of long standing'. Noblemen came to Moscow in considerable numbers and, together with the metropolitan nobility, fulfilled three functions in the Muscovite state: military, administrative, and economic. They formed the main military force of the country; they were the govern-

---

[1] A reference to the *Ulozhenie* of 1649. See James Mavor, *An Economic History of Russia*, J. M. Dent & Sons Ltd., 2nd edition, 1925, Vol. I, pp. 88-91.

ment's principal executives, and made up the personnel of the administration and the tribunals; finally they held the largest proportion of the country's capital, including land, which, in the seventeenth century, meant peasant-serfs as well. This multiplicity of functions made the proper fulfilment of duties impossible; each of the three functions impinged on the other two. During intervals between campaigns the urban men of service went back to their homes; the metropolitan nobility either went on short leave to their estates, or, like some of the provincial nobility, were employed in civil administrative posts, or were sent on administrative or diplomatic missions, when, in a contemporary phrase, they were 'in business' or 'on mission'.

In this way civil and military duties were mixed, and civil affairs were undertaken by soldiers. Certain duties and missions exempted these men from fulfilling their military service in war-time, but obliged them to send serfs in their stead, in proportion to the number of peasant homesteads on their estates. Permanent secretaries and under-secretaries who worked in state departments were considered to be on indefinite leave from the army, or on an indefinite mission, and, like widows and minors, were allowed to provide replacements if they owned well-populated estates. This system encouraged evasion and was much abused. The dangers and unpleasantness of life during campaign, together with the harm done to estates by neglect during their owners absence, encouraged those who had well-placed relations to solicit for positions which would exempt them from military service. Others simply 'escaped' by not replying to a summons, which was particularly easy because of the immense distances which separated the estates from the capital. A soldier or clerk would be sent with a mobilisation order, and would find an empty house — and strangely enough, nobody would know where the owner was, or how to find him.

Peter did not exempt these provincial nobles from personal and indefinite obligatory service. He did nothing to alleviate the burden, but, on the contrary, overwhelmed them with new obligations, and issued very severe instructions in order to put an end to the existing abuses, and make the nobility leave their estates. Peter wanted to establish the exact number of reserves among the nobility, and ordered them to furnish the War Office, and later on the Senate, with complete lists of all young men, relations, and children over the age of ten, living with them. Orphans had to come to Moscow in person to be inscribed on the lists. The lists were frequently revised and altered. Thus in 1704 Peter personally interviewed over eight thousand youths who had been summoned to Moscow from the provinces. The interviews were followed by the distribution of the youths among regiments and schools. In 1712 those living at home or studying in schools were ordered to present themselves at the chancellery of the Senate in Moscow; from here they were sent by carriage to St. Petersburg to be examined, and there were divided into three categories according to their ages. The youngest were sent to Reval to study navigation; the next group were sent to Holland for the same purpose; the eldest were turned into soldiers. 'For my sins I was included among those who were sent abroad,' piteously wrote V. Golovin in his memoirs. Being of noble birth did not exempt anybody from this examination. In 1704 the Tsar personally examined the offspring 'of the most illustrious persons', when between five and six hundred young princes, including Golitsyn, Cherkasky, Khovansky, and Lobanov-Rostovsky, were inscribed as soldiers in the Guards regiments, 'and they perform their duties well,' wrote Prince Boris Kurakin.

Nor were the personnel of the departments left alone. Because of the advantageous character of this type of employment the numbers had grown out of all reason. In 1712 a revision of all clerks was carried out, not only in the provincial departments, but even in the Senate. Those who were redundant, and who were fit to serve, were removed and turned into soldiers. In order to prevent absenteeism, which Peter punished severely, adult noblemen were ordered to appear at reviews either together with the youths or separately. Peter thus hoped to prevent them from going into hiding, and ensure their availability for service.

In the autumn of 1714 Peter ordered all noblemen between the ages of ten and thirty to appear in the course of the winter and register themselves at the Senate. This order was accompanied with the promise that whosoever denounced an absentee would receive all his wealth and estates, even if the informer was the nobleman's own serf. An ukaze of January 11th, 1722, goes even further: a defaulter was 'degraded' or suffered 'political death'; he was excluded from the society of honest men and declared an outlaw; he could be robbed, wounded, or killed with impunity. The public executioner affixed his name to the gallows in the market place, to the rolling of drums, so that 'the public learn that this man disobeyed an ukaze and is a traitor'. Whoever apprehended a defaulter and turned him in was to receive half his possessions, movable and immovable, even if he were the defaulter's own serf.

These severe measures were unsuccessful. Pososhkov, in an essay on *Poverty and Wealth* written during the last years of Peter's reign, vividly describes the deceptions and expedients indulged in by the nobility in order to evade service. On the eve of a military campaign both the metropolitan nobility and the courtiers would clutch hold of some 'trumped-up business' or insignificant police mission, under cover of which they spent the rest of the war living on their estates. The vast number of new commissaries and high officials helped the nobility in their subterfuges. 'There is,' wrote

Pososhkov, 'an unlimited number of slothful gallants each of whom would have been capable of chasing five of the enemy, but who have secured lucrative positions, live peacefully and increase their wealth. Others escape service by judicious bribery or by feigning illness or holy imbecility (yurodstvo). "He jumped into the lake and stood there with the water lapping at his beard. Anybody who wants him is welcome." There are noblemen who have grown old on their estates and have never served. The poor and the old serve while the rich try to escape. Some idlers even mock at the Tsar's severe ukazes. The nobleman Zolotarev "when he is at home seems like a lion to his neighbours, but when it comes to the army he is worse than a goat". When at last he could no longer avoid service he sent a needy nobleman in his place and gave him a horse and servant. He himself rode through the villages in a carriage drawn by six horses despoiling everything. The fault lies with the entourage of the Tsar. They give him false reports on the basis of which the Tsar issues his orders, do what they like and distribute favours to their immediate friends. Nowhere,' remarks Pososhkov sadly, 'has the Tsar got an honest counsellor. All the judges are corrupt; those who ought to serve are left alone, those who are unfit for service are forced to serve. The great monarch works hard and accomplishes nothing; there are few who help him. The Tsar pulls uphill alone with the strength of ten, but millions pull downhill. How then can his work prevail? If you cannot change the old order, however hard you work, then you might as well forget about it.' In spite of his pious veneration for the Tsar, the self-taught publicist has quite unconsciously shown us a pitiful, almost ridiculous Peter.

Pososhkov's observations are particularly valuable in as much as they show what actually happened to the ideal organisational system created by Peter's legislation. Even such details as, for example, the way in which the nobility fulfilled their military obligations, must be seen in their proper perspective. The nobility had always begun their state service at the age of fifteen, and Peter did not change this, but instituted a new preparatory obligation: compulsory primary education. According to the decrees of January 20th, and February 28th, 1714, children of noblemen, civil servants, secretaries and under-secretaries had to learn 'ciphers', that is, arithmetic and elementary geometry, and 'are forbidden to marry until they have done so'. A marriage licence was not issued until the teacher had granted a certificate of scholastic achievement. Decrees stated that schools were to be built in all the provinces, near churches and large monasteries. These schools were to be staffed by pupils of the mathematical colleges which had been founded in Moscow about 1703, who were to receive an annual salary of three hundred roubles (in the roubles of 1900).

The decrees of 1714 introduced a totally new conception in the history of Russian education: compulsory secular education. The scheme itself was modest enough. Each Province was allotted from the mathematical colleges two teachers who had studied geography and geometry. Arithmetic, elementary geometry, and a smattering of religious instruction from the religious primers of the time were considered sufficient preparation for service. Any extension of this programme was considered harmful. These studies were compulsory for all children between the ages of ten and fifteen, when military service began. A decree of October 17th, 1723, stated that pupils over the age of fifteen were forbidden to remain at school 'even if the pupils so desire, in order to prevent them from using their studies as an excuse for avoiding reviews and their military service'. This was not likely to happen.

The danger came from another quarter. Pososhkov says that as late as 1723 only one episcopal school had been established, and that was at Novgorod. The cipher schools, which were to be established on a separate basis, and which were to be open to all classes of society, were barely in existence. The school inspector of Pskov, Novgorod, Yaroslav, Moscow, and Vologda wrote in his report of 1719 that only twenty-six pupils, all sons of priests, had been sent to the school at Yaroslav, and 'no pupils had been sent to any of the other schools', so that the teachers were getting paid for doing nothing. The nobility found this compulsory study burdensome and pointless, and did everything possible to avoid it.

One day a crowd of young noblemen, who did not want to go to one of these cipher schools, had themselves enrolled at the Zaikonospassky Theological Seminary in Moscow. Peter sent these devotees of theology to the Naval Academy at St. Petersburg, and made them drive piles in the Moika Canal as a punishment. General-Admiral Apraxin, faithful to the old traditions of family honour, was offended and showed his displeasure in an ingenious way. He went down to the Moika and, seeing the Tsar approach, took off his Admiral's uniform with its riband of St. Andrew and hung it up on a pole. He then joined the other noblemen and began to drive piles. When Peter came up he said in surprise, 'How is it Theodore Matveevich, that you, a General-Admiral and a nobleman, are driving piles?' Apraxin replied cheerfully, 'Sire, these labourers are my nephews and grandchildren;[1] who am I then and by what right should I be privileged?'

At the age of fifteen a nobleman joined a regiment as a private. The young noblemen of important and wealthy families generally joined a Guards regiment, while the young men of the poorer and lesser nobility joined a line regiment. Peter's theory was that a nobleman should be an officer in a regular regiment, but that it was imperative for him to serve

[1] They were not in fact his relatives at all; but it was the custom for an old nobleman to refer to young noblemen in this fashion.

in the ranks for a few years before getting his commission. A law of February 26th, 1714, categorically prohibited young men 'of noble birth' who had not served in the ranks of a Guards regiment, and who 'did not know the fundamental duties of a soldier', from receiving commissions. The Army Regulations of 1716 say that 'the Russian nobility have no other way of becoming officers than by serving in the Guards'. This explains why under Peter the Guards regiments were composed entirely of noblemen. Towards the end of Peter's reign there were three Guards regiments, a 'leib-regiment' of dragoons (later on the Horse Guards) being added to the two existing Guards regiments in 1719. These regiments acted as practical military training schools for the offspring of princely and other noble families, as well as nurseries for officers. After serving in the ranks of a Guards regiment, a nobleman was given a commission either in a line regiment, in an artillery regiment, or in the dragoons. The ranks of the dragoons, who were entirely composed of 'noblemen's children', included three hundred princes. In St. Petersburg it was not an uncommon sight to see a Prince Galitsyn or Gagarin doing sentry duty, musket on shoulder. A nobleman in the Guards lived like an ordinary soldier in barracks, received the same rations, and performed the same fatigues. Derzhavin[1] tells in his memoirs how he, a nobleman and a colonel's son, joined the Preobrazhensky regiment as a private in the reign of Peter III. He slept in barracks with men of humble extraction, did fatigues, cleaned out ditches, mounted guard, carried supplies, and ran errands for the officers. Thus in Peter's military organisation the nobility was to provide the trained cadres — to furnish the officers who passed via the Guards to the line regiments, or through the Naval Academy to officer the fleet. During the interminable Northern War military service had become, in the real sense of

[1] Gabriel Derzhavin (1743–1816) is mainly known as a poet.

the word, perpetual. When peace came the nobles were given leave, usually once every two years, to visit their estates for six months at a time. Only the injured and the old were allowed to retire from the army, but even they were not allowed to retire properly. They were either sent to garrison towns or given posts in local civil administration. Only the hopelessly incurable and disabled men were either awarded pensions from 'hospital funds' or sent to monasteries to be fed at the monastery's expense.

This was how Peter planned a nobleman's normal military career. But the nobleman was needed everywhere, in the civil administration as well as in the army. Moreover conditions of both military service and civil service in the new judicial and administrative institutions became more and more stringent, so that a more specialised preparation was required. It became impossible for an individual to fulfil both functions simultaneously, which had remained the privilege of those Guards officers and senior generals who, even after Peter, were considered capable of filling any post. Gradually the personnel of the civil administration was separated from the personnel of the military administration. No freedom of choice between the two types of service was allowed, since the nobility would have all chosen the easier and more lucrative civil service. The division of the noblemen between the services was arranged by an instruction in 1722 to the Heraldmeister within whose competence the nobility came. He was ordered to see that 'no more than one third of a family be allowed to join the civil service, lest the land and sea forces suffer'. There was also another motive for distinguishing between the military and civil services. Whereas previously ignorance and conceit were considered sufficient qualification for the civil service, the instructions now laid particular emphasis on specialised knowledge. Because of the almost total absence of specialised training in administration, and especially economics, the Heraldmeister was ordered to 'maintain a school with a brief course of instruction in economics and civics' for the statutory third of the offspring of illustrious families and families of modest condition who entered the civil service.

This division was a technical improvement. Peter also changed the system of promotion, thereby introducing a new element into a structure based previously on genealogy alone. In the Muscovite state men of service held positions which depended primarily on their ancestry and degree of nobility. Only a limited number of tasks was open to a member of a particular family, and a man of service in climbing this ladder reached the highest level open to one of his birth, more or less rapidly, depending on his capacity and talents. As a result, a man's career depended on his family origin and on merit, but in practice merit was the less important and ability alone was less likely to lead to promotion than family origin. The abolition of *mestnichestvo* destroyed the old traditions on which the genealogical organisation of the serving classes was based; but the hereditary principle remained customary. Peter intended to stamp it out completely and gave more weight to ability than to claims of birth. He was constantly repeating to the nobility that service was their most important duty, wherein 'lies their nobility and by which it is distinguished from baseness of origin'. Peter informed the nobility that, origins notwithstanding, they must always cede pride of place to an officer. Peter's measures opened the ranks of the nobility to men of humble origin. A nobleman beginning his service as a private was destined to become an officer; but, by a decree of January 16th, 1721, a private of humble origin who was commissioned because of his abilities was simultaneously created an hereditary nobleman. Peter's theory was that if a nobleman could become an officer because of his origins, then an officer automatically became a nobleman 'by right of service'; he laid this rule down as the basis for the organisation of military service.

The ancient hierarchy of boyars, great officers of the Crown, *stol'niks*, and *striapchie*, based on birth, on court position, or on membership of the Duma, lost its original importance; the old Court of the Kremlin disappeared with the transference of the imperial seat to the banks of the Neva, and the Duma vanished when the Senate was created.

The register of grades of January 24th, 1722, in fact the Table of Ranks, introduced a new classification of men of service with new ranks which, with very few exceptions, were given foreign names, generally Latin and German. These ranks were arranged in the Table in three parallel columns, civil, military, and court, each divided into fourteen ranks or classes. The Table of Ranks in the reformed Russia substituted a bureaucratic hierarchy based on ability for the aristocratic hierarchy based on birth and genealogy. One of the articles annexed to the Table specifically emphasised that nobility of birth in itself, without service, was of no importance and did not qualify anybody for high office. Members of illustrious families could not qualify for a rank until they had shown both their sovereign and the state that they were capable men, 'and they will not receive rank and honours until they have done so.' The children of Russians and foreigners who were inscribed in the first eight ranks (down to and including the rank of major and college assessor) 'whatever their birth, become the equals of the best and most ancient noble families, and enjoy the same dignity and advantages'. For this reason government service opened the ranks of the nobility to everybody, and the hereditary structure of the nobility was completely altered.

Unfortunately it is impossible to estimate how many people were ennobled under Peter. Towards the end of the seventeenth century there were about 2,985 ennobled family

H

names amongst whom there were 15,000 landowners, not counting their children. Vockerodt, Secretary of the Prussian Embassy in Russia towards the end of Peter's reign, who had collected a great deal of material on Russia, wrote in 1737 that at the time of the first revision there were about 500,000 members of noble families, from which it is possible to deduce that there were approximately 100,000 noble families. Unfortunately these figures give no idea of the proportion of commoners who became noblemen through the Table of Ranks.

The transformation of the local militia of the nobility into a regular army in which all classes were represented led to three important changes in the nobility's service. First, civil and military service, hitherto one and the same thing, were now separate. Second, both types of state service were preceded by a compulsory course of preparatory education. Third, and perhaps the most important for the future of Russia, Peter's regular army lost its territorial composition. Previously during campaigns 'regimental service' was performed, not only by garrisons, but by entire detachments of noblemen drawn from the same district. Regiments of foreign organisation recruited from different parts of the country dealt the first blow to territorial recruitment. The enrolment of volunteers, and later on conscription, finally destroyed the territorial basis of military organisation, and gave the regiments a heterogeneous composition which deprived them of local allegiance. A man from Ryazan, absent for a long time or forever from his native Pekhlets or Zimarov, forgot that he was from Ryazan, and knew only that he was a dragoon in a fusilier regiment commanded by Colonel Famendine. The barracks successfully extinguished any territorial allegiance. It was the same in the Guards. The ancient metropolitan nobility, cut off from their narrow, almost provincial, court life, joined forces with the indigenous Muscovite nobility.

Permanent residence in Moscow or on estates close to the capital, and daily attendance at the Kremlin, led the new courtiers to associate Moscow with home, in the same way that Kozelsk was home for the Kozelskian noblemen and their sons. Transformed into guardsmen of the Preobrazhensky or Semenovsky regiments, and sent to the Finnish marshes on the Neva, these noblemen forgot that they came from Moscow, and felt only that they were guardsmen. This exchange of local for regimental or barrack ties could result in the Guards becoming a blind instrument of force in the hands of a powerful sovereign, or Praetorians or Janissaries under a weak ruler. Thus in the Time of Troubles in 1611, a natural ambition was conceived in the militia of the nobility commanded by the Princes Trubetskoi, Zarutsky, and Liapunov, who had come to deliver Moscow from the Poles: to win Russia for themselves by pretending to defend her against external enemies. The Romanov dynasty, by consolidating the institution of serfdom, was responsible for this idea; Peter by creating a regular army, but more particularly a Guards regiment, gave the dynasty an armed force but cannot have foreseen how or to what purpose it would be used by his own male and female descendants.

The nobility's complicated new service obligations made it imperative to improve their material situation in order to ensure efficient service. This led to an important change in the position of the nobility as a landowning class. It has already been noted that in old Russia there was a juridical distinction between two systems of land tenure. A *votchina* estate was hereditary while a *pomestie* was an estate held in service tenure on a temporary basis, generally only for one life. Before Peter, the two systems of land tenure had begun to approximate to one another; certain features of the *pomestie* were incorporated into the *votchina* system and vice versa. The reason for this lay in the very nature of the *pomestie* as a landed estate. In the days when the peasantry was free, the main purpose of a *pomestie* was to reward the beneficiary for his services to the State with the yield, in money and kind, of the estate. In these conditions there was no difficulty in transferring a *pomestie* from one person to another. The recipient of a *pomestie,* however, naturally took an interest in its management — he established a farm with his own materials and workmen, cleared woodlands, tilled the land, and settled peasants to whom he advanced money. In this way new assets, which tended to become the *pomeshchik's* personal property, were created on Crown lands which had been given to a man of service on a temporary basis only.

Law and custom came into opposition with one another as the position of the peasants developed into serfdom and serfdom became legalised, so that the customary relationship between *pomeshchiks* and tenants overwhelmed the original meaning of the *pomestie* estate. How could a *pomestie* estate remain a temporary possession once the peasants had become the *pomeshchik's* own serfs? The difficulty was met without actually altering existing tenure rights. The law gave way before the new situation in so far as it extended a *pomeshchik's* right to dispose of his estate. Although outright sale was still expressly forbidden, a *pomestie* estate could be given away or bequeathed on special terms. It could go to a son or other relative, as a dowry to the suitor of a daughter or niece, or even to a person outside the family on condition that he supported the owner for his lifetime, or, if the owner were a widow, until she remarried, or he discharged this obligation by payment of a lump sum. Hereditary succession to a *pomestie* estate was sanctioned, as was sole succession to the property, and its indivisibility. In contemporary registers this is expressed as follows: 'When two sons accede to service the eldest shall be inscribed separately and the younger shall serve with his father on the *pomestie* estate;'

after the father's death the estate passed to the younger son alone.

In Tsar Michael's time decrees had spoken of *pomesties* as hereditary, although the law did not yet recognise this. A Michaelian edict states that 'a *pomestie* estate shall not pass out of the possession of the family'. This virtual acceptance of hereditary succession to a *pomestie* estate resulted in a further difficulty. The size and value of *pomestie* estates increased in proportion to a *pomeshchik's* rank and capabilities. Hence the question: how could a son inherit a *pomestie* estate, especially an important one, if he had as yet not earned through service the right to as large an estate as his father died possessed of? This problem was solved by the Muscovite bureaucracy in the ukaze of March 20th, 1684,[1] which permitted the heirs to inherit whether they were serving or not, while the division of estates among relatives or strangers was forbidden, and if no direct heirs existed the property could on certain conditions be left to collateral relations. This ukaze changed the system of land tenure. While it did not wholly establish legal or testamentary hereditary succession to a *pomestie* estate, it did ensure what might be called the *familisation* of estates, i.e., that the estate remain in the possession of one family. What in fact followed was the division of *pomestie* estates among the numerous heirs, whether direct or collateral, and the principle of sole succession was abandoned. The creation of a regular army meant the decay of estate possession dependent on service. When the service of the nobility became not only hereditary but also perpetual the tenure of *pomestie* estates followed suit, and became indistinguishable from the *votchina* system of tenure. It followed therefore that the granting of *pomestie* estates was gradually replaced by the

[1] That is to say during Peter's minority. For the effects of this ukaze see James Mavor, *An Economic History of Russia*, J. M. Dent & Sons, 2nd edition, 1925, Vol. I, pp. 107–8.

granting of *votchina* estates together with tenants living on them.

In a surviving list of Crown towns and villages distributed to monasteries and individuals between 1682 and 1710, the expression 'in *pomestie*' is rarely used, and then only until 1697; generally the estates were given 'in *votchina*'. During these twenty-eight years nearly 44,000 peasant homesteads and 1,350,000 acres of tilled land, not counting woods and pastures, were distributed from Crown property. In this way the *pomestie* and *votchina* types of tenure had become practically indistinguishable one from the other by the beginning of the eighteenth century, and the *pomestie* estate as a distinct form of tenure had nearly disappeared. Three main features marked the merger between *pomestie* estates and *votchina* estates; *pomestie* estates could be inherited, as were *votchina* estates; *pomestie* estates could be divided among direct and collateral heirs, as were *votchina* estates; and the gifts of *votchina* estates took the place of temporary possession of *pomestie* estates.

This state of affairs was responsible for Peter's decree of March 23rd, 1714 on the law of inheritance. The main features or 'clauses' of the decree were:

(1) Immovables — *votchina* estates, *pomestie* estates, houses, shops — were not to be alienated but were to 'remain in the family'.

(2) Immovables were to pass from a testator to one of his sons, selected by the testator. Movables were to be divided by the testator as he wished among the remaining children. Failing sons, the same system was to be applied to daughters. In cases of intestacy, immovables were to go to the eldest son, failing whom, the eldest daughter, and movables were to be divided equally among the other children.

(3) A childless testator could leave his immovables to 'any

member of his family he pleased', and could dispose of his movables as he liked, either to relations or to strangers. In cases of intestacy where there were no children, the immovables went to the nearest relation, and the movables were to be divided 'in equal parts to whosoever may be thought proper'.

(4) The last surviving male of the family was to leave his immovables to one of the women of his family, on condition that her husband or her betrothed undertook in writing to add the name of the extant family to his own.

(5) Should a cadet of a noble family become a merchant, or should he after the age of forty enter the 'white clergy',[1] the act should not be regarded as dishonourable to himself or to his family.

The motive behind this decree is clear; the sole heir of an undivided property shall not be in a position to ruin his 'poor underlings' the peasants by imposing fresh impositions on them, as was done by the numerous heirs of a divided estate who wished to maintain the same standard of living as their father. The sole heir was to do everything possible to lighten the tax-paying burden of his peasants. In this way noble families would not be extinguished, 'but would continue to be illustrious and eminent,' whereas the division of estates would lead to the ruin of noble families, and turn them into simple countrymen 'of which there are already numerous examples in the Russian people'. The decree contains the observation that any nobleman who received even a piece of bread free, however small, would render indifferent service to the state, or would try to avoid it altogether and live in idleness. The new decree obliged the cadets 'to seek their own bread' through State service, study,

---

[1] i.e., the secular clergy.

commerce, etc. The decree is an honest one; the all-powerful legislator admits his incapacity to protect his subjects from the rapacity of impoverished *pomeshchiks,* and considers the nobility to be a class of idlers.

This decree introduced important changes in the class of land-owning men of service. But the decree did not introduce a system of primogeniture inspired by the feudal system of Western Europe, as is frequently believed, even though Peter did investigate the inheritance laws of England, France, and Venice, and inquired about them from foreigners living in Moscow. The decree of March 23, 1714, did not award exclusive rights to an eldest son; primogeniture was established only for cases of intestacy. If he so desired, a father could bequeath his properties to a younger son and completely ignore the elder. The decree established, not primogeniture, but the principle of sole succession and the indivisibility of immovables. This same principle was an attempt to put an end to the division of estates which had been increasing as a result of the decree of 1684, and which was responsible for inefficient service among the *pomeshchiks.* The juridical structure of the decree of March 23rd, 1714, was quite original. Having merged *pomestie* estates with *votchina* estates, the decree established for them an identical system of succession. But did the decree convert *votchina* estates into *pomestie* estates or vice versa? In the eighteenth century the latter view was taken, and the decree of 1714 was described as 'abounding with grace' since it was thought that Peter intended to convert *pomestie* estates into personal property. As a matter of fact the decree did neither of these things. What it did do was to combine the juridical peculiarities of *pomestie* estates and *votchina* estates, thereby creating a totally new and unprecedented system of land tenure which is best described as 'a system of hereditary, indivisible and perpetually obligatory ownership', in which the owner was bound to serve. All these features had existed in previous systems of land tenure in Russia. Until 1714, however, two of these features had never been combined: heredity belonged to the *votchina* system of tenure, and indivisibility to the *pomestie* system. *Votchina* estates were not indivisible, *pomestie* estates were not hereditary, and compulsory service was attached to both systems of tenure. Peter joined these distinctive features together, extended them to all systems of land tenure in the country, and made all estates inalienable from the family. These are the changes introduced by the decree of March 23rd, 1714.

This decree clearly illustrates the procedure Peter adopted in order to reorganise society and the administration. He accepted the existing systems without trying to put them on any new principles; he merely adjusted and combined the various systems in a different way. He abolished nothing, but modified the laws to make them conform with the new requirements of state. The new combinations may have given the new order an original aspect, but for all that it was based on old forms.

The decree of March 23rd, 1714, by providing for sole inheritance, relieved the now landless cadets, the heir's brothers and often nephews, from any service obligations, and left them free to choose other occupations. By 1714 Peter no longer needed all noblemen for the army, though hitherto the militia had been composed primarily of noblemen. At this stage Peter only wanted the sole successors to estates to become officers, and wanted them to be so placed that they could be efficient without finding it necessary to overburden their peasants with excessive exactions. This was entirely consistent with the position Peter expected the nobility to fill in his new, all-class army: that of commanding officers. This decree, like so many other of Peter's social reforms, failed to take into account contemporary customs and ideas. It divided the nobility into two classes: comfortable owners of

inherited estates, and dispossessed, homeless, landless, pro-
letarian brothers and sisters who either lived as pensioners in
the owner's house, or 'flitted miserably from one house to
another'. It is not hard, therefore, to imagine the complaints
and family quarrels which arose as a result of this decree, particularly as it was not an easy one to put into application.
The decree itself was badly drafted, failed to foresee certain
possibilities, and is full of ambiguities: Clause 1 forbids the
alienation of immovables, clause 12 permits their sale in cases
of necessity. The decree drew a sharp distinction between the
conditions on which movables and immovables might be bequeathed, but failed to define these terms; not unnaturally
this led to abuses and misunderstandings.

Subsequent Petrine decrees attempted to clarify the position, but it became more obscure when the decree of 1714
was submitted to a detailed revision in a decree of May 28th,
1725. The decree of 1714 was considered by Peter himself to
be a temporary measure only. He condoned important devia-
tions from the law, and in a supplementary decree of April
15th, 1716, ordered one quarter of a deceased nobleman's
immovables to be left to the widow for the remainder of her
lifetime, adding, 'This is to remain in force until further
notice.' Compulsory service by cadets was not in fact abrogated; they were enrolled as before, and both eldest and
younger sons were commanded to appear at 'inspections'.
Moreover estates granted to noblemen prior to the decree of
1714 were continually being divided in accordance with the
decree of 1684. It is probably to these divisions that Pososhkov is referring in his *Poverty and Wealth*. Apparently the
nobility behaved as if the decree introducing the principle of
sole inheritance had never existed. Pososhkov vividly describes how they proceeded to divide amongst themselves,
after the owner's death, both tenanted and untenanted estates,
subdividing villages into insignificant lots — which was, of

course, harmful to the Treasury — quarrelling among themselves, and even committing crimes which carried the death penalty. These divisions were later recognised and accepted in a decree of 1715. In brief, the decree of 1714 completely failed to achieve its purpose; it merely succeeded in complicating property rights and in bringing economic chaos to agriculture.

Peter's essential principle could be summarised thus: every nobleman serving the state in the capacity either of a civil servant or of an officer must own property if he was to be in a position to discharge his duties efficiently, and this property must be indivisible.

Chapter Five

★

BOTH ECONOMICALLY and juridically the position of the nobility was becoming more and more dependent on the condition of the peasantry. Those Petrine reforms which affected the rural population were aimed primarily at consolidating the military reforms, and at solving a problem which they had made specially pressing: how to increase the resources of the Treasury.

The Code (*Ulozhenie*)[1] had divided society into three main classes, and had defined their rights and obligations. The classes were: (1) men of service; (2) townsmen, i.e., those engaged in trade and industry; (3) the rural population, i.e., the peasantry. The last class was sub-divided into bonded peasants, free 'black-ploughing' (*chernososhnye*) peasants, and state and court peasants. Between these three main classes, or four if the clergy are included, come a number of intermediary, hybrid, groups, which did not form integral parts of any of the main classes, and lacked cohesion, though they overlapped into some of the main classes. These groups were not burdened directly with state obligations but served private interests. There were four of these groups: (1) *Kholopy polnye*, permanent bondsmen, *kabal'nye*, serfs bound temporarily by contract, and *zhilye*, whose bondage was also temporary. (2) *Vol'nitsy*, a group of free men consisting of freed bondsmen, townsmen, and peasants who had abandoned

[1] The Code of 1649 was the first Russian attempt at codification in the broad sense of the term. It remained in operation until 1833.

their occupations and stopped paying state tax (*tyaglo*), and even men of service who were either landless or had abandoned their estates — in general all those men who had neither domicile nor occupation. These people formed an intermediary class coming between the serfs and the free men who paid state tax. Because the distribution of alms, by the clergy and by charitable laymen, was so badly organised, there was a large number of professional beggars who must be included in this intermediary class. The genuinely pious, and the aged of both sexes who were sheltered by churches or private foundations, are not, however, included in this class. (3) Episcopal and monasterial servants and attendants; of these the servants acted as stewards of church land and closely resembled civil servants; they received land from ecclesiastical institutions on conditions of *pomestie* estate tenure, and sometimes were transferred into the civil service. The attendant was a sort of ecclesiastical serf but did not come under the existing serf laws. (4) A large body of children of the clergy, *tserkovniki*, as they were called, whose hopes of finding employment as sacristans had not yet been fulfilled. They lived from hand to mouth near the churches where their fathers had the living, sometimes engaging in urban pursuits such as trade or industry, sometimes entering the service of a private individual.

It is possible to distinguish all these groups according to their position in the state. Bondsmen (*kholopy*) and episcopal and monasterial attendants were serfs, not for a limited period but for life, and were exempt from paying the state tax; vagrants and the children of the clergy were free men, but were similarly exempt. 'Black-ploughing' peasants who were free, and household serfs who were bonded, both paid the state tax. The multiplicity of these intermediary classes gave the social structure a heterogeneity which impressed contemporary foreign observers who were astounded at the number of idlers in the state of Muscovy. This idle, non-productive mass of people was dependent for support upon those tax-paying classes who supplied the Treasury with its revenue. Moreover these people were rivals of the state in as much as they used up those resources which were badly needed to supplement the revenue of the Treasury. Peter, with his natural instinct for economy, wanted to see these people employed, and useful to the state both in service, and as taxpayers. By conscription, and, later on by the census, he instituted a general purge of society and simplified its composition.

When the regular army was first established the most eager and numerous recruits were the *vol'nitsy* and the serfs. Originally these classes constituted the rank and file of the Guards regiments, and it was not until later that they were replaced by the nobility. In order to maintain the strength of his forces Peter openly violated bondage-right by allowing serfs to enrol without obtaining their masters' consent. The newly formed regiments that fought at Narva in 1700 were mainly recruited from these two classes. Moreover, just before Narva, an order had been issued ordering the recruitment of any *kholopy* and serfs who were fit for service. Prince Boris Kurakin mentioned in his autobiography that 'volunteers to the army were promised their freedom, those who wished could leave their domiciles, and a great many took advantage of this', and when the Baltic fleet was being created 'three thousand of these youths were enrolled'. In the same way work was found for a large mass of useless and unemployed men. The purge of society was moreover very thorough; of the tens of thousands of volunteers, few returned to their previous miserable existence. Many of those who had not had time to desert either fell at Narva, Riga, Erestfer, or Schlüsselberg, or died of hunger, cold, or disease. With the establishment of conscription the army no longer confined itself to urban and rural taxpayers, but accepted house serfs, vagabonds, children of the clergy, monastery servants, and even clerks. In this way a principle, hitherto unknown in Russia, was established — the obligation of all classes to perform military service.

The second and more effective way of simplifying the structure of Russian society was the introduction of the census which Peter carried out in a characteristic manner, and which is a good illustration of the methods and resources he had at his disposal. After the conquest of Livonia, Esthonia, and Finland, the pressure of the Northern War was diminished, and Peter had time to consider how best to maintain his regular army on a peace-time basis; even after the end of hostilities this army would have to remain under arms, housed in barracks, and maintained at the state's expense. The army could not be disbanded, and it was not easy to know what to do with it. Peter evolved a complicated billeting and maintenance scheme, and, on November 26th, 1718, during the negotiations for peace with Sweden at the Aland Congress, issued an ukaze couched in the first words that entered his head.

Phrased in Peter's usual hurried, careless, and laconic style, the first two clauses of the decree state that 'it is necessary to exact from everybody within the period of one year the truth concerning the number of male souls belonging to whom and where. Should anybody conceal anything then his possessions will be given to whomsoever informs against him. State how many tax-paying souls are required to maintain a soldier and fix a mean rate'. The ukaze continues in an equally confused way to say how all this is to be done, and threatens defaulters with confiscation of property, the sovereign's most terrible anger, ruin, and even death — expressions commonly found in Peter's legislation. This decree meant more work for the urban and rural administrations as well as for the landowners. A period of one year had been considered sufficient for the compilation of the lists, but by the end of 1719 only a few had been drawn up, and most of these were inexact. The Senate therefore ordered guardsmen throughout the country to put the civil servants, and even the governors, who were responsible for the lists, in fetters, and to keep them there until the newly created chancellery at St. Petersburg had received all the lists and the total returns. But even this severity did not expedite matters, and lists were still being sent to St. Petersburg in 1721. The main reason for the delay was that this confused decree was so difficult to understand that further clarification and explanatory supplements were required. At first it was thought that the census was to apply only to the agricultural peasants; later on it was ordered that rural household serfs were to be inscribed as well, and supplementary depositions had to be made. This gave rise to yet a further difficulty: the landowners guessed that all this was going to lead to the imposition of a new and burdensome tax, so they and their subordinates only inscribed a proportion of the actual numbers. At the beginning of 1721 over twenty thousand souls were discovered 'salted away'. Governors and *voevodas* were ordered to go on tour, and verify all the lists personally. The Holy Synod appealed to the parish clergy to help with these verifications and revisions, and threatened not only to relieve them of their benefices, rank, and possessions if any more cases of concealment occurred, but also to inflict 'merciless corporal punishment to be followed with forced labour, even in cases of old age'. After having resorted to the issue of severe decrees, to torture and to confiscations, to get the rusty administrative machinery into motion, the government finally calculated that, according to the rolls, there were in 1722 about five million peasant souls in the country.

The second clause of the November decree was now put into effect — 'the dispersion of the army throughout the country,' and the distribution of the regiments among those who were to maintain them. Billeting officers — ten generals or colonels, each accompanied by a corporal — were sent to the ten districts in which the census had been carried out. It was intended to billet the regiments in companies in 'permanent dwellings', that is to say, in cantonments built specially for this purpose, instead of billeting the soldiers in the peasants' homes, in order to avoid conflicts between hosts and guests. The billeting officer was ordered to assemble the nobility living in his district and persuade them to build barracks for the soldiers and houses for the officers and general staff. New difficulties arose, however; the billeting officers had also been told to verify the number of peasant souls. In effect, this was a second census which brought to light enormous frauds, and showed that in some districts more than half the number of peasant souls had been 'salted away'. It therefore became impossible to use the original figure of five million as a basis for distributing the regiments about the country. Peter and the Senate alternately threatened and cajoled the landowners, billeting officers, and elders, and fixed a new time limit for further revisions — which was never observed. Moreover, the officials themselves, owing either to their confused instructions or to innate stupidity, made a complete muddle of the classifications. They were not sure whom to inscribe on the lists and whom not to inscribe; they bombarded the government with requests for information; they did not even know the size of the army, and it was only in 1723 that the exact numbers were ascertained.

Meanwhile all the officials were ordered to finish their work at 'whatever cost', and return to the capital by the beginning of 1724, the date Peter had fixed for the poll-tax to come into effect. None of the officials arrived within the time limit, and they all warned the Senate that they could not possibly finish by that date. The time limit was extended to March, and the collection of the poll-tax proper was put off until 1725. By that time the affair had been going on for six years, but Peter himself never saw the end of it. The officials had still not arrived in the capital by January 28th, 1725, when Peter died.

The regiments found themselves awkwardly placed. Most of the landowners had refused to build barracks, and preferred to billet the soldiers in the peasants' homes. The landowners were then compelled to build barracks, which resulted in new 'heavy burdens' being laid on their peasants. Building was begun hurriedly and everywhere at once by peasants who were taken away from their usual occupations. In order to buy the necessary land on which the new buildings were to be built, a new tax was levied, which delayed the collection of the poll-tax. These barracks were supposed to be finished by 1726, but soon after Peter's death the finishing date was put back four years. A start had been made, but nowhere was anything finished, and enormous quantities of material provided by the peasants had been wasted; only the officers' houses were finished. The plan had been badly conceived from the start. Soldiers and officers were billeted on peasants both in towns and in the country.

But the regiments were not allowed to remain mere parasites dependent on the census-souls for their upkeep. By some curious whim, Peter had decided that these regiments were a convenient administrative instrument. As well as helping with the building of their barracks, they were given complicated duties to perform as policemen and overseers. In order to maintain the regiments the nobility were told to organise themselves into associations which every year were to appoint commissaries who were to tour their respective districts, and who were empowered to collect the poll-tax, act as judges, and impose fines. The commissaries, in conjunction with their superiors, the regimental officers, were made responsible for the maintenance of law and order in their respective districts.

The regimental commanders and officers were ordered to apprehend thieves and brigands, prevent the peasants from absconding, arrest runaways, root out illicit stills and contraband, restrain civil servants from exploiting the peasants, and afford protection to all and sundry. They enjoyed such vast powers that, together with governors and *voevodas*, they could prosecute the commissaries, supervise the application of imperial decrees by the governors and *voevodas* themselves, and report directly to the capital in cases of irregularity and negligence. Had the regiments conserved their territorial composition and been billeted in their own districts they might have served a useful purpose. But they were strangers to the districts, and had been injected by force into local society and administration; they could not live in peace with the local population since they imposed new burdens, not only on the peasants, but on the landowners as well. A peasant could not go to work in another district even when he had been given a discharge paper signed by his landowner or parish priest; he had to present himself at regimental headquarters where an officer certified and recorded the letter, and issued the peasant with a permit signed and sealed by the colonel. The peasant, moreover, had to pay stamp duty. The government under Catherine I was forced to admit that the unfortunate peasants fled, not only because of harvest failures and the poll-tax, but because 'of the discord that existed between the officers and local administrators and between the soldiers and the peasants'. The peasants found the collection of the poll-tax by the regiments extremely painful. The original census decree of 1718 had empowered the commissaries to collect the poll-tax, and no mention was made of military participation.

In 1723 Peter showed his extraordinary faith in the capacity of army officers by issuing a short decree which stated that 'to prevent the commissaries from causing confusion' because of inexperience in collecting the poll-tax, they must collaborate with army officers in the first year 'in order to make a good beginning.' But this collaboration continued for many years, and was long remembered by those who paid the poll-tax. The presence of the military caused greater hardship than the tax itself. Armed visitations were made three times a year and each visitation lasted for two months: for six months of the year the towns and villages were in a state of panic. Moreover the inhabitants had to maintain the soldiery while they carried out searches and even executions. It is hardly likely that the Tartars under Batu Khan behaved worse when they conquered Russia.

Only after Peter's death did the Senators and a few other dignitaries state that the mere coming and going of officers, soldiers, commissaries, and others, brought terror to the villages because they took the last means of the peasants in taxes in order to advance themselves; the peasants not only realised all their belongings and cattle for what prices they could get but their sowing grain as well, and 'fled beyond the frontiers'. These official protests remind one of Pilate washing his hands; why did not these high officials say something to Peter during his lifetime, and face to face? The regiments had hardly settled into their permanent quarters when it was noticed that the number of census-souls had greatly diminished, partly as the result of increased mortality, and partly because more of them were fleeing. Soon after Peter's death an infantry regiment in Kazan found it could only account for half the number of taxpayers responsible for the regiment's upkeep — thirteen thousand census-souls were missing. In all this it is difficult to recognise the Peter who created the victorious army of Poltava; Peter transformed the army into one hundred and twenty-six police posts which then terrorised the population of ten provinces.

Leaving aside for the moment fiscal considerations, let us look at the poll-tax from the point of view of its social and economic effects. It hardly seems likely that Peter, who had been hasty in formulating his ideas on the poll-tax and incorporated them in his first decree, foresaw the magnitude of the undertaking, which in time grew in complexity. It is probable that, in imposing a poll-tax, Peter had in view exclusively the bonded serfs — peasants and house-serfs. But having created a new unit of taxation, the census-soul, to cover these classes, it became impossible to continue levying the old tax on households on the other classes. For this reason State and Court peasants, free single householders (*odnodvortsy*), and townsmen were added to the tax-rolls. Especially important was the extension of the census registration to the intermediary classes. In this particular instance Peter surpassed his ancestors in the arbitrary disposal of human beings. A decree of 1722 ordered the following to be inscribed on the poll-tax registers: the sons, grandsons, nephews, and other relatives of 'all those who had been, but are no longer employed by the Church, namely priests, deacons, cantors, or sextons'. Moreover all these people were bound 'for nothing' to the proprietors of the land on which the churches stood. If the church 'stood apart' from privately owned land, then these people might choose to whom they should be bound; the decree does not, however, state on what conditions.

The law was no more lenient towards the *vol'nitsy*. By a decree of March 31st, 1700, those serfs who had fled from their masters and wished to become soldiers were enrolled into the army. A decree of February 1st, 1700, had authorised the enrolment of free men and serfs bound by contract (*kabal'nye*) who had been set free at their masters' death, and who, after examination, were pronounced fit to serve. According to the decree of March 7th, 1721, those who had not been examined since 1700 were now to present themselves; those who were considered fit were enrolled as soldiers, and those not found suitable were threatened with the galleys unless they 'went into one of the other public services or bound themselves anew to some proprietor'. In this way Peter hoped to rid the country of vagrants and unemployed. Provision was also made for those who, rather than enrol as soldiers, preferred to remain serfs, in which case the owners had to send healthy replacements to the army in their stead. A serf bound by contract (*kabala*) to an aged master, and himself over military age, already looked forward to the freedom that would be his at his master's death. But if his master took on another serf bound by contract who was of military age, then the older serf, both against his will and despite the existing contract, became a soldier for an indefinite period, which was no improvement over his life as a serf. Soldier, serf, or galley-slave — these were the alternatives open to a whole class of free men.

Peter's measures concerning the serfs were equally peremptory. Within this class two groups of people, both of whom rented land, the courtyard serfs (*zadvornye*) and the *delovye*, who were small tradesmen, had been registered as state tax-payers a long time before the introduction of the census, in exactly the same way as the rest of the peasantry. With the reform, all the remaining economic and legal categories of serfs, servants of the clergy and the laity, agricultural peasants, and household serfs both urban and rural, were fused into one legally uniform mass. A resolution of January 19th, 1723, stated that all these people were to pay poll-tax (as did the peasantry), and as a class they were transformed into serfs bound to their masters in perpetuity. The *kholopstvo* as an independent class of serfs who did not pay state taxes disappeared; the personal bondage of the serf and the land bondage of the peasant were amalgamated — the result was a single class of bonded people (*krepostnye lyudi*) who were subject to personal and land bondage alike, and who could be exploited and controlled at will by their masters.

The census concluded the arbitrary simplification in the structure of society which Peter's other reforms had started; all intermediary classes were, in contradiction to existing law, forced to belong to one of the main rural classes, either to the state peasantry or to the bonded people (*krepostnye lyudi*). The small class composed of the freeholders (*odnodvortsy*), the 'black-ploughing' peasants (*chernososhnye*), the Tartar, Yasash, and Siberian 'agricultural labourers' (*pashennye sluzhilye lyudi*), the pikemen, cavalrymen, dragoons, etc., were all incorporated into the state peasantry.

The extent of serfdom had increased considerably. But was serfdom juridically altered? What took place was a revolution, but it was a revolution of a negative order. The abolition of the serfs (*kholopstvo*) as a non-contributing class did not abolish their bondage, but both made them liable to state taxation and removed the existing limitations on their bondage. The limitations had been equally applicable to serfs bound by contract and serfs bound for a definite period of time (*zhilye*). Now registration of a 'census-soul' on the landowners' list automatically entailed serfdom, and abrogated any existing contracts. This revolution had been in preparation over the seventy years preceding the first revision. It has already been shown how badly the Code had defined the nature of peasant serfdom, and the distinction it made between the serfdom of the peasant and the servitude of the serfs (*kholops*). The development of serfdom after 1649 was determined by the vagueness of its definition in the Code itself. According to the Code of 1649, the serf was bound to the person of the landowner on condition that he was given a plot of land. The serf was not bound to the land on condition of dependence upon the landowner. Hence later legislation did not elaborate the limitations and conditions of serfdom, *qua* serfdom, but developed ways and means of doubly exploiting serf labour in the interests of both the Treasury and the landowner.

As far as serf ownership is concerned, from 1649 onwards landowners and agricultural labourers cease to be contracting parties and become owners and owned. The latter paid arbitrarily imposed taxes first of all to their masters and then to their masters' superior, that is to say, to the government. For this reason the government gave the landowners wider legal powers over their serfs; the landowners became the government's financial agents and inspectors of serf labour, and were made responsible for law and order in the villages where the serf inhabitants were always prepared for flight. The landowners, on their part, bombarded their local governments with petitions that more drastic measures be taken for the recovery of runaway serfs. The imperfections of the law resulted in a great deal being left to the arbitrary powers of the stronger side, in this case the landowners.

After 1649 practice revealed a complex process of change in the condition of serfdom: the earlier juridical forms of serfdom blended with the later economic conditions in which the serfs (*kholops*) found themselves, until those features which distinguished serf from peasant had completely disappeared. In contravention of the Code, some peasants were taken from the land into household service. The law said that the children of peasants taken into household service were to receive their freedom, as were the children of serfs bound by contract upon the death of the master. But now household serfs taken from among the permanent bondsmen (*kholopy polnye*), and from serfs bound by contract were tied even closer to their masters by written bonds of the same type, and, together with those household serfs who had by a reverse process settled on the land, became liable to state taxes. Thus bonded household serfs appeared from amongst the peasantry, while serfs bound by contract and 'old men of service'[1] were settled on the land under conditions which gave the land-

[1] These were freeholders charged principally with military duties.

owner the right to move them and their animals in the event of the estate changing hands.

The relations of the rural population were changing towards the end of the seventeenth century as the different systems of servitude were slowly being converted into one single and general class of serfdom. The imposition of the poll-tax both exposed and encouraged the practices of the landowners, who were not subject to any control. Again, in contravention of the Code of 1649, the landowners assumed criminal jurisdiction over their serfs, and the right of discretionary punishment. Private documents dating from the end of the seventeenth century show that, for stealing two vedro[1] of wine from the steward, or presenting a petition to their master on behalf of all the peasants in the village saying that, since they were poor and had only a little land, would the master please impose dues that they could pay, and would he please get another steward, or saying that one was not bound to his master, the following sentence was pronounced: 'the offender is to be mercilessly beaten with the knout until there is scarcely any breath left in his body.' The peasant community still existed, but it had no effective power, and merely served in a subsidiary capacity to uphold the *pomeshchik's* authority: in judicial matters, for instance, the master gave the order 'all serfs are to be questioned'; the peasant community itself carried out the enquiry, but the master pronounced sentence.

This unchecked growth of *pomeshchik* power showed that some legislative control over them was imperative, and towards the end of Peter's reign Pososhkov was not alone in being convinced of this. Pososhkov, who was a peasant by birth, looked on the enserfment of the peasants as only a temporary evil. 'The *pomeshchik*' he wrote, 'is not going to own the peasant for ever. He will only own the peasant tempor-

[1] About five and a half gallons.

arily since the true lord of the peasant is the Autocrat of
Russia.' Some thinking peasants, whose opinion Pososhkov
shared and recorded, developed the idea that the *pomeshchiks*'
power over the peasants was not permanent, as it was over a
beast of burden, but a trust given to them by the government
which in its own time the government would take away, just
as it retired an aged or redundant civil servant. Pososhkov
was very disturbed about the way in which the *pomeshchik*
arbitrarily disposed of peasant labour and property. He insisted on the absolute necessity of legislation 'in order to
decide how much a *pomeshchik* shall be allowed to levy in
taxes or in kind, and for how many days of the week a
peasant shall be required to work for his master'. Pososhkov
also drew up a plan in which he suggested some sort of all-
Russian convention of 'eminent noblemen and lesser noblemen' to consider the extortionate practices of the landowners
and the rate of peasant assessment; this was somehow supposed to make the peasant feel 'that decisions were emanating
from a joint council or from a proclamation by His Majesty'.
This was the earliest manifestation of the idea that a committee of provincial noblemen should be appointed to consider how the condition of the peasantry might be improved;
one hundred and thirty years were to elapse, however, before
this was done.

Pososhkov had further ideas on this subject, and proposed
that the peasants' land should be separated from the *pomeshchik's* estate, so that it would cease altogether to belong to
the *pomeshchik*. Pososhkov also wished to arrange *pomeshchik*-peasant relations through 'government decrees', and his
suggestions are reminiscent of the 1861 Act of Emancipation's
clauses concerning peasants whose bondage was temporary.
It appears that people were thinking about the abolition of
serfdom. During the last years of Peter's reign it was ru-
moured that he had been advised, on several occasions, to

abolish serfdom, and to stimulate and encourage the majority of his subjects by granting a moderate amount of freedom. Because, however, the Tsar understood his people and knew that they would not work without compulsion, this advice was rejected. Thus Peter maintained the old system although he knew that it was fundamentally unsound. The Code of 1649 had allowed the alienation of peasants and bondsmen from the land, and even their sale, with the break-up of the family. At the beginning this happened only rarely, but later on the practice became general. This traffic in serfs, as if they were cattle, disturbed Peter: 'this cannot be seen anywhere else in the world, and is responsible for not a few popular protestations.' In 1721 Peter told the Senate that 'this sale of men must be stopped, or if this is not possible then they must be sold not singly, but together with their families or households'. This was not, however, a peremptory order, but good-natured advice given to my Lord Senators 'for their consideration'; the Senate was at this time deliberating a new Code. The truth was that the autocratic monarch was not sure how extensive his powers were, and did not feel himself strong enough to put down the lesser nobility who were primarily responsible for the retail trade in serfs.

Not long before Peter gave his advice to the Senate, he had allowed serfs to volunteer of their own free will for the army, and had said that they were to be allowed to take with them their wives and any children below the age of twelve; children older than this were to remain behind and remain serfs. Peter was concerned not with the equity of serfdom, but with its economics, and he was well aware of his Treasury's interests. Previously, government and *pomeshchik* had owned peasant villages between them, 'in strips' (*cherespolosno*). The government was interested in the agricultural peasants and serfs as taxpayers, paying their taxes through the *pomeshchik* who acted as the government's police agent. The non-tax-paying household serfs were left in the *pomeshchik's* care in conformance with the conditions of the various forms of bondage. Under Peter a mutual (*sovmestnoi*) system of possession was substituted for the *cherespolosno* system. The ancient forms of bondage, with their limiting and differentiated conditions, disappeared: the only distinctions that remained were economic, and these were rearranged at the wish of the landowner.

But, having increased the *pomeshchiks'* power, the government now demanded a share of the labour of the non-tax-paying serfs. What happened? Did the *kholopy* become bonded agricultural peasants or vice versa? Neither one nor the other. Exactly the same thing happened as with the *votchina* and *pomestie* estate systems of tenure. From a new combination of the old systems of bondage and from the fusion of agricultural peasants, bonded serfs (*kholopy*), and free people (*vol'nitsy*) emerged an entirely new status, that of the '*krepostnye lyudi*'. They and their children after them became absolutely bound to their masters, as had been the earlier permanent bondsmen (*kholopy polnye*), and were liable to State taxes as were the former bonded peasants.

Peter's innovations neither intensified bondage as such, nor limited it. Medieval Russian law had begun with the complete slavery of the *Russkaya Pravda* which was similar to the Greco-Roman system, though in time conditions of slavery were somewhat ameliorated. In the seventeenth century the weak and greedy government of the new dynasty allowed the landowners complete freedom, thereby making it possible for the ruling classes to take full advantage of the peoples' impoverishment. The ruling classes ignored those contracts which they found particularly irksome, ceased to differentiate between the various forms of serfdom, and even managed to enserf a large proportion of the free peasants. Peter's legislation did nothing to prevent these harmful tendencies; on the contrary it amalgamated all previous forms of bondage into one type of absolute bondage. This had the effect of returning Russian society to the long familiar Greco-Roman rule, that 'Slavery is indivisible; one cannot differentiate between conditions of slavery; nothing can be said about a slave, except that he is a slave'.

On the other hand Peter made the ownership of serfs taxable by imposing a state tax, for which the owner was responsible, on each male serf. Peter was concerned with revenue, not with freedom, with taxpayers, not with citizens. Though contrary to all law and justice, the effect of the census-registration was to increase the number of taxpayers by more than one hundred thousand. In spite of the apparent irrationality of the poll-tax, it did lead to an improvement in agriculture in the eighteenth century. The old direct taxes, the tax on ploughs and the tax on households, which it replaced, were really taxes on land, and had forced the peasant and the landowner to reduce the amount of cultivated land. In order to make up for these losses, they both took to subterfuge of a sort which naturally tended to reduce the tax yield. It was because of this that in the sixteenth and seventeenth centuries peasant holdings grew smaller and smaller. The government of the new dynasty tried to prevent this rapid reduction of peasant holdings by abolishing the tax on ploughs, and introducing in its stead a tax on households. Instead of increasing the amount of tilled land, both landowner and peasant began to reduce the number of dwellings, either by cramming into each the largest number of people possible, or by amalgamating three, five, or ten peasant dwellings, leaving only one common entrance, and nailing up all the other doors. Agriculture suffered and state revenue declined. When the tax on households was replaced by a tax on souls (which was a direct tax on manpower), all incentive to curtail tillage disappeared: the peasant paid seventy kopecks whether he tilled two desyatins or four.[1] The improvement in agriculture, clearly seen in the eighteenth century, was thus partially, if not wholly, due to the imposition of the poll-tax. At the same time that the poll-tax was introduced, Pososhkov was dreaming about an ideal situation in which each peasant household would have at least six desyatins under cultivation, giving one and a half desyatins to each peasant since, on the average there were four peasants in each household. Towards the end of the eighteenth century a holding of this size was thought small; holdings on the average were larger, and each peasant household cultivated ten desyatins and sometimes more. It was mainly owing to the imposition of the poll-tax, though perhaps indirectly, that in the eighteenth century the land was cultivated as never before.

The significance of the poll-tax is thus explained. Though in itself it did not alter the legal status of the peasant, it was responsible for effecting important changes in agriculture. The decrees which imposed the poll-tax were not intended to produce this particular consequence.

[1] 1 desyatin = 2.7 acres.

Chapter Six

★

THE NUMBER OF persons registered as taxpayers and as serfs was increased by the census. The object of Peter's industrial and commercial legislation, with which, after the army, he was mainly concerned, was to improve the quality and increase the quantity of goods. Peter's talents were well suited to this work, and his activity was as great as it had been when he was engaged on the military reforms. He was a far-sighted, tireless, and resourceful organiser, and was not only a true successor to the acquisitive, property-owning Muscovite Tsars, but also a creative statesman and an economist capable of finding new resources and turning them to a profit. Peter's predecessors had bequeathed to him their theories and timid beginnings: Peter made a plan, and found the means to implement it.

Muscovite statesmen of the seventeenth century had realised that the financial system of the state was unsound. Taxation had been increased haphazardly according to the requirements of the Treasury, and its burden was heavy, while nothing had been done to raise the level of production. Peter's economic policy[1] was based on the assumption that an increase in production would increase the tax yield. He aimed at teaching his subjects improved techniques and giving them better tools, at creating new industries and at developing the country's untouched natural resources. It was with this in

[1] For a detailed work on Peter's economic policy see E. Pernet, *La Politique Economique de Pierre le Grand,* Paris, 1913.

mind that Peter began to investigate every aspect of the national economy. There was hardly an industry, however modest, in which he did not show an interest and in which his influence was not felt: farming in all its branches, the breeding of cattle, horses, and sheep, hop growing, silkworm culture, horticulture, viniculture, pisciculture, etc. He expended most of his energy, though, on developing the country's manufacturing industries, and in particular mining [of ores], which was of such military importance.[1]

No activity, however, was ignored by Peter, who always examined everything in detail. One day when he was in a small French village he saw a priest gardening. Peter was immediately full of questions and of practical lessons for himself. 'I will persuade my idle priests' he said, 'to cultivate their gardens and plots so that they will be assured of their daily bread, and will lead a better life.' The aspect of Western European civilisation which attracted Peter was its technical achievement, and, having once seen it for himself, he remained forever fascinated. He inspected factories and workshops in Amsterdam, Paris, and London, and made careful notes on everything he saw. Peter's first acquaintance with Europe was made at a time when mercantilist theories were popular. As is known, the mercantilists held that, to avoid impoverishment, a nation must be self-sufficient, while to become wealthy it must export as much, and import as little as possible. Impressed by what he had seen abroad, Peter accepted the mercantilist theory, and at once acted upon it. Accordingly he tried to introduce into Russia a great variety of industries, paying little attention to installation costs in his eagerness to exploit Russia's natural resources and reduce her dependence on imports.

His admirer, Pososhkov, seems to have understood what Peter had in mind when he said that even if at first it cost

[1] See Roger Portal, *L'Oural au XVIIIe siecle*, Paris, 1950.

more to produce a new good in Russia than to import it, once the enterprise had consolidated itself it would compensate for all losses. Peter was influenced by two considerations: first, that in undiscovered and untapped natural resources Russia was not inferior to any nation, but was richer than most; and second, that the state must itself be responsible for the development of this wealth, and take any steps necessary to make the Russians play their part. More than one ukaze shows the importance Peter attached to these matters. Thus he wrote 'Our State of Russia is richer than other countries in metals and minerals, which till this time have never been used'; and he encouraged new industries, such as sericulture and viniculture, and the discovery and development of new and hitherto dormant sources of revenue, so that 'God's blessings shall not be idle in the earth'.

Peter was also very thrifty; he encouraged the exploitation of the country's natural resources, but at the same time was careful to prevent pillaging and unnecessary devastation. He was especially careful with shipbuilding timber, particularly since he knew how reckless the Russians were with it. He made a great fuss about looking for peat and coal for fuel; he thought out various uses for hitherto useless materials, and ordered all branches from trees used for shipbuilding to be made into axles or burned for potash. This petty saving is reminiscent of the Grand Duke of Moscow, Ivan III, who sent some sheep for a foreign ambassadors' banquet and ordered the skins to be returned! Peter's desire to preserve shipbuilding timber led him to supress a custom, sanctioned by law and practised by the pious, of using coffins cut from a single block of oak or pine. In 1723 Peter sent to his Chief Superintendent of Forests (who was attached to the Admiralty) an instruction that henceforth coffins were to be made from solid blocks of fir, birch, or alder; pine coffins were only to be made from planks of a specified length, and

K

oak coffins were strictly forbidden. Everybody was closely supervised by Peter who, in his attempt to stir his lethargic country to action, left little to voluntary private initiative. He knew that the Russians baulked at innovation, and, realised that nothing could be achieved in industry without compulsion. 'Even if it is good and necessary, yet be it novel and our people will do nothing about it unless they are compelled.' Peter ordered the college of Manufactures not only to help the manufacturers 'with suggestions, but if necessary to use force, to exhort them and help with machinery and by other means', thereby giving the manufacturers so much support that 'having seen the measure of the Tsar's benevolence, all manner of men will voluntarily and without fear enter into new undertakings'.[1] Comparing his subjects to children, Peter said that unless the master used force his pupils would never learn the alphabet, and that, though they might sulk at first, they would be grateful when they had learned it. 'Was not everything done by force,' exclaimed Peter in 1723 looking back over thirty years, 'and are not people grateful for what has resulted?' As a result of his personal experiences and observations in Western Europe, Peter introduced a series of measures to develop Russian industry which we shall now discuss.

1. *The employment of foreign master-craftsmen and manufacturers*

Soon after Peter's return to Russia in 1698, a large number of artists, craftsmen, and artisans who had entered Russian service began to arrive in the country. Peter had engaged at Amsterdam alone more than one thousand master-craftsmen and artisans. Russian Residents at foreign courts were primarily occupied with finding local craftsmen willing to

[1] Some aspects of Russia's industrial growth is discussed in Roger Portal, 'Manufactures et classes sociales en Russie au XVIIIᵉ siecle', *Revue Historique,* Avril-Juin, Juillet-Septembre, 1949.

enter Russian service. In 1702 a proclamation of Peter's was published throughout Germany inviting foreign capitalists, manufacturers, and artisans to come to Russia on highly advantageous terms.[1] From this date an ever increasing number of industrialists and artisans went to Russia, tempted by the generous terms offered to them, and the scrupulous care of the Russian government in keeping its promises.[2] Peter particularly valued French craftsmen and artisans, who had enjoyed a very good reputation since the days of Colbert. When he was in Paris, Peter showed great interest in the

[1] A translation of this document has been printed in E. Schuyler, *Peter the Great*, London, 1884, Vol. II, pp. 176-7. 'It is sufficiently known in all the lands which the Almighty has placed under our rule, that since our accession to the throne all our efforts and intentions have tended to govern this realm in such a way that all of our subjects should, through our care for the general good, become more and more prosperous. For this end we have always tried to maintain internal order, to defend the State against invasion, and in every possible way to improve and to extend trade. With this purpose we have been compelled to make some necessary and salutary changes in the administration, in order that our subjects might more easily gain a knowledge of matters of which they were before ignorant, and become more skilful in their commercial relations. We have therefore given orders, made dispositions, and founded institutions indispensable for increasing our trade with foreigners, and shall do the same in future. Nevertheless we fear that matters are not in such a good condition as we desire, and that our subjects cannot in perfect quietness enjoy the fruits of our labours, and we have therefore considered still other means to protect our frontier from the invasion of the enemy, and to preserve the rights and privileges of our State, and the general peace of all Christians, as is incumbent on a Christian monarch to do. To attain these worthy aims, we have endeavoured to improve our military forces, which are the protection of our State, so that our troops may consist of well-drilled men, maintained in perfect order and discipline. In order to obtain greater improvement in this respect, and to encourage foreigners, who are able to assist us in this way, as well as artists and artisans profitable to the State, to come in numbers to our country, we have issued this manifesto, and have ordered printed copies of it to be sent throughout Europe.'

[2] This is rather a sweeping statement, and indeed many exceptions can be found. See in particular John Perry, *The State of Russia*, London, 1716. Captain Bruce remarked on 'the difficulties strangers have to encounter in endeavouring to get out of this country'. See Captain Peter Henry Bruce, *Memoirs*, London, 1782, pp. 114-15, 172, 210, 223, 350, 364.

Gobelin tapestries, and decided that he would like to build a factory for their production in St. Petersburg. The chief of the four master-craftsmen who were invited to Russia in 1716 was the famous French architect Leblond, 'that marvel' as Peter called him, who was given a state apartment at St. Petersburg for three years, a salary of five thousand roubles, and permission to leave Russia at the end of five years without having to pay any duty on his possessions. A tapestry factory was established, but owing to the absence of the right type of wool the master-craftsmen had nothing to do.

Peter did not look after his own subjects nearly as well as he looked after the foreigners. Thus in an order to the college of Manufactures he provided that, if a foreign master-craftsman wished to leave Russia before the expiration of his contract, the college was to find out whether he had been offended, even if he had not made a complaint but merely seemed discontented. Those Russians who had actually offended a foreigner were to be severely punished. Privileges were granted to foreigners on one condition: 'that they instruct our Russian people properly and conceal nothing.'

2. *The sending abroad of Russians in order to learn crafts*

During Peter's reign batches of young Russians were sent to the main industrial towns of Europe, where their instructors received very generous payment for their training. Russian sailors were sent to study in Holland, and from there went to Turkey, the Indies, and elsewhere, so that, in the words of Prince Kurakin, 'they were dispersed throughout the universe'. Similarly, in accordance with the government's policy, Russians were sent all over Europe to study a variety of arts and crafts, from 'medicine and philosophy' to methods of furnace-building, interior decoration, or bed-trimming. Peter wanted them to learn manufacturing trades in particular. Unfortunately, the foreigners who had been engaged on short contracts were unwilling and negligent in their teaching, and, when their contract expired, returned to their own countries leaving their 'Russian pupils imperfectly taught'. The Russians suspected that the foreigners were deliberately concealing their professional secrets. Peter therefore ordered the college of Manufactures to send abroad those young men who wished to study, to subsidise them at the Treasury's expense, and to give their families privileges in proportion to the progress they had made.

3. *Legislative inducements*

In medieval Russia those in state and church employ were forced to develop a double conscience — one for public life, the other reserved for private and personal use. The first required his public conduct to be honourable and dignified; the second allowed him to do as he pleased in private provided he went to confession once a year. This dichotomy hindered industrial progress in Russia. The urban industrial and commercial classes paid heavy 'industrial and commercial' taxes; they paid a direct tax on buildings and industrial establishments, and a five per cent turnover tax, as well as fulfilling onerous and unpaid duties imposed on them by the Treasury. According to the Code of 1649, every urban trader was obliged either to be a member of a tax-paying society or to help to meet the town's taxes. But the privileged classes, the men of service, the clergy, and especially the wealthy monasteries, also engaged in trade, and they paid no taxes. Thus an economy which was already hampered by a primitive commercial system and an impoverished rural population was further restricted. The privileged classes despised the merchants whom they regarded as 'inferior people',[1] so that, while they

---

[1] It is interesting to notice how little this attitude changed. When, in 1825, one of the Decembrists suggested that merchants should be admitted to the Northern Society, the retort was: 'Impossible! Merchants are ignoramuses!'

had nothing against trading, they disdained the name of merchant. The merchants themselves resorted to dishonest practices, giving short measures and false weight in an attempt to extricate themselves from their difficulties. In the writings of foreigners this dishonesty was proverbial: 'No cheating — no sale.' Nevertheless, it is obvious that, at meetings of the Zemsky Sobor in the seventeenth century, for example that of 1642, and during the conferences between representatives of the different social classes and the government, it was the representatives of the merchants and industrialists who alone showed a modicum of political and social sense and an understanding of what was necessary for the public good. Pososhkov, who, as a merchant of peasant origin, was aware of many considerations beyond the grasp of the upper classes, showed the irritation natural to one of his calling when he wrote that nobles, boyars and their servants, church dignitaries, civil servants, soldiers, and peasants were all trading without paying any of the taxes, and were taking the bread out of the mouths of the tax-paying merchants, Russian merchants had also to compete with an astute and well-organised body of foreign merchants who were protected by the corrupt Muscovite administration. It was high time, said Pososhkov, referring acidly to those foreign merchants who had established themselves in Moscow, to put away their pride; they had given themselves airs enough, he complained, when the monarchs were not interested in trade and the boyars were in power. When foreigners came, he wrote, they 'give influential people a gift of one hundred roubles, because of which they make a profit of half a million roubles. And all because the boyars look on the merchants as they look on an egg shell; they would cheerfully sell the merchants for a groat'. If Peter ever read these lines, which appeared in an essay written specially for him, he was probably very pleased with them. Throughout the whole of his reign

Peter preached dignity, 'honesty,' and the usefulness to Russia of industry and trade; he constantly affirmed that commercial and industrial occupations were as useful and as honourable as public service or teaching. Probably more than one nobleman disliked Peter's decree on sole succession, which stated that a cadet who received no patrimony might not remain in idleness but must 'seek his own bread through State service, study, etc., and that this act should not in any way be regarded as dishonourable to himself or to his family'. In his private journal of legislative projects, side by side with his major reforms, Peter made a special note to send men to England to learn bootmaking and carpentry. In 1703, during the construction of St. Petersburg, he ordered that a workhouse be built in Moscow in which trades were to be taught to the vagrants. He also ordered illegitimate children to be taught a variety of crafts in houses specially built for this purpose in Moscow and other towns, which shows that Ivan Betsky,[1] a businessman of Catherine II's reign, was not the first to think of making illegitimate children the basis of a middle class.[2] Faced with the existing state of understanding and knowledge, and the lack of interest of previous rulers, Peter had to display considerable vehemence in his civil ordinances to gain recognition for the ideas and standards of the industrial and commercial middle class that he was

[1] Ivan Betsky (1704–95) was an illegitimate son of Prince Ivan Troubetskoi. He had been educated abroad, and knew Jean-Jacques Rousseau. Catherine the Great appointed him president of the Academy of Arts and Director of the St. Petersburg Military Academy. His peculiar ideas on education were inspired by the theories of Locke, Fenelon, and Rousseau. The Moscow Orphanage was founded in 1763, and its inmates were expected to become 'middle class'.

[2] There, as in other passages, the term 'middle class' is used in a way which may cause confusion. The middle classes, to Peter, probably meant the skilled workmen, independent 'small masters' or 'yeomen of trade and industry', whose economic significance had so impressed him in Western Europe, not the professional men and senior executives who are commonly called middle class in Western Europe today.

endeavouring to encourage and promote. Peter insisted that a well-planned and well-run industry was beneficial to the state because it increased the national product and fed the hungry. Here Peter's economic sense led him to appreciate the basic necessities of society. Later on, during Catherine II's 'philosophical' reign, Peter was heavily criticised by refined pedants like the Princess Dashkov for having devoted so much time to such trifles as artisans, commerce, and industry. These critics would have been more indulgent if they had remembered that Peter had had to send abroad for master-craftsmen to teach his subjects how to make brooms and boxes, or that the Russian Church in its seven hundred years had been so intent on saving souls that it founded neither schools for peasants nor of iconography. 'Instead of painting a head, eyes and mouth, it was sufficient merely to paint in some dots and the result was called an ikon,' wrote Pososhkov about contemporary ikon painters.

4. Industrial companies, loans, subsidies, and exemptions

Concerned as he was with industry and commerce, one of Peter's objects was to teach the upper classes not to treat the industrialists and their work with scorn. Already, side by side with simple traders, men of rank and dignity, and great office-holders were becoming entrepreneurs, factory owners, and manufacturers. The most effective way of interesting men in commerce was to grant privileges, subsidies, and loans; Peter, however, wanted to see such an organisation of industry as would justify these policies. Having taken note of Western European industrial habits and methods, he tried to make his own capitalists copy them, combine their capital, and form companies.

Even before Peter certain types of industrial association had existed. Wealthy merchants generally belonged to a 'trading house', which was a special form of indivisible association be-

tween members of the same family, and usually consisted of a
father or an elder brother, with children, nephews, and cousins.
The control of these associations did not depend on capital,
nor were they managed by a council of the associates: they
were administered by the head of the family, who was responsible to the government for their common capital on behalf of his subordinates and the members of his household
(who were later called 'trading sons, brothers, and nephews').
Towards the end of the sixteenth century one of the most
famous trading houses was that of the brothers Stroganov,
salt miners, whose capital amounted to 300,000 roubles. Towards the end of the following century an equally famous
establishment was the Archangel trading house of Bazhenin, the shipbuilders, whose wharves were to be found on
the Northern Dvina. During the seventeenth century other
types of association appear, designed for the distribution and
not for the production of goods. For example, a merchant
who was to visit a fair would make an agreement with
manufacturers to take their goods for sale along with his own
and share the profits. An attempt had been made by Ordin-
Nashchokin to establish another type of association, this time
between the smaller and the larger merchants. The purpose
of a combination of this sort was to keep up Russian export
prices. In contrast with the trading houses, which were based
on kinship, the new types of association were based on mutual
trust.

The *artels*,[1] which were associations of labour and capital,
are another matter, since although he looked into them,
Peter left them to their own devices. He did not, however,
think them capable of competing successfully on the international market. In 1699, at the same time that urban taxpayers were removed from the jurisdiction of *voevodas*

---

[1] The *artel* was a sort of mutually-guaranteeing, mutually-protecting company of artisans.

and granted municipal self-government, a decree was issued (October 27th) ordering the merchants to transact their business 'in the manner of other countries', in companies, and calling on them 'to form merchant councils in which they might discuss methods of carrying on commerce to the greatest advantage'. This measure frightened the Dutch merchants, who then had a strong footing on the Moscow market; the Dutch Resident at Moscow relieved them by insisting that, since the Russians had exhibited no capacity for association or for the adoption of any new idea, the scheme must fail. Peter, however, had a way of making this scheme prosper: he could use force and he could grant privileges. The privileges with which Peter encouraged industrial enterprises were awarded principally to companies. Founders of factories or workshops were exempted from the various duties imposed by the Treasury and the towns, and sometimes their sons, brothers, foremen, master-craftsmen, and apprentices were exempted too. Moreover for a specified number of years they were allowed to sell their goods and purchase raw materials duty free; and they received subsidies, and could borrow free of interest. The college of Manufactures was responsible for looking after the manufacturing companies: as soon as a company showed signs of being in difficulties an enquiry was to be instituted 'as quickly as possible', and if the reason was found to be a lack of working capital then the college was to 'assist by making the necessary capital available'. Industrial enterprises were protected from foreign competition by prohibitive duties which were increased as indigenous production developed; in certain cases the duty equalled the price of the merchandise.

Prior to the foundation of the college of Manufactures in 1719, employers had the right to judge their own workers and servants in factory and other civil matters. This right was later transferred to the college, which sat in judgement not only on the employees but on the employers as well. In order to encourage industrial development, Peter even counter-manded his own decrees. Thus, although he had always in-veighed against runaway peasants, and ordered that they be fined and returned to their owners, in a decree of July 18th, 1722, he categorically forbade them to be returned to their owners if they had found work in a factory. In another de-cree of January 18th, 1721, he granted to factory owners and manufacturers from the merchant class one of the rights of the nobility, that of buying 'villages', i.e., land peopled by serfs, for their factories and workshops, subject to the condi-tion 'that the villages would be attached always to these factories';[1] thus the merchant-industrialist acquired a labour force which was obliged to work for him. It is now evident that Peter had placed the manufacturing and industrial classes in an extremely privileged position. He put their occupation on a par with state service, and in certain circumstances even above it; he gave owners of factories and workshops the right to harbour runaway peasants, a right denied even to land-owners in state service, and he endowed the capitalist of peasant origin with a nobleman's privilege of owning land with a serf community living on it. Under Peter, the fac-tories and workshops appear as the successors to the medieval monasteries as institutions for discipline and correction. In several decrees on the same subject, Peter ordered 'women and girls in sin' to be sent to the factories and workshops to be re-formed. Thus the old order of boyars was replaced by a nobility of loom and foundry in the Table of Ranks.

To what extent did Peter succeed in achieving the objects of his economic policy — to stimulate Russian industrial enterprises, to develop her natural resources, and to end the domination of the home market by foreign goods? Peter

[1] For a description of 'possessional' manufacture, see P. Lyashchenko, *History of the National Economy of Russia,* Macmillan, New York, 1949, pp. 293–4.

believed that these aims were attainable, and the more patriotic of his contemporaries shared this view. Pososhkov, for example, courageously believed that Russia could do without foreign goods, but that foreign countries could not have existed for ten years without Russian goods, and for this reason 'it is better for us to be their masters and for them to be our slaves'. Evidently Peter hoped to inject new life into business by the formation of industrial companies in which not only the commercial classes should participate but also noblemen and high officials of state. His excellency, Prince Menshikov, who could pluck the most important merchant's beard with impunity, even joined some of them in forming a company to catch cod, walruses, and other creatures of the White Sea. 'Interesents', or associates in industry and business, now came together from different social classes, but a prominent case will show that one must not exaggerate the practical usefulness of the noblemen.

During his stay in France in 1717 Peter had become very enthusiastic about the silk industry. The Vice-Chancellor, Baron Shafirov, and Count Tolstoy, a Privy Councillor, both shrewd courtiers, proposed to form a company for the manufacture of silk, and they were then joined by Prince Menshikov himself. Peter granted them extensive privileges and generous subsidies. The promoters organised everything on a grandiose scale, but, before long, they quarrelled amongst themselves, and Menshikov had to resign; he was replaced by Admiral Count Apraxin. The company was then granted new privileges, including the right to import silk duty free, which was promptly sold to private merchants for 20,000 roubles. Then, having cost the Treasury vast sums and lost its original capital, the company wound itself up. This fate overtook more than one of Peter's factories. Peter himself, while showering favours on his companies, made them look less like their Western European counterparts and reshaped them on traditional Muscovite lines, which did not encourage enterprise.

Russian enterprise did not meet Peter's expectations; hence the capitalists were to build factories, form companies, and appoint partners by ukaze. It was usual for Peter to build the necessary factory or workshop at the Treasury's expense, and then lease it on particularly advantageous terms to a chosen entrepreneur. Thus when, in 1712, the Treasury paid for the building of cloth factories which were to be run by a group of merchants in association, the order read: 'If they do not wish to do this of their free will then they must be forced; grant them facilities to defray the cost of the factory so that they may take pleasure in trading.' Thus merchants were obliged, as a matter of duty, and were indeed forced, to build factories and form companies; and both factories and companies became state institutions.

Peter also used the old Russian system, but altered its conditions to meet the Treasury's new requirements. Hitherto the Treasury had exploited its sources of revenue, such as customs and excise, either by auctioning them to the highest bidder, or by letting chosen agents manage them. Now, however, new industries and new sources of revenue were appearing which promised, as the decree on companies indicated, 'to increase the receipts of the Treasury', but which called for revised fiscal methods. The method Peter introduced to organise his companies and factories was to grant a monopoly and compel people to undertake the new enterprise. This method of industrial promotion in a Treasury-controlled hothouse naturally led to that government interference throughout which, with its detailed regulation, cavilling supervision, and lack of experience, frightened people away.

There was yet another obstacle to industrial progress: private owners of capital were unwilling to take risks. The lack of common justice, and the excessive power of people in authority, made timid people unwilling to put their savings into circulation; peasants and small traders buried their savings in the ground in order to hide them from the landowners and the tax-collectors, while the nobility adhered to their usual practice of shearing their peasants like sheep, and not wishing to display their spoils to the envious, either hid the gold in their coffers, or, if they were more intelligent, banked it in London, Venice, and Amsterdam. This information comes from Peter's contemporaries, who added that Prince Menshikov had more than one million roubles banked in London.[1] Thus vast amounts of capital were kept out of circulation. These hoards were regarded by the government as parasitical because they earned nothing, and therefore deprived the Treasury of its lawful revenue of 'tenth money' (actually, a five per cent turnover tax); tax evaders found that their capital was treated as contraband and seized by the police. An ukaze issued at the beginning of the Northern War stated that 'the hoarding of money is forbidden; informers who discover a cache are to be rewarded with one third of the money, the remainder to go to the state'. All traders and industrialists were obliged to make a declaration on demand, to the relevant department, of their assets and current income, which served as a basis for the assessment of taxes. Informers were the state's principal agents of control, and were highly favoured by the Treasury.

In a village called Dedinov, on the river Oka, there lived the brothers Shustov, peaceable folk who had no trading interests and lived comfortably. They declared that they possessed no more than two or three thousand roubles. But in 1704 a rogue of a merchant denounced them, saying that in reality they were extremely wealthy, and that they had inherited vast sums from their grandfathers which were earning

[1] I have tried to verify the truth of this assertion with the Bank of England, who inform me that they are unable to find any records of such a deposit.

nothing, but were being spent on drink. Moscow therefore ordered a search, and between the ceiling and the floor in the uninhabited part of the house, a hoard of gold coins was found which weighed 4 puds, 13 funti,[1] as well as 106 puds of Chinese gold and old muscovite silver coins.[2] Translating this mass of silver and gold into Petrine money, and then into modern currency, it will be found that the brothers Shustov had inherited more than 700,000 roubles. The government confiscated this capital on the grounds that it had not been lawfully declared. The point of the case is that the capital, instead of being put to a use of which Peter approved, was in danger of being squandered.

In other cases, materials which had been prepared for use were wasted because Peter was either unable, or did not have sufficient time to dispose of them. Harness and other military stores, for example, which had been ordered for a campaign, were stored in two warehouses in Novgorod, and there left to rot because no order was issued for their disposal, until eventually, mouldy and rotten, they had to be dug up with spades. Yet again, in 1717, great quantities of oaks, some of them worth more than one hundred roubles, which had been brought to St. Petersburg through the Vishni-Volochok Canal for the Baltic Fleet, were washed up on the islands and shores of Lake Ladoga where they were left half covered with sand, all because the original order for bringing them had contained no instruction to remind Peter of them, and, as it happened, he was away touring Germany, Denmark and France trying to settle the Mecklenburg affair. That shows us the bad side of Peter's methods. Large-scale building invariably leaves a lot of litter behind it, and in his hastily conceived schemes much was wasted.

His industrial enterprises strongly impressed certain superficial foreigners; it seemed to them that Russia was one large

[1] About 155 lbs. avoirdupois.   [2] About 3,810 lbs. avoirdupois.

factory in which hitherto hidden riches were everywhere being extracted from the earth, and in which axe and hammer resounded everywhere. Scholars and craftsmen came from abroad bringing books, tools, and machines, and in their midst was Peter directing and supervising. Even those foreigners who were suspicious of Peter's efforts to establish industry admitted that, though some enterprises had failed, in general factories and workshops were not only producing enough to satisfy internal demand, but were sending goods to foreign markets, as was the case, for instance, with iron and sailcloth. By Peter's death two hundred and thirty different factories and workshops were established in Russia.[1] Peter was above all interested in industries which had military utility, such as linen, canvas, and cloth. In 1712 he ordered the cloth factories to be so organised that within a period of five years 'we no longer have to purchase uniforms from abroad', but this had not been achieved when he died.

He had more success with mining. In his time metal working was mainly carried on in four important centres: Tula, Olonetz, the Urals, and St. Petersburg. The industry had originally been established in the first two areas under Tsar Alexis, but had failed in both. Peter revived it. Iron works were built by the Crown, and by the ironmasters Batachev and Nikita Demidov. Later on a Crown armaments factory was built at Tula to provide arms for the entire army. A huge arsenal sprang up, surrounded by suburbs populated by the armourers and smiths. On the banks of Lake Onega, in the province of Olonetz, smelting and iron works were built in 1703 which subsequently developed into the town of Petrozavodsk. Soon after this iron and copper works were built by the Crown and by private concerns at Povientz, and at other

[1] For a general description of the manufacturing industry in the eighteenth century, see P. Lyashchenko, *History of the National Economy of Russia*, Macmillan, New York, 1949, pp. 283–99.

places in the neighbourhood. The metallurgical industry in what became the Perm Province of the Urals expanded so enormously that it can be said that the opening of the Urals was due to Peter. He had ordered prospectors to search the Urals before he even went for his first foreign tour, from which he returned with a crowd of mining engineers and miners. The results of research were favourable. Russian ore yielded up to one half of its own weight in good iron. In 1699 Peter built an ironworks on the banks of the Neva, near St. Petersburg; this cost the Treasury 1,540 roubles, and another 10,347 roubles was collected from the peasants to pay the workers' wages. As early as 1686 hundreds of muskets had been sent to Peter at Preobrazhensky as equipment for his 'poteshnie', and those had come from the Tula workshops of Demidov. In 1702 Peter leased the Neviansk ironworks to Demidov on the understanding that he kept the army supplied with munitions. By 1713 Demidov had more than one million hand grenades lying in his Moscow warehouses. He organised his business so well that he could afford to charge remarkably low prices, and the income from his business gave his son 100,000 roubles a year in the reign of the Empress Anne.

Further expansion in the Urals both by the Crown and private enterprise closely followed the building of the Neviansk ironworks. Indeed, the Urals were now a vast industrial and mining area, the administrative centre of which was Ekaterinburg,[1] the town named in honour of the Empress Catherine I, built on the river Isset by General Henning, a mining and artillery expert, and one of Peter's ablest collaborators. To provide the labour for the factories, and to guard them against the hostile Bashkir and Khirgiz tribes, twenty-five thousand serfs were assigned to the region. In the neighbourhood of Ekaterinburg there were, towards the end of

---

[1] Sverdlovsk.

Peter's reign, nine iron and copper foundries belonging to the
Crown, and twelve belonging to private concerns, of which
Demidov owned five. The total smelting production of the
Russian foundries in 1718 came to six and a half million puds[1]
of iron, and nearly 200,000 puds[2] of copper. This sort of mining exploitation allowed Peter to equip the army and navy
with fire-arms of Russian materials and manufacture. Peter
left at his death, a total of 16,000 guns in Russia, beside the
naval pieces.

At the same time that Peter was energetically developing
the country's manufacturing industries, he turned his attention
to markets, to domestic trade, and especially to the problem
of external trade in which Russia was helpless in the hands of
the Western European seafarers. The main object in going
to war with Sweden had been to establish a trading port on
the Baltic Sea, even a single one. Hitherto Peter's schemes
had foundered on the problem of communications. Thus it
had been necessary to build a network of new roads before
Peter could get his troops and supplies from Moscow to Azov,
for the campaign of the Pruth. These roads imposed un-
believable sacrifices on the local peasantry. With the founding
of St. Petersburg a winding road, 750 versts long, was built
between the two capitals. Because of the mud and the dilapi-
dated bridges, even foreign ambassadors going from Moscow
to St. Petersburg had to allow five weeks for travelling, and
had to wait eight days at an inn for fresh horses. Peter wanted
to straighten the road out and shorten the distance by at least
100 versts, and to do this he built 120 versts of new road from
St. Petersburg, but the plan had had to be abandoned because
of the insurmountable difficulties presented by the swamps
and forests of Novgorod.

The difficulties of the overland routes made Peter turn his
attention to the rivers, the unique network of waterways

[1] 104,464 tons.   [2] 3,214 tons.

needing no maintenance, which nature had bestowed on Russia. After careful study he conceived a brilliant plan. He would provide a complete canal system to link the country's magnificent rivers.[1] Unfortunately the vagaries of his foreign policy interfered with the scheme. Early in his career, after he had captured Azov and wished to consolidate his position in the area, he wanted to organise commercial traffic with the Azov ports, and even thought of building a fleet on the Black Sea. He therefore set about linking the central waterways of the country to the Black Sea by two sets of canals, one between two tributaries of the Volga and Don, the Kamishinka and the Ilovlia, and the second through the small Lake Ivan (in the district of Epifan) from which issues on one side the Don and on the other the Shat stream, a tributary of the Upa which flows into the Oka. To do this it was necessary to dredge, deepen, and canalise the lake and rivers. For years tens of thousands of men worked in both places using an immense quantity of material. Twelve stone locks were completed on the Ivan Canal. But the Northern War made Peter turn his attention to other matters, while with the loss of Azov in 1711, the costly constructions of Azov and on the Don had to be abandoned.

With the foundation of St. Petersburg the possibility of linking the new capital to the central regions by waterways naturally presented itself. Peter dreamed of being able to embark on Lake Moskva and disembark on the Neva without trans-shipping *en route*. Together with a well-informed peasant called Serdukov, Peter surveyed the wild regions about Novgorod and Tver, explored the lakes and rivers, and then had the Vishni-Volochok network built by digging a canal linking the Tvertsa (a tributary of the Volga) with the river

---

[1] For an interesting contemporary account of canal building in Russia, see John Perry, *The State of Russia,* London, 1716. Perry's first assignment in Russia was the project for linking the Don and the Volga.

Tsna (which eventually widens into Lake Mstino, and, issuing under the name of Msta, finally flows into the Ilmen). In 1706 this job, which had taken 20,000 workers four years, was finished; but ten years later the stone lock gates were blocked by sand, due entirely to carelessness, and the canal was only dredged with great difficulty. The difficulty of this route, linking the Volga to the Neva, was the turbulent Lake Ladoga, on which many vessels were lost. Many of the flat-bottomed boats which navigated the shallow waters of the Vishni-Volochok network were not capable of riding out the storms of Lake Ladoga, and many of them were lost. In 1718 Peter decided that it should be possible to avoid the dangers of the passage of Lake Ladoga by cutting a canal round it which would allow the traffic to go straight from the mouth of the Volkhov, near the Lake, to the Neva near Schlusselberg.

He entrusted the matter to Prince Menshikov, who was completely ignorant of such affairs but who as usual, was poking his nose into everything. Menshikov and his companions managed to spend more than two million roubles. Excavations were carried on according to no plan, thousands of workers died from privation and sickness, and nothing was achieved. The enterprise was then handed over to an experienced engineer called Münnich[1], who had just entered the Russian service, and he succeeded in finishing this hundred-verst canal, although not in Peter's lifetime. Peter's plan involved yet another canal which was to connect the Volga with the Neva. The watershed between the Vitegra, a tributary of Lake Onega, and the Kovzha, which flows into

[1] Burkhard Christoph von Münnich served in the armies of France, Hesse, and Poland. He entered Russian service in 1721. In 1728 he was made a Count, and in 1732 a Field Marshal and Governor of St. Petersburg. During the Palace revolution of 1741 he was arrested, tried, and sentenced to death, but reprieved and exiled to Siberia. He was recalled to St. Petersburg when Peter III ascended the throne. See R. N. Bain, *The Pupils of Peter the Great*, Constable, 1897, pp. 188–92.

Lake Bielo, was to be cut through at the place where, in the nineteenth century, the Mariinsky Canal system was dug. Surveys were also made with a view to linking the White Sea with the Baltic. No work was done on any of these, and of the six canals Peter had had surveyed but one was finished — a modest enough success.

Rivers and canals were used to send shipments to the new capital, and Peter's acquisition of Baltic ports resolved the problem of Russia's foreign trade. As a result of the Northern War Peter gained seven Baltic ports: Riga, Pernov, Reval, Narva, Viburg, Cronstadt, and St. Petersburg, of which he himself built the last two. The question of diverting the flow of trade arose in 1714, if not before. Till then trade with Western Europe had passed through the White Sea and Archangel, pre-Petrine Muscovy's sole port. After the foundation of St. Petersburg, and as Peter consolidated his position on the shores of the Baltic, so he determined to divert foreign trade from the circuitous White Sea route to the Baltic, and make it converge on his new capital.[1] This commercial revolution affected many vested interests and national habits: the Dutch opposed Peter because they had long been comfortably established at Archangel; Russian merchants because they had become used to the well-worn route of the Northern Dvina. The senators supported both parties, and General-Admiral Apraxin even told Peter personally that his scheme would ruin the merchants and that the results would forever be on his conscience. To this Peter replied that the application of principles is notoriously difficult, but that in time all parties would accept the change. The struggle continued for eight years before his opponents finally came round. St. Petersburg prevailed over Archangel, and became Russia's leading port in foreign trade. In 1710 one hundred and fifty-three foreign

[1] J. J. Oddy, *European Commerce*, London, 1805, Chapter XI, pp. 200–11, shows how successful Peter was in diverting foreign trade to the Baltic.

ships entered Archangel: as early as 1722 one hundred and sixteen were using St. Petersburg, and in 1724 two hundred and forty. In 1725 a total of nine hundred and fourteen Western European merchant vessels entered Russia's Baltic ports, excluding Pernov and Cronstadt. This means that the interests involved had adjusted themselves to the change.

Peter addressed himself to two of the problems of Russia's foreign trade, but resolved only one: he achieved an increase of exports over imports, and, within two years of his death, Russian exports came to 2,400,000 roubles, compared with imports at 1,600,000 roubles.

He had less success with his second problem: he failed to create a Russian mercantile marine to take the country's foreign trade out of foreign bottoms because he could find no interested Russian entrepreneurs. His insistence on diverting maritime commerce from Archangel to St. Petersburg is perfectly comprehensible. St. Petersburg, with its fortifications at Cronstadt, had originally sprung up as a military outpost against Sweden; with the end of the war, St. Petersburg would have lost the right to be called a capital had it not retained its importance by acting as a centre for commercial and other relations with Western Europe, and indeed, by strengthening those relations, to secure which the war itself had been fought. For St. Petersburg could not have remained merely a town peopled by bureaucrats, or a billet for the two Guards Regiments quartered on the Moscow side of the town and the four regiments on the Island of St. Petersburg.

The cost of the new capital was enormous.[1] It was paid for partly by levying heavy taxes and partly by using the forced labour of people driven in from all parts of the country, even from Siberia, and more neglected than looked after. In 1712,

[1] One of the most vivid accounts of the first days of St. Petersburg can be found in Christopher Marsden, *Palmyra of the North*, Faber & Faber, 1942, pp. 45–79.

after nine years of hard work, another round-up was conducted in all the eight Provinces into which Russia was then divided and nearly 5,000 more workers were sent to St. Petersburg. It would be difficult to find anywhere in military history, a massacre which accounted for more men than St. Petersburg and Cronstadt. Peter called his new capital his 'paradise', but for the people it was a mass grave. See how it was built and with what it was nourished! High dignitaries of new or existing government institutions which had been transferred here were obliged to build themselves houses; nobles, merchants, artisans, and all their families were sent here, or, to be more accurate, were driven here by ukaze, and they had somehow to find lodgings and food; the settlement looked like a gypsy encampment, and even Peter himself lived in a hut with a leaking roof. The barren wastes around St. Petersburg were unable to provide food for this multitude. Thousands of carts from Crown villages and *pomeshchiks'* estates travelled incredible distances along the winter roads carrying bread and other supplies for the Court and the nobility, while thousands of others came from towns in the interior with general merchandise.

This hazardous hand-to-mouth bivouacking lasted until the end of Peter's reign, and had a lasting effect on living conditions in the capital on the banks of the Neva. Peter had the reputation of sparing neither life nor money to achieve his purpose: hundreds of thousands of workers (the numbers are probably exaggerated) perished while building the port of Taganrog, later demolished by treaty with the Turks. The same thing happened at the ports on the Baltic. The ports of Cronstadt and St. Petersburg had serious disadvantages: they were ice-bound for months at a time, their freshness of water was harmful to wooden ships, and the channel between the two towns was very shallow. In vain did Peter spend money and effort on trying to overcome the two disadvantages of ice and shallowness. He still had to find a more suitable harbour than Cronstadt, and this he found in the excellent roadstead at Rogervik near Reval, which unfortunately had to be protected with breakwaters from the westerly gales. At the cost of devastating the forests of Livonia and Esthonia, large numbers of tree trunks were brought to Rogervik where cribworks were made, filled with rocks, and lowered on to the bed of the roadsteads, but they were destroyed by a violent tempest. Another attempt was made, again unsuccessfully, and the ruinously expensive enterprise was abandoned.

Chapter Seven

★

WE HAVE ALREADY surveyed the measures Peter took to increase the quantity and improve the quality of the tax-payers' work in order to increase the revenue; we must now turn our attention to the financial results of these measures. In his financial policy Peter met great difficulties. Sometimes he created new difficulties, sometimes he mishandled old ones; and he showed a singular lack of financial ingenuity. He admitted himself that he found no part of government business so hard to understand as trade, and that he had never been able to think clearly about it. He might well have said the same thing about the management of the government's revenue and expenditure. Although he saw clearly where the nation's sources of wealth lay, and acknowledged that the burden of taxation should not be too heavy, he was incapable of anything more useful in practice than the simple but useless truism contained in an instruction to the newly-created Senate: 'gather ye money where ye may, for money is the artery of war.'

In 1710 Peter ordered an investigation into government income and expenditure. The results showed that, for the triennium 1705–7, average yearly receipts had been 3·33 million roubles. The army and navy had cost 3 million roubles and other expenditure had been 0·824 million roubles. The annual deficit was 0·5 million roubles or 13 per cent of expenditure. The deficits had been met by drawing on the small reserves accumulated by the Treasury in past years which were now exhausted. It was estimated that in 1710 there would again be a deficit of half-a-million roubles. The government decided to meet it by levying an additional tax of 50 kopecks on each taxable household. Under Peter, as indeed under previous rulers, this was what internal credit usually looked like — a non-recoverable 'loan' on which no interest was paid; no other way of raising money existed because neither at home nor abroad was there any confidence in the Russian Treasury.

To meet his future needs Peter relied on the revision of the taxpayers' roll. Until then, direct taxation had been based on the household census of 1678, but complete and consistent totals are not to be found in any of the records: the number of households quoted varies between 787,000 and 833,000; the taxes moreover were imposed unequally. In any case a roll more than thirty years old was bound to be wrong, and only a Russian exchequer could have been satisfied with basing its direct taxes for 1710 on the assessments of 1678. Now, faced with these substantial deficits, Peter ordered a new census of households, assuming that after thirty years the number of taxpayers would have increased, but he sustained a financial defeat equal to his military defeat at Narva. The Senate calculated in 1714 that, according to the census of 1710, the number of taxpayers had decreased by one quarter during the preceding thirty years. That the decrease was exaggerated, however, appears from Miliukov's detailed review of the evidence in his *State Economy in Russia in the Time of Peter the Great*;[1] the decrease was probably a fifth. Peter himself was responsible: hundreds of thousands of healthy men were withdrawn from the tax-paying population by the recruiting system; tens of thousands were sent to work on wharves and canals, and in

---

[1] Paul Miliukov, *Gosudarstvennoe khozyaistvo rossii v pervoi chetverti XVIII stoletiia i reforma Petra Velikogo,* 2nd edition, St. Petersburg, 1905. See Miliukov, Seignobos and Eisenmann, *Histoire de Russie,* Paris, 1932–3, Vol. I, where Miliukov's findings are summarised.

building the new capital; tens of thousands had fled in order to escape taxation and other burdens imposed on them by the state, or had escaped the census entirely because of the incompetence of the officials. Peter, of course, had his own ideas on the ability of his people to pay taxes: the more sheep that are sheared, the more wool will the flock give. The next household census, of 1716–17, showed, however, a further decrease; and the Senate itself testified in 1714 that, in the Province of Kazan alone, more than 35,000 households, or nearly one-third of the tax-paying population, had vanished since the census of 1710.

Financial difficulties were aggravated by the beginning of the Northern War. In the reign of Peter's elder brother direct taxes had been divided into two classes: the 'yamskoi and polonianichny' which were paid by the serfs, and the heavier 'streletskaya' which was paid by the rest of the tax-paying population. Both these direct taxes were continued under Peter. The existence of a regular army and navy, however, called for more money, and new war taxes were introduced: dragoon tax, recruit tax, ship tax, and conveyance tax. The first, which was to provide horses for the dragoons, was two silver roubles for country households, nine for town households, and was levied on the clergy as well. Although indirect taxation had been thoroughly exploited by earlier Muscovite administrations, Peter did not neglect it; indeed, he found novel methods of exploiting it which involved him in political innovation. To do this he had to make a new political departure. He had to give up the view, which he had learnt in the nursery of the Kremlin and held for most of his life, that the state, enjoying absolute power by right, was the sole instrument in the conduct of public affairs. He had to look for help outside the apparatus of the state, and appeal to the native wit and ingenuity of his people. His appeal was answered because his own activities had stimulated political thinking, and produced, in one generation, a group called, in Peter's day, the 'projectors', whom we should call publicists. They came from all social classes: thus Saltykov was the son of an aristocrat, Yurlov was an army colonel, Zotov was the son of Peter's tutor, Muromtsev was a trader, and Pososhkov was a peasant industrialist. In their 'projects' they discussed many different subjects, from abstract notions of order within the state to conditions in the rope-making industry, on which Maxim Mikulin wrote a memorandum. Pososhkov presented the Tsar with a large volume containing a vivid, but unnecessarily gloomy, picture of Russia, with suggestions for improvement. He was also, as should be remembered by those who enjoy their leisure, one of the first manufacturers of playing-cards in Russia.

With the 'projectors' there appeared the 'revenue finders' whose function was so similar to that of the 'projectors' that it is hard to separate them. We know at least twenty names which belong in both categories, while there must be many more whose names are unknown. A special decree defined the duty of the revenue-finders who were specially appointed, and made up a distinct financial department: they were to 'sit and repair the nation's finances', that is to say, they were to discover new sources of revenue. An interesting point is that most of these officials came from the *kholopy* class, for some of the men employed in boyars' households were, as we have shown above, better educated and more intelligent than their masters. Kurbatov, for instance, who was the boyar Sheremetiev's major-domo, heard about a new stamp duty when travelling abroad with his master; on his return home, in 1699, he wrote an anonymous letter to Peter, suggesting its introduction in Russia. According to Prince Kurakin's wildly exaggerated estimate, its introduction brought in 300,000 roubles; in fact, in 1724, it only brought in 17,000 roubles. For this suggestion Kurbatov was appointed to a special post resembling that of a director of a department of industry and commerce. He was subsequently appointed vice-governor of Archangel, and died while awaiting trial on a charge of embezzling public funds. Others, all boyars' *kholops*, followed Kurbatov; they included Ershov, sometime vice-governor of Moscow, Nesterov, an 'ober-fiscal', i.e., a controller general, one of the most ruthless denunciators of aristocratic embezzlers, who was himself convicted of misappropriation and broken on the wheel, and Varaxin, Yakovlev, Startsov, and Akinshin. Every revenue-finder spent his time busily looking for something new to tax, some source which had escaped the Treasury's notice; as soon as he had devised a new tax, direct or indirect, he was put in charge of the new department created to administer it. In this way the tax-free statutory rents of private landowners, and their appendages and trading establishments, were either alienated to the Crown and transformed into Treasury property, as was done with fishing rights, or were taxed at rates up to 25 per cent, as happened with inns and mills, while revenues which had previously been taxed were taxed yet again at a higher rate. The revenue-finders served their sovereign well: new taxes were poured on to the taxpayers like water from a watering can. From 1704 new taxes were imposed one after the other, on land, on horse collars, on hats and boots, on vehicles plying for hire at 10 per cent of the charge, on horse hides and sheep skins, on beehives, on hot baths, on inns, on rented houses, on 'corners',[1] on cellars, on chimney stacks, on watering places, on loading and discharging timber, on driftwood and firewood, and on the sale of foodstuffs, from water melons, cucumbers and nuts to the 'other small things' which bring the list to an end. Taxes appeared which even the Muscovite taxpayer, for all his experience of past impositions, resented and found difficult to understand.

[1] Rent was paid for the 'corners' when several people shared a room.

Taxes were imposed not only on trades and land, but even on religion, not only on property, but also on conscience. The old belief was tolerated but its adherents were subjected to a double tax as if it were a barely tolerated luxury. By an ukaze of 1705, beards and moustaches, which medieval Russia considered divine attributes, were also taxed. The rate varied according to the class of the wearers: nobles and civil servants paid 60 roubles, the merchants of the first class paid 100 roubles, ordinary traders paid 60 roubles, *kholops*, church servants, etc., paid 30 roubles; a peasant was exempt so long as he only wore his beard in his own village, but had to pay a tax of 1 kopeck on entering or leaving a town. In 1715 this was replaced by a uniform tax of 50 roubles on all wearers of beards, whether orthodox or Old-Believers. We read with dismay the ukaze Peter himself presented to the Senate in 1722, when he made up his mind about freedom of conscience — how seriously and with what insistance does he order 'the old ukaze on beards to be strictly enforced, the wearer to pay 50 roubles a year, and the bearded and Old-Believers to wear only old-fashioned dress, i.e., a peasant's coat with a high-standing collar, and a coloured smock with a girdle'! When a man presented himself at a government office in a beard, but without the dress prescribed to go with it, his petition was to be ignored and he was 'to be kept in the office' and forced to pay his fifty roubles again, even though he had already paid his annual tax. Those who were unable to pay were sent to the galleys at Rogervik to work off their debt. Whosoever met a bearded man not dressed in the prescribed fashion could seize him, bring him in front of the authorities, and receive half the fine as well as the clothes the victim was wearing.

The projectors proved themselves to be highly inventive, and an enumeration of the taxes for which they were responsible shows that they had organised a general raid on the public, particularly on the small traders, the artisans, and the labourers. In their eagerness they attained real virtuosity and almost insane ingenuity: they even suggested taxes on births and marriages. Indeed a marriage tax was levied on the Mordvins, the Tcheremis, the Tartars, and other non-Christian peoples whose 'heterodox marriages' came under the jurisdiction of the department run by Paramon Startsov, the projector, originally set up to collect a tax on beehives that he had devised. Yet it is strange that the projectors and revenue-finders overlooked the possibility of putting a tax on funerals. A marriage tax had already been imposed in medieval Russia, in the form of a tax on two items of wedding regalia, the 'oubrous' or sash, and the coat of marten fur. This on its own is perhaps understandable — after all, marriage is a bit of a luxury — but to tax a Russian for having the audacity to be born, and then to refrain from taxing him when he dies, is a financial inconsistency which, by the way, the Church remedied. Revenue was collected by specially created departments, one each for fisheries, private bathhouses, inns, honey, and all the other articles subject to tax, and these taxes were naturally called 'departmental taxes'. The departments were all subordinated to the main department of the Province of Izhera, the director of which was the Governor of Izhera, Prince Menshikov. The government looked on these taxes as trifles. According to Prince Kurakin, the fishery tax brought in about 100,000 roubles a year, and the honey tax about 70,000 roubles.

Towards the end of Peter's reign the double inconvenience of the system of projectors (if one can call it a system) was made clear: it was not really productive, and it caused bad feeling among the people. Pososhkov recorded both these faults, and, after an enumeration of some of the taxes, remarked bitterly that the Treasury could not be filled from the proceeds of a jumble sale, and that these things 'only aggravate the people: small change is always small change'. The taxpayer not only suffered the weight of some of the taxes, but was irritated by their excessive number. There were some thirty in all, pursuing him like gadflies in July. They gradually realised less and less, and arrears began to accumulate. According to the roll of 1720, total receipts were lower than the figures quoted by Prince Kurakin, so that, except for the tax on bathhouses, no tax produced its estimated yield, and only 410,000 roubles were collected instead of an estimated 700,000 roubles. The tax on beards, and the fines on those who failed to wear prescribed dress with them, were the least profitable: only 297 roubles 20 kopecks was realised out of an estimated 2,148 roubles 87 kopecks. As a result the Treasury was forced to moderate its demands. An ukaze of 1704 stated that councillors and merchants of the first class were to pay 3 roubles for their private bath-houses, courtiers, other merchants, and other persons of rank 1 rouble, and peasants 50 kopecks. The poorer members of the middle class, such as soldiers and deacons, were quite unable to pay for their baths, even when urged on by a cudgel, so that after the first year their baths were taxed at the same rates as those of the peasants. Finally Peter himself was compelled to cross out some of the taxes which appeared on the register of 1724. If the schemes of the projectors told us nothing else, they reveal that a basic principle of his financial policy was to ask for the impossible in the hope of getting as much as possible.

The great estates of the Church were an important source of revenue, to which the government was compelled by the war to pay increased attention before the projectors got to work, although the latter were made responsible for some of the collection. After Narva, Peter melted down many church bells for cannon. An ukaze of December 30th, 1701, deprived the monasteries of the incomes they had received from their *votchina* estates. Peter justified himself by asserting that the monks, in spite of the example of their predecessors, and against their vows, were eating up their wealth instead of using it to help the poor. This revenue was collected from the monasteries by the *Monastyrskii Prikaz*,[1] a government department responsible for the administration of the lay affairs of the Church. It was founded by Tsar Alexis in 1649, closed by Tsar Theodore, and re-established in 1701. Later it was put in charge of the peasants and *votchina* estates of the patriarchs and bishops. From the monastery revenues it collected the Prikaz gave each monk his money and grain, ten roubles and ten quarters[2] of grain to each, and, according to the ukaze, devoted the rest to the almshouses and the poor of those monasteries that did not have *votchina* estates. Nonetheless, if Prince Kurakin is to be believed, the Treasury still benefited by an amount between one and two hundred thousand roubles a year. Only in the last year of the war with Sweden was the *Monastyrskii Prikaz* subordinated to the new Holy Synod,[3] whereupon the management of their own revenues reverted to the ecclesiastical authorities. It was the assistance extracted by Peter from the monasteries in time of necessity that prepared the way for the subsequent expropriation of church lands.[4]

Peter also endeavoured to add to his revenues by increasing the number of state monopolies. To a list including pitch, potash, rhubarb, and glue, he added salt, tobacco, chalk, tar, cod liver oil, . . . and oak coffins. After 1705 the last luxury of

[1] For details of the powers enjoyed by the *Monastyrskii Prikaz*, see Florinsky, *Russia*, Macmillan, New York, 1953, Vol. I, pp. 279, 292, 410, and E. Schuyler, *Peter the Great*, London, 1884, Vol. II, pp. 180–5.

[2] 279·4 lbs.

[3] For the organisation of the Church under Peter, see B. H. Sumner, *Peter the Great and the Emergence of Russia,* The English Universities Press Ltd., 1950, pp. 144–50. See also N. Zernov, 'Peter the Great and the Establishment of the Russian Church', *Church Quarterly Review*, Vol. CXXV, 1938.

[4] Church lands were finally expropriated under Catherine the Great by an ukaze of February 26th, 1764.

the well-to-do Russian gentleman, his oak coffin, could no longer be got from the usual tradesman, but only from the Treasury, which sold it at four times its normal price. When the Treasury had sold the whole of the stock confiscated from the original merchants, the use of oak coffins was prohibited. The Treasury was similarly instructed, by an ukaze of 1705, to buy up all the salt on the market and re-sell it at twice the previous price. This monopoly, although it gave the Treasury a hundred per cent profit, was so badly organised that it even upset Pososhkov, who was in favour of a free market in salt. 'In the villages,' he wrote, 'salt has become so rare and expensive that it sometimes costs more than one rouble a pud, while in Moscow at the old price, a pud of salt cost no more than 24 kopecks; many go without salt, fall ill of scurvy and die.' Even men's pleasures were exploited to raise revenue: playing-cards, dice, chess sets, and other games, in addition to tobacco and vodka, were added to the list of State monopolies and farmed out. A contemporary remarked that 'having paid the tax one is free to play'. In the first year farmed taxes brought in 10,000 roubles.

The Treasury made considerable sums by a reissue of the coinage — actually by debasing it. Before Peter the currency consisted of small silver coins called dengi,[1] kopeck, and half-kopeck pieces. Common multiples of the kopeck (three, ten, twenty-five, and fifty) had their own names, but were only units of account, as was the rouble itself (one hundred kopecks). From 1700, small copper and large silver coins were issued, the latter bearing the names of the old units of account. Since, in fact, their weight and silver content were gradually diminished, this meant the acceptance of token money.

Actually the Russians of the time shared the bold and patriotic faith of contemporary financiers in the power of the government to determine the value of its currency. Pososh-

[1] Now the ordinary Russian word for money.

kov actually supposed that, in Russia, unlike other countries, the value of money depended solely on the sovereign's will; he had only to order a kopeck to become a grivna for it to be so. One projector even suggested an outright fraud in order to pay for the war: a secret ten-per-cent currency depreciation. This, he said, 'without harming anybody', would prevent money from leaving the country. But the money market was neither so simply organised, nor such a faithful subject. Towards the end of Peter's reign the Mint gave the Treasury 300,000 roubles a year, but this was purely nominal because money was depreciating in value, and the price level was rising. By the end of Peter's reign the silver kopeck bought only half as much bread as it had in the 1670's and, in terms of our [i.e., of 1900] money, its value had fallen from fourteen or fifteen to eight kopecks.

Under Peter the system of direct taxation was fundamentally altered. For a long time the 'household unit' had been a useless basis for the system, and Peter's new chancellery made matters even worse. The inconvenient fact was that the censuses of 1710 and 1717 showed a considerable diminution in the number of households since the census of 1678. In order to protect the interests of the Treasury official statistics were juggled about, and, when the new division of Russia into Provinces in 1719 was based on the register of households, an ingenious combination was produced. The best figures were selected from the censuses of different years, and naturally the results were brilliant: the number of taxable households which, according to the census of 1678, did not exceed eight hundred and thirty-three thousand (according to other findings eight hundred and eighty-eight thousand), now exceeded nine hundred thousand, not counting taxable urban dwellers, in spite of the decrease which had appeared in two other counts. The consequence of this statistical jiggery-pokery was to deprive the register of households of any practical value as a basis of taxation and force the bureaucrats to look for a substitute. Furthermore the situation revealed by the censuses of 1710 and 1717, discussed in Miliukov's book, suggested the same thing. The paradoxical fact emerged that the number of households in some areas was decreasing while the population was increasing. The explanation, of course, was that the average size of household was increasing (five and a half males instead of three or four). In these circumstances the Treasury could not benefit from the increase in population as long as the basis of assessment was the household. The only remedy it suggested was a poll-tax, which had already been discussed in the time of Sophia and Prince Golitsyn; and it was hoped that this new method of taxation would remedy the wastefully uneven incidence of the tax on households. On these grounds Nesterov had agitated for the poll-tax in 1714, believing that it would be more equal in its effects; and he was followed by others who wrote of the advantages of substituting a tax on 'persons', or at least on the family, for the household tax. Peter, it seems, was indifferent to the economic and legal elaboration of the new system of taxation; he was more interested in the effects of the new tax on his commissariat, that is, on the well-being of his army and navy. He did not realise that his military expenditure had to be regulated by the nation's ability to pay; in fact he optimistically believed that the Russian taxpayer was an inexhaustible source of revenue.

Though his projectors had written to tell him that 'his low-born subjects were heavily overburdened with taxes', and that, if there were further increases, the land would be depopulated, Peter wrote from France in 1717 to tell the Senators that 'it is possible to find the money without overburdening the people'. He told them that, if more money were needed, they were to increase temporarily the taxes on all manufactured articles and were to put a 'poll-tax on urban dwellers, and use other devices, and this will not ruin the state'; and he directed that speculation was to be 'investigated immediately and on the spot, and the guilty executed'.

Peter did not stop to consider the relative merits of different bases of taxation such as the household, the family, the worker, or the soul, but left the decision to the Senate. His interest was centred on the soldier, who was to be provided for, and on the peasant, who was to foot the bill. In November 1717, Peter attended the Senate, and rapidly drafted an ukaze which was only made intelligible by the exegetical skill of the Senators. 'The army and the naval reserve shall be maintained, in addition to their pay, by the peasants, each household or equivalent number of souls whichever shall be more convenient, to support one man, a soldier, a dragoon, or an officer, generals excepted, according to the tax each now pays, and when this is done they will be absolved from all other taxes and from forced labour.' Thus all direct taxes were to be replaced by a single military tax, but whether the tax, the amount of which was to depend on the cost of maintaining a soldier, a dragoon, and an officer, was to be on households or on souls was a matter of indifference which had not even been decided. A few days later, however, it was decided to tax individuals, that is 'souls' or the 'working people', rather than households, but the Senate, interpreting, ordered a census of the entire rural male population 'not omitting old men and the latest babes'. The difficulties and delays, the revisions and amendments connected with the census have been mentioned before. It is difficult to make much sense of the different totals, all from different periods, which have survived: the number of 'souls' varies between five million and nearly six.

On the instructions of the Supreme Privy Council to the college of State Revenue in 1726, the actual accounts of poll-tax receipts for 1724 were appended to the Estimates made by the Senate for that year; a list of arrears, drawn up Province by Province, was also included. The labour of collecting this information had been undertaken so that the Senate might organise the billeting of the regiments, and fix the incidence of the poll-tax. Hence, we can obtain some idea of how the poll-tax system worked in its first year, after which Peter died, and soon afterwards the system was modified. There were, according to the documents, 5,570,000 'souls', of whom 169,000 lived in towns. The tax rate per 'soul' fell from 95 kopecks to 74 kopecks on the revision of the census. In order that the same burden should be imposed on all 'souls' the State peasant was charged an additional 40 kopecks, corresponding to what the privately owned serf paid to his landowner; urban taxpayers paid 1 rouble 20 kopecks per 'soul'.

This new poll-tax, which involved a fiction called 'the revisional soul', shocked many people. Even such a warm defender of Peter as Pososhkov saw no good in it, and refused to understand it. 'The soul is something intangible and incomprehensible, and has no price,' he wrote, 'prices should be fixed only on tangible goods' such as landed estates. Pososhkov related this problem to the national economy, which Peter did not understand. The economy consists of capital and labour, not 'souls'— only productive workers could actually pay taxes (not children and ancients). Peter had at hand an example, in the Baltic provinces peasant tax or 'hak', of a tax imposed on workers (in this case the tax was imposed on groups consisting each of ten workers between the age of fifteen and sixty). But Peter was more interested in receipts which would not fall in arrears than in a rational tax assessment. Moreover with the contemporary system of administration and understanding of finance, no rational system was likely to succeed. It was impossible to assess accurately the productive capacity of the country, so that the only possible calculation was to add up the male population, including male babies. The 'revisional soul' was such a calculation, a divisible tax unit which was purely fictitious. It had nothing to do with economics, nor even with financial policy, but was merely the college of State Revenue's accounting unit. The attempt to give this fictitious unit practical interpretation was left to the taxpayers who, in time, managed it. By a 'revisional soul' the peasant came to understand a certain amount of labour, and goods (such as beasts) to be used in such labour, which he must devote to the cultivation of land, or the pursuit of a craft, according to the assessment made upon him. It was in this sense that the peasant spoke of a half, a quarter, or an eighth of a 'soul', without in the least meaning to quarrel with psychology.

The poll-tax succeeded the household tax, but was assessed, even under Peter, according to the out-of-date register of 1678. The fictional nature of this new tax unit, which lasted until the middle of the nineteenth century, was bound to have an effect on people's thinking. The perplexities it occasioned lasted for two centuries. Pososhkov had written of the household tax that even the nobility did not understand what sort of a tax-paying unit it was. Some counted households by the number of doors, others by the number of chimneys, but neither realised that a peasant household was 'landed property'— a share in the land. The 'revisional soul' was an even greater mystery than the household, and whatever interpretation was used, the question still remained: why did the Treasury officials create taxpayers who could not pay for themselves? The authorities made arbitrary requirements of what had formerly been normal obligations to the state. The goverment, surrounded by its many departments, was kept aloof from the people as if it were something strange and special, which hardly encouraged in them a feeling of responsibility to it. Chichikov's dead souls were a worthy epilogue to Pososhkov's bitter description of the taxes as 'soul-destroying'.

The way the poll-tax worked under Peter only made matters worse. Two justifications were offered: taxes would be levied equally, and there would be an increase in revenue without the taxpayers being overburdened. The ukazes dealing with the poll-tax, did not, however, define the 'revisional soul': was it only a unit of account, or was it a tax assessment? The ukaze of 1722 on the taxes of urban dwellers states 'that they shall be assessed according to the wealth of their towns'. The poll-tax was imposed on the rural population as its name implies; it was not only imposed on those who appeared in the estimates as 'souls' but, in fact, on all individuals, whether they worked or not. There were complaints of 'oppression and inequalities among the people', for example that a poor peasant with three small sons had to pay twice as much as a wealthy peasant with one son. In fact the tax which was supposed to be uniform in its application only increased the natural differences between families of different sizes and circumstances.

It is difficult to compare the burden of the poll tax with that of the household tax because of the incommensurability of these units of account, and the lack of data. It is quite probable that Manstein, who heard and remembered a great deal about the last few years of Peter's reign, accurately recorded in his notes contemporary opinion on the poll-tax. He said that Peter collected twice as much from the poll-tax as from the household tax, but this was only a superficial guess, and not an exact reckoning. The household tax varied considerably in different localities, and according to the category of taxpayer. Urban and court households were taxed at a higher rate than the 'black-ploughing' and church peasant households, who in turn paid more than households of peasants belonging to the landowners. Moreover identical peasant households paid at different rates in different Provinces: a peasant household belonging to a landowner in the Province of Kazan paid on the average 49 kopecks, while a similar household in the Province of Kiev paid 1 rouble 21 kopecks.

This inequality was in some measure evened out by the differences in local economic conditions. Equal taxation had in fact been made impossible by the big decrease in the number of households in the central and northern Provinces only revealed by the census of 1710. In the central and northern Provinces taxes were still being assessed according to the returns of the census of 1678, and the surviving households had to pay nearly twice as much in order to compensate for the lack of numbers, while in the Provinces of Kiev, Kazan, Astrakhan, and Siberia, where an increase had occurred, the household tax had been considerably decreased.

As a result of the complicated and confusing demographic changes that were taking place, the poll-tax fell unequally on different taxpayers; in general, it raised the level of direct taxation, sometimes by an infinitesimal percentage, and sometimes by 2 per cent, 3 per cent and even more. The average household tax imposed on peasant households in the three Provinces of Archangel, Kazan, and Kiev in about 1710 was less than half the poll-tax subsequently collected from an average household of four souls. Those who suffered most were in any case the most miserable peasants belonging to the landowners, to whom the household tax had not applied because of the heavy liabilities imposed on them by their masters. The poll-tax, however, did apply to them, as it did to the more prosperous court and church peasants, with the result that in some areas the taxes were doubled and even quadrupled. Equity demanded that the landowners proportionally lower the dues owed to them, and indeed it seems that the government expected them to do so. In the interests of equality, the government proposed to make the state peasants, who were free from the exactions of private landowners, pay an additional amount over and above the general poll-tax, so that 'the landowners may receive what they are owed by their peasants without causing them distress'. This additional tax was fixed at 40 kopecks. But the landowners were not to be satisfied with a mere 4 grivni. On the contrary, their own expenditure had gone up because of their state service liabilities and obligations to the Treasury. They had, for instance, to make payments to the Treasury on behalf of their non-income earning domestic serfs. Any increase on the landowners own expenditure was passed on to their peasants in full, and sometimes with interest; the landowners even increased the peasant's *obrok*[1] to an unprecedented level, thereby taking advantage of the absence of any legal regulation of the *obrok*. At the time the tax system was changed, a peasant household, says Pososhkov, paid the landowner 'eight roubles or more'. Weber, the Brunswick Resident who collected valuable information about Russia during his term of office there from 1714–19, wrote in his work *Das Veränderte Russland* that it was rare for a peasant to pay his master an *obrok* of more than 10 to 12 roubles. It follows that it was common for a peasant to pay up to 10 roubles. Assuming that a peasant household paid a little over 7 roubles, and that there were four souls to a household, then the *obrok* per soul was twice the poll-tax, and nearly five times the normal payment of 40 kopecks per soul due by ukaze to the landowner. At least half the payments were made in grain and labour, but one wonders where the peasants, with their limited opportunities for earning money, found the remainder.

While the poll-tax did away with some of the existing anomalies, it increased others, and, of course, created new ones. The departments drew up an all-inclusive scheme

[1] *Obrok* were annual payments, either in money or in kind, made by serfs to their masters for the use of the land which they farmed on their own account.

which, because of the different taxable capacities of different regions and classes, actually increased the burden imposed by direct taxation; taxes were not uniformly imposed, and the increase in revenue was not obtained without overburdening the people. There is official evidence to substantiate this. In 1726 a report of the college of State Revenue (mentioned above) stated that in 1724 the arrears of the poll-tax amounted to 843,000 roubles, or 18 per cent of the total which they estimated should have been paid. The college of State Revenue adds plaintively: 'with respect to the above mentioned arrears owing the college of State Revenue, governors and vice-governors, and *voevodas*, and Kamerers, and District commissaries report that: souls tax moneys can nowhere be collected in full, the peasants are poor, the harvest is bad, entries have been made twice and thrice in the tax-book, and large numbers are excluded because of recruitment to the army, ruin by fire, death, escape, physical disabilities due to age or disease, and landless peasants themselves sons of landless soldiers.' Indeed this is in some measure a posthumous testimonial to Peter on his poll-tax, by the very financial institution responsible for its administration.

Other taxes, both direct and indirect, produced exactly the same effect: on the one hand there was the Treasury, forced by necessity to exaggerate its demands, believing that money would always be found, and on the other hand were the large arrears which were the silent answer of the taxpayers. The revenue-finders had busily invented new excises and taxes on industry and land, and had increased the revenue from these taxes from one and a half million roubles at the beginning of the eighteenth century to nearly 2,600,000 roubles by 1720. Nevertheless the returns from the new taxes showed a deficit of half a million roubles, or nearly 20 per cent of the total. Peter's financial progress is revealed in his last Budget for 1724, which includes receipts from the poll tax, collected for the first time, as well as receipts from customs and from taverns, industries, etc. On the expenditure side it will be sufficient to quote the chief item, military expenditure.

REVISIONAL SOULS

Serfs	4,364,653	78%
State peasants	1,036,389	19%
Urban dwellers	169,426	3%
	5,570,468	100%

Poll-tax collected from the above at a rate of 40 kopecks[1]	4,614,637 roubles
Other revenues	4,040,090 roubles
	8,654,727 roubles

Military expenditure

Army (paid for by the poll-tax)	4,596,493 roubles
Navy	1,200,000 roubles
	5,796,493 roubles

These incomplete figures quoted from the documents for 1724 illustrate some of the significant results of the financial reform. The returns in later years show an increase in all the figures, but the proportions changed very little. The connection between tax reform and the military reform which inspired it is clearly illustrated: the cost of maintaining the army and navy amounted to 67 per cent of the estimated budget revenue, and to nearly 75·5 per cent of the actual revenue. The army was costing the country much more than it

---

[1] These figures are obviously inconsistent. To obtain a yield of 4.6 million roubles from 5.57 million taxpayers requires a tax rate of approximately 80 kopecks. From the figures given on pp. 170 and 174, however, we may judge that this is just about what the average poll-tax rate was.

had done forty-four years before, when less than half the
revenue was spent on it. Moreover receipts for 1724 were
nearly three time those of the deficit year 1710. The share
of the poll-tax in this improvement was an increase of more
than two million roubles in Treasury receipts, although, as we
have seen from the college of State Revenue's report, collection was so difficult that as much as 848,000 roubles due
were not collected in the very first year of the new tax. Thus
the struggle with the deficit which had been going on for
fifteen years had not prevented the 13 per cent deficit of 1710
from becoming 18 per cent, to the impediment of the war
effort.

Towards the end of his reign, Peter's budgets came to three
and a half times those of his elder brother. In the money of
1900, the budget of 1680 came to twenty million roubles, and
that of 1724 to seventy million roubles. But Peter benefited
from the rapid change in the system of taxation which was
radically altered by the poll-tax. Before the poll-tax, direct
taxes were less productive than indirect taxes. Peter's concern
to develop industry and trade suggested that the yield of indirect taxes might increase. But exactly the opposite took
place: the poll-tax became the most important, accounting
for 53 per cent of all receipts. Thus, in the absence of sufficient
capital accessible to taxation, further hardships were imposed
on the poverty-stricken labouring classes, the 'working
people' who were in any case nearly exhausted. Yet native
and foreign observers both considered that, in view of the
size and natural resources of his vast empire, the Tsar should
have obtained larger revenues without overburdening his
people. Peter himself was of this opinion; at any rate in his
Reglament to the college of State Revenue in 1719 he expressed the idea, whether original or borrowed, that 'there is
no state in the world which is unable to bear the taxes which
are imposed, given that equality and justice are observed in

the matter of taxes and expenditure'. It was Peter's misfortune that he was never able to observe the 'given that', which was so essential to success.

The same observers agreed unanimously that Peter had to deal with two enemies to sound finance and the public welfare, enemies who cared neither for justice nor equality, and who were too powerful for his heavy and ruthless hand — the nobles and the civil servants, who were the creatures of the very authority they served so badly. The observers commented that nothing so concerned a nobleman as a reduction of his peasant's obligations to the Treasury, not because he was concerned to see the burden on his peasants reduced but because he wanted to increase his own exactions and did not care how he did it. As for the civil servants, they were virtuosos. There were so many opportunities for corruption that, as Weber said, it would be as difficult to examine them all as to drain the ocean. The most outstanding practitioners were the Provincial councillors elected by the nobility, the directors of departments, and the tax-collectors. Weber compared them to birds of prey, and said that they looked on their duties merely as opportunities to suck the marrow from the peasants' bones and build their fortunes on others' ruin. A clerk, on taking up his appointment, would have barely the clothes to dress in, and a salary of only forty or fifty roubles a year, yet in four or five years he would build himself a stone house while the villages under his charge would be depopulated.

So much for the evidence of squeamish and prejudiced foreigners. Pososhkov, a Russian who had seen much, was himself of the opinion that the judges and bureaucrats were worse than the thieves and brigands to whom they were too lenient. Russians who were familiar with the trickery of civil servants calculated, whether in jest or in earnest, that only thirty roubles out of every hundred collected reached the

Treasury, and that the civil servants divided the remainder among themselves as a reward for their troubles. Russians as well as foreigners, amazed at the scope of Peter's activities, were astonished that so much fertile land should remain un-populated, uncultivated, or badly cultivated, and generally unexploited. People explained this by pointing to the number of war casualties, and to the oppression of the peasants by the nobility and bureaucracy which had left them without the enthusiasm for new undertakings. Weber believed that the oppressions of serfdom had so demoralised the peasants that they had neither the understanding nor the energy for any-thing beyond getting their miserable daily livings.

In financial matters Peter was like a coachman who whips on his emaciated horse while pulling constantly at the reins. He himself probably put the biggest obstacles in the way of his own poll-tax. Although this tax was heavier than the household tax, it was not excessive. A peasant household of four people, which was then the average size, would have paid about 3 roubles poll-tax in all. Pososhkov, who resented the poll-tax, and greatly preferred a household and land tax, admitted that it was possible for an average peasant house-hold with six desyatins of land to pay three or four roubles in tax. He was speaking, of course, only of the peasants' money payments which, when the household tax was in force, con-stituted but a part of their burdens; their obligations to their masters, in labour and kind, and the special taxes which showered on them during the war, were even heavier. What did the building of St. Petersburg alone cost! Year after year thousands of workers were drafted from the Provinces, and tens, even hundreds, of thousands of roubles were collected from the Provinces for their maintenance, so that Egyptian pyramids could be erected on the swamps of the Neva. The peasants and domestic serfs (for whose upkeep the peasants had actually to pay in any case) were constantly required to

furnish bread, horses, wagons, and yet more money for harness and for the transport of the men and horses. In some Provinces payment of these new impositions fell into arrears by
as much as one third, and an extra tax was imposed on all
households to make up the deficit. Prince Kurakin, himself a
large landowner, calculated in his autobiography that in 1707
'on the average, sixteen roubles a year were collected from
every household'. Taxes of 120 to 130 roubles (in the money
of 1900) from every household would seem quite incredible,
were it not for the evidence of Kurakin who was responsible
for the payment. The poll-tax, which was introduced after
the end of the war with Sweden, was supposed to reduce the
burden of the taxes imposed during the war, and to replace
all other direct taxes. The large arrears of the first year of the
poll-tax showed how far the capacity of the peasants to pay
taxes had already been exhausted.

When Peter died the state did not owe a kopeck, although
one industrialist, who had been abroad, suggested that the
government borrow five million roubles against the issue of
credit tokens which were to be made of wood instead of
paper because the former was more solid! In 1721 Peter
thought of inviting John Law, the famous speculator whose
bank had just collapsed, to establish a trading company in
Russia on advantageous terms, and of asking him one million
roubles for the privilege, but nothing came of it. The damage
done by the decline in the moral strength and tax-paying
capacity of an overstrained people would hardly have been
paid for had Peter conquered not only Ingria and Livonia but
even Sweden — or five Swedens.

THE BUILDING OF ST. PETERSBURG BY SERF LABOUR

From the watercolour by A. V. Moravov

Chapter Eight

★

OF ALL PETER'S reforms, the reform of the administration has
been particularly admired. This, indeed, is the most striking
aspect of his work; but far too much emphasis has been laid
on the administrative institutions as they finally appeared at
the end of Peter's reign, and not enough on their slow and
difficult evolution. The chief object of the administrative reform was to create conditions favourable to the success of the
other reforms; but it was not until the military and financial
reforms had been introduced that the administration itself
was suitably reorganised. There is therefore a discrepancy between the object of the administrative reform and its timing;
and we must see how the progress of reform was affected by
this discrepancy. The usual features of the Petrine reforms,
their lack of coherence and general plan, their dependence
on ever-changing conditions and demands, make a study of
the administrative changes particularly difficult. If we take
them in their chronological order we are likely to lose sight of
their relations with the rest of Peter's reforms, while if we
take them systematically we are likely to see in them a cohesion and unity which for a long time they did not have. It
will therefore be better, in the interests of learning, to pass
haphazardly from one part of the administration to another,
than to follow our own inclination and try to be systematic.
Our impressions will be confused, but we will be able to cor-
rect this at the end by looking over the subject once again,
and following methodically the administrative divisions

between central and local government, and the further sub-
divisions as prescribed by constitutional law. The course of
events, moreover, allows us to begin properly with the
central administration.

For nearly twenty years, from the fall of the Tsarevna
Sophia until the Provincial Reform of 1708, there was no
radical change in either central or local organisation. The
twenty years were difficult years in which very drastic steps
were taken to equip the country for war, and to improve the
organisation of industry and finance. At the centre of the administration was the Boyar Duma whose sessions the Tsar
sometimes attended. Here the only innovation was that the
boyars were no longer to 'deliberate alone', but to 'join in
Council'. Some of the ancient Muscovite prikazes were amalgamated, others were divided, they were generally given new
names, and new prikazes were created, modelled on the old,
to deal with new affairs: the Preobrazhensky Prikaz dealt with
the guards and the secret police, the Admiralty Prikaz dealt
with the fleet, and the Military-Naval Prikaz dealt with foreign mercenary seamen. Attitudes, not new perhaps, but animated by a new force, pervaded the archaic administrative
bodies. A result of the struggles between the Court parties led
by the different Tsarevnas, the internecine feuds of the military classes, the struggles of the impoverished nobility with
the parvenus, and the conflict between the traditional and the
Western political tendencies, was that power came to depend
on the peculiar position of individuals, to the detriment of the
proper institutions of government. During the regency of the
Tsaritsa Natalia, for example, her brother Leo, a nonentity
who was nonetheless the head of the Possolsky Prikaz, was
put in charge of all ministers but two. The exceptions were
Streshnev, Minister of War and Internal Affairs, and Prince
Boris Golitsyn who, as head of the Prikaz of Kazan, 'ruled
absolutely' over the Volga region, and according to Prince

Kurakin, was responsible for its utter ruin. Moreover when the favourites were in power, the boyars in the Duma 'were only spectators'. Thus in 1697, when Peter was preparing to go abroad, all boyars and heads of Prikazes were ordered to wait upon the head of the Preobrazhensky Prikaz, Prince Romodanovsky, and to 'hold council with him at his request'. Prince Kurakin commented that he was 'an evil tyrant, drunk most of the time', and Kurbatov that 'though a man of bad judgement he was all-powerful in his ruling'. Prince Romodanovsky was, in fact, endowed with extraordinary powers: he was made head of the Cabinet, and even President of the Duma although, as a mere 'stolnik' his rank did not permit him to sit in it. The ancient legislative formula 'the sovereign has ordered, the boyars decreed' could have been replaced by 'Streshnev (or Prince Romodanovsky) has ordered and the boyars remain silent'. Another change, dictated by necessity, altered the activities of the Boyar Duma itself.

Faced with so many new expenses, Peter wanted to know how much money was held by the Prikazes. In 1699 he therefore re-established the Prikaz of Accounts, or 'Privy Chancellery', which was to control all state finance. To the Prikaz of Accounts all other Prikazes had to submit weekly and yearly statements of receipts and expenditure, reports on their staff, buildings, etc., from which it prepared its complete statement of the accounts. These statements, the series of which for 1701–9 is in P. Miliukov's book, provide excellent material for the study of Peter's financial administration. The Duma was mainly concerned with economic problems, and particularly with the economic problems of the war, while Peter took personal control of foreign and military affairs. As the Privy Chancellery was concerned with similar business, it became a department of the Boyar Duma, which in fact began to meet at the offices occupied by the Privy Chancellery.

All these changes were gradually altering the composition, jurisdiction, and character of the Boyar Duma itself. From time immemorial it had consisted of men of rank, but, on the decline of their power, it ceased to be the council of the boyars. It was changed into a council of limited size which was no longer recruited simply by birth, and which exercised different functions. It invariably worked with the Tsar, and under his presidency, at its legislative functions. With the Tsar frequently abroad, however, it had to deal with the current business put before it by the Prikazes and the detail and execution of Peter's hasty suggestions on internal administration; it therefore became an administrative body. Moreover Peter insisted that when he was away the council should act independently, without waiting for his opinion. So long as the Duma and the Tsar acted together, it had not been necessary to separate the responsibilities of each; the new independence of the former required some definition of its responsibilities. In 1707 Peter ordered the Boyar Duma to keep minutes of its meetings which were to be signed by all members, and confirmed his order with the words 'no resolution is to be taken without this, so that the stupidity of each shall be evident', which hardly shows much respect for the councillors he had called upon to handle such important business. The evolution of the Prikaz of Accounts into a department under the Boyar Duma, and the change of that body, which now had a negligible boyar element, into a deliberative and executive council of ministers responsible for the economic problems of the war, gave a clear indication of the direction of administrative reform, the object of which would plainly be to look after the regular army and navy by looking after the Treasury.

The first step in this direction was the attempt to use local autonomy for fiscal purposes. In the seventeenth century, at the request of the local communities, the function of the *voe-*

vodas, who had become too tyrannical, were sometimes transferred to the *gubnye starosty*[1] who were elected by the local nobility. According to Tatishchev's evidence, it was because the district *voevodas* 'thieved daringly' that it was decided in the reign of Tsar Theodore to allow the nobility to elect *voevodas* in the pious hope that they would be able to control the rapacity of the local officials who were supposed to keep order. What actually happened, however, was that the responsibility for collecting the Streltsy tax and the indirect taxes was transferred past the *voevodas* to the elected *starosty* who were responsible to their electors, in an attempt to protect the taxes from the ravages of the *voevodas*.

The ukaze of January 30th, 1699, went even further: in view of the prejudices of the *veovodas* and the hardships they imposed on the traders and industrialists of the capital, the latter were to be allowed to elect annually from among themselves 'Burmisters',[2] 'as many good and honest men as they wish,' who were not only to administer the collection of taxes, but also to try civil and commercial cases. Other towns, associations of 'black-ploughing' peasants, and of court peasants were told by ukaze that they could free themselves from the offences and bribes of the *voevodas*, who were no longer to be in control, and, 'if they so wish', their own elected officials would collect the taxes and try cases, provided that they paid double the tax assessment. It can be deduced from the above, therefore, that, as far as the taxpayer was concerned, there was not much to choose between the *voevoda* and the government. The ukaze now proposed that the provincial tax-paying associations rid themselves of these secondary monarchs by paying double the tax assessment, in exactly the same way that with the introduction of the *zemstvo* institu-

[1] Elders.
[2] 'Burmister' was a corruption of burgomeister. Peter frequently used German names for his newly invented offices.

tions[1] under Tsar Ivan,[2] the taxpayers could get out of the clutches of the *kormlenshchiki*[3] by paying a special State tax. In a century and a half, therefore, the government had not produced any new ideas in administrative reform. The new gift, with its conditional clause, seemed a very expensive one to the taxpayers; only eleven cities out of seventy accepted, and the remainder replied that they would not pay at twice the rate, and that they did not have anybody whom they could appoint as *burmister*. Some even said that they were satisfied with their 'honest' *voevodas* and officials![4] As a result the government dropped the double assessment, and made the election of a *burmister* compulsory. Indeed it seems from some ukazes that the autonomy of the towns was more important to the government than it was to the towns. The *voevodas* by their 'waywardness and unjust exactions' were responsible for the large arrears in Treasury receipts, and it was to be hoped that the use of unpaid and responsible *burmisters* would result in an improvement. The reform of 1699 clearly reflects one of the many symptoms of the malady which, for centuries, had afflicted Russian administration. This malady was represented by the perpetual struggle between government and institutions whose quality the government was unable to improve. Thus the *voevodas*, having lost their judicial and administrative power over the commercial and industrial communities of the towns, and over the free rural populations, had only the men of service and their peasants to administer,

[1] The *zemstvo* were institutions of local self-government, whose organisation and functions varied throughout the centuries.

[2] See Florinsky, *Russia,* Macmillan, New York, 1953, Vol. I, pp. 192–4.

[3] *Kormlenie* means 'feeding', and the *Kormlenshchiki* means 'the fed'. These officials were not paid directly by the government but lived at the expense of the population who paid them dues, which were mostly in kind. See Kucherov, *Courts, Lawyers and Trials under the last three Tsars,* Praeger, New York, 1953.

[4] Florinsky adds that thirty-five rejected the proposal, while twenty-six elected the new officers but said nothing about the doubling of the assessments. See Florinsky, *Russia,* Macmillan, New York, 1953, Vol. I, p. 366.

and in the northern regions of Russia, where these social classes were non-existent, the office of *voevoda* disappeared completely.

The government, however, still found it necessary to use noble associations to check the rapacity of the surviving *voevodas*. An ukaze of March 10th, 1702, abolished the *gubnye starosty*, elective officials chosen by the local nobility to enforce the law. The government however, did not want the local nobility to remain inactive in local government, and the ukaze continued: 'the *voevodas* together with the nobles, *pomeshchiks* and *votchiniks*, and good and knowledgable people, who are to be elected by the *pomeshchiks* and *votchiniks* of the towns, are to govern the towns,' and two to four men were to be elected from each district. Having granted the commercial and industrial population of the towns the right to participate in a representative collegiate administration, the logical sequence of events would have been for the government to widen the system to include the rural land-owning class who, by virtue of the ukazes of 1699, were still governed by the *voevodas*. But unfortunately administrative logic broke down completely, and failed to grasp what was going on. When the regular army was created, the old Muscovite district associations of noblemen, which were based on the territorial organisation of their detachments in the militia, were dissolved. All noblemen capable of performing military duties were dragged from their native districts, and sent to join the new regular regiments which were stationed in remote areas. The only noblemen to remain were those who had been retired due to their unfitness for service, and the shirkers who had gone to earth. There was not much hope for the establishment of rural self-government if it was to depend on the invalids and the shirkers who were, in any case, liable to the loss of their civil rights. The whole problem had been dealt with very superficially, as the documents on the *voevoda* associates published by M. Bogoslovsky[1] show. The rural associations of the nobility, or rather their remains, displayed almost complete indifference to the right conferred upon them, and only in a few places were councils elected for the *voevodas* to consult. Elections were therefore replaced by direct nominations either from the capital or by the *voevoda* — who was supposed to be controlled by his nominees. Not unnaturally, the *voevoda* quarrelled with his council, and after eight or nine years this odd reforming experiment destroyed itself by its own futility.

More important and more successful were the changes in the financial organisation of the commercial and industrial classes of the towns. The tax-paying associations of the towns had been linked only to the Prikazes in Moscow; since their liberation from the rule of the *voevodas*, the towns paid their indirect taxes to the Prikaz of the Great Treasury (Bolshoi Kazni), and their direct 'Streletsky' tax to the Streletsky Prikaz. Now, however, the government wanted to place the wealthy merchants of Moscow in positions of authority over all the towns, and use them as its financial general staff. Thus in 1681 a commission of wealthy Moscow merchants was charged with settling the rate at which the towns of different means were to contribute to the Streletsky tax. The reform of 1699 turned this commission into a permanent institution, and the ukaze of January 30th, 1699, provided that, for taxation purposes, the urban offices and their elected *burmisters* were to be subordinated to the *Burmisterskaya Palata* or *Ratusha*,[2] which consisted of the *burmisters* elected by the wealthy merchants of Moscow. Local *burmisters'* offices were to be accountable to the *Ratusha* for revenue received from

---

[1] M. Bogoslovsky, *Oblastnaya Reforma Petra Velikogo*, 1902. (Local Reforms of Peter the Great).

[2] The *Burmisterskaya Palata* was soon called the *Ratusha*, from the German word *Rathaus*.

customs dues and the tax on inns, and were also to send it all the revenue they had collected from other taxes. In this way the *Ratusha* in Moscow became the central office for the political organisation and taxation of the merchant and industrialist class. By-passing all the other departments, it presented its reports directly to the Tsar and in time became a sort of Ministry of Towns and Urban Taxation. A number of taxes, including the Streletsky tax, the Inns tax, and the Customs tax, together yielding more than one million roubles, which had previously been collected by thirteen Moscow Prikazes, were now transferred to the *Ratusha*.

In 1701, when the actual receipts proved larger than the estimated amount, the taxes paid into the *Ratusha* came to 1·3 million roubles, which was more than one-third — nearly a half in fact — of the total estimated tax receipts for that year. The *Ratusha's* revenue went to maintain the army. Its activities were considerably extended when Kurbatov, the projector, was appointed as inspector of its administration, and he became the President of the Council of Moscow Burmisters. Originally a household serf, Kurbatov showed anything but a servile attitude on his appointment; on the contrary, finding himself surrounded by bribery and corruption, which had increased out of all proportion during Peter's frequent absences, he waged a constant and remorseless war in the interests of the state. Every letter he wrote to the Tsar contained a complaint against embezzlement, or a denunciation of some highly placed thief. He reported that in Moscow and in other towns large sums were abstracted from taxes which had already been collected, that the *Ratusha's* clerks were robbers in the grand scale, and that the elected *burmisters* were no better. 40,000 roubles were stolen in Yaroslav, and 90,000 in Pskov. Naryshkin was sent to expose them but he was bribed, and protected the thieves. In his reports to the Tsar, Kurbatov castigated men of the highest rank, such as Prince Romodanovsky, one of the worst offenders; the only exception was his own patron, Prince Menshikov, who was the biggest swindler of all. Kurbatov asked the Tsar for absolute authority, and the power to sentence the embezzlers to death, in order to root out the evil. He wrote that he had increased the *Ratusha's* revenues by hundreds of thousands of roubles, and that they now amounted to almost 1·5 million roubles. Yet in spite of this success, the *Ratusha* barely managed to cover the military expenditure, and the Provincial reform put an end to Kurbatov's financial activities, and indeed to the *Ratusha* itself.

The Provincial reform came about as a consequence of Peter's own activities, which were stimulated by internal and external events connected, directly or indirectly, with the war. Previous Tsars had remained in the capital, except for the rare occasions when they went on a pilgrimage or on campaign, and the administration of the country had been highly centralised. Direct and indirect taxes, collected throughout the country, were sent through the *voevodas* to the capital, where they were distributed among the Moscow Prikazes who used most of the money themselves, returning only a small proportion to the provinces to pay the salaries of the provincial men-of-service and meet other local expenses. Peter completely overturned this antiquated and rigidly centralised system. First of all he freed himself from the capital and travelled, visiting the most distant parts of Russia, and causing turmoil wherever he went either by his own furious activity or by the risings it provoked. At the end of a frontier campaign in some distant Province, Peter did not leave it in peace; on the contrary, he at once urged it to some new and arduous enterprise. After the first Azov campaign, for instance, Peter started to build a fleet at Voronezh. A number of towns in the Don basin were ascribed to the Admiralty Department at Voronezh, and thousands of men

were driven in to forced labour, while the taxes collected
in the region were diverted at once to this undertaking instead
of being sent to the Prikazes in Moscow. Similarly, after the
fall of Azov, the labour and taxes of other towns were used
to build a port at Taganrog. After the conquest of Ingria, on
another frontier, the same thing happened with the building
of St. Petersburg and the Olonetz shipyards in which the
Baltic Fleet was built. In 1705 there was a revolt in Astrakhan
directed against Peter's innovations;[1] in order to pacify and
reorganise the region, its taxes were transferred from the
control of the central departments to the regional authorities
who were to use the money for local needs. The same thing
happened at Smolensk and Kiev when King Augustus was
forced to make peace with Charles XII, and sign the Altranstaedt Agreement[2] of 1706, as a result of which Charles, who
had occupied Poland, threatened Peter's flank. All these
events showed that it would be better for the taxes to go
directly to the regional administration instead of indirectly
through the Prikazes in Moscow, where the funds melted
away. They also led to an increase in the powers of the
regional administrators, who were given the new title of
gubernator although the region they administered was not yet
called a *guberniya* — a Province. What had already been done
made it easier to carry out these changes. A number of departments in Moscow were concerned in the financial, and even
in some of the military, affairs of vast regions such as Kazan,
Siberia, Smolensk, and Malorossia. It was now only necessary
to send the head of the relevant department to the area under
its control, and to bring him into closer contact with the
people, to make his task a great deal easier.

[1] It was provoked in particular by heavy taxation.
[2] This was a secret agreement by which Augustus was forced to end his
alliance with Russia, and by which he was forced to recognise Leszcynski as
Poland's legitimate king.

The real need for decentralisation was made more obvious by the situation Peter found himself in after the war. He appreciated that his preoccupation with diplomatic and military affairs, and his continual movement, made it impossible for him to give sufficient attention to internal affairs, and that he would therefore be a bad administrator. He wrote to Kurbatov, justifying the Provincial system, that 'It is difficult for a man to understand everything, and govern from a distance'. He did not believe that the central departments and the *Ratusha* were capable of producing enough money to cover his military expenditure, but he thought that if he appointed powerful vice-regents to vast areas, they would be able to find the money. Peter was the sort of man who placed more reliance on men than on institutions; hence his plan to make specific areas pay for the army, and indeed his military budget was planned with this in mind. Peter had great difficulty in understanding the advantages of centralised government and the single Exchequer which Kurbatov had discussed with him, for he shared the prevailing opinion that every item of expenditure had to be linked to its own special source of income. Later on, when explaining the purpose of the Provincial Reform, he wrote that he had made the Provinces share between them military and other expenses, so that 'everybody should know from where the required receipts were coming'. It was this idea which was the basis for the division of Russia into Provinces in 1708.

The reform was initiated by a typically short and obscure ukaze of December 18th, 1707, which put many towns under the jurisdiction of Provincial centres such as Kiev and Smolensk. The following year, after many alterations, the boyars of the Privy Chancellery divided three hundred and forty one towns between the eight enormous new Provinces of Moscow, Ingermanland (later called St. Petersburg), Kiev, Smolensk, Archangel, Kazan, Azov, and Siberia. In

1711 the Province of Voronezh was constituted from the group of towns which had been assigned to help with the naval construction programme at Voronezh. This brought the total to nine Provinces, which happened to be the same number of territorial divisions which had been planned in the reign of Tsar Theodore. The coincidence of number, and, perhaps, the general idea of a single military and administrative territorial unit, are the only features the two ideas had in common. The territorial configuration of the Provinces corresponded neither to the Theodorian plan nor to the territorial arrangements of the regional departments in Moscow. In some cases whole territories were incorporated into a Province, in others a territory was divided among several Provinces. In the fixing of boundaries the distances and communications between the towns and the Provincial centres were taken into account. Thus all the towns lying on the nine main roads leading out of Moscow, the roads to Novgorod, Kolomna, Kashira, etc., were included in the Province of Moscow. The influential men such as Prince Menshikov, Streshnev, and Apraxin, who knew they were to be governors, were not indifferent to the administrative rearrangements on which their interests depended. When the boundaries had been settled, the army had to be divided among the Provinces for maintenance and, so that each Province would know the size of its share, total military expenditure had to be divided up likewise.

The main purpose of the reform was to put the responsibility for the maintenance of the army on this territorial basis. The Privy Chancellery and the nominated governors worked together on this problem, which was also discussed during sessions of the Duma, and at meetings of the governors. Discussions went on until 1712, when it was decided that it was possible to put the new administrative machinery into operation. Four years of hard preparatory work were spent on the reform, but even so errors were made: thanks to its inaccurate knowledge, the Privy Chancellery, which was the co-ordinating authority, overlooked nineteen of the regiments when it was allocating them among the Provinces. After Poltava, Peter himself thought not only of dividing the maintenance costs of his regiments among the Provinces; he thought that the war was nearly over, while in fact, it was to last for another eleven years.

The Provincial reform added an extra layer of officials to the local administration. In 1715 the establishment consisted, besides junior officials, of a governor, a vice-governor who either assisted his superior or governed part of the Province himself, a 'landrichter' who was an official in charge of the administration of justice, and an 'ober-proviant' and 'proviantmeister' who were in charge of grain collection. The governor, moreover, was not to be the highest authority in the Province. Although the experiment of persuading Provincial associations of nobles to take an interest in local administration by electing some of their number to supervise the *voevodas* had proved a complete failure, Peter now repeated this experiment on an even wider basis. An ukaze of April 24th, 1713, provided for the creation of boards of landraty of eight to twelve men according to the size of the Province, who were to take their decisions by a majority vote, and with whom the governors were obliged to consult. The governor was to have two votes, and be not the 'chief of this "consilium" but its chairman'. The landraty were chosen by the Senate from two lists of candidates drawn up by the governors, and were, in fact, modelled on the landraty of the Baltic provinces of Sweden conquered by Peter. Later on, however, no doubt realising the drawbacks of nominating councillors recommended by the governors, Peter changed his mind, and on January 20th, 1714, ordered 'the nobility to choose the landraty in every town or district'. But the

Senate never gave effect to this order, and continued to choose the candidates from the governor's lists. In 1716 Peter changed his mind again, and instructed the Senate to choose landraty from officers retired due to age or wounds. Thus the landraty were not elected representatives of the Provincial nobility nominated to assist the governors, but officials whose powers derived from the Senate and the governor himself. By the time of this ukaze, however, the functions of the landraty had already altered completely from those of the original plan. The episode of the *voevodas* and their council had been repeated.

The Provinces into which Peter divided the country were so vast that each included several of the Provinces into which it was divided in the late nineteenth century. Thus the Province of Moscow in Peter's time included the whole, or parts, of the late nineteenth-century Province of Moscow, as well as its surrounding Provinces of Tula, Vladimir, Yaroslav, and Kostroma. These enormous Provinces were subdivided into districts which were comparatively small, and there were in consequence so many of them in each Province that the administration had to group the districts and organise another administrative unit between Province and district. This grouping of districts into *Provintsii* or sub-provinces, which started in 1711, was not done uniformly but only for particular and local reasons. In the Province of Moscow, for instance, most of the districts were grouped into eight sub-provinces.

A third sub-division, however, was still to be added. There were great disparities in the wealth, and above all in the number, of taxable households in the different Provinces. There were, for instance 246,000 households in the Province of Moscow and only 42,000 in the Province of Azov. Peter, who liked simple mathematical schemes, wanted to reduce the variations between the Provinces to a single financial denominator, but thought the calculation household by household would be too laborious. He therefore invented a large accounting unit called *dolia*,[1] which for no apparent reason he fixed at 5,536 households, and took the total number of households to be 812,000, a completely arbitrary figure, supposedly taken from the census returns for 1678. The contribution of each Province to the expenses of the government was to depend on the number of *dolia* in it. Peter then turned the *dolia* into an administrative unit by dividing into *dolia* not only the households on the financial register, but also the Provinces themselves, and put the landraty to run the *dolias*. We have already mentioned that the experiment of administration by *voevodas* and councils elected by the provincial nobility had failed. With the Provincial reform of 1711, however, the *voevodas* who had survived the reform of 1699 had been fully reinstated with wide financial and legal powers not only over the rural population but also over the trading communities of their districts, and with the new name of 'kommendant'. It is difficult to ascertain whether the suppression of urban self-government was accomplished by order from above, or by custom and usage below. As we have seen, the districts had been grouped into sub-provinces, which were administered by *ober-kommendants* to whom the *kommendants* had been subordinated.

The ukaze of January 28th, 1715, however, suppressed the territorial divisions into districts and sub-provinces and the *ober-kommendants* and the *kommendants*. It provided instead for the division of Provinces into *dolia* which were to be administered by landraty vested with fiscal, police,[2] and judicial powers, which, however, were limited to the rural population, for the ukaze denied the landraty any jurisdiction

---

[1] The literal translation of the word *dolia* is 'fraction'.

[2] This word is not here used to mean 'police' in our narrow sense. It was used to cover economic and financial functions, as well as what we would now call the social services. See B. H. Sumner, *Peter the Great and the Emergence of Russia*, English Universities Press Ltd., 1950, pp. 131-3.

whatever over the trading community. This ukaze effected a complete change in the provincial administration of the country when it abolished the old unit of the district. In defiance of history and geography, but in the name of arithmetic, the *dolia* of the landraty sometimes coincided with the old districts, sometimes combined several of them, and sometimes divided them. Moreover it proved impossible to divide each Province into a series of squares each containing 5,536 households, so the ukaze left the governors free to increase or decrease the size of the *dolia* 'as it shall prove convenient, having regard to distances'. Sometimes, therefore, a *dolia* would consist of 8,000 households, while its neighbour would have only half as many, and evidently the number in a *dolia* could differ very widely from the average. Yet it was by the number of its *dolia* that a Province's contribution to state expenses was fixed, and the number of *dolia* was determined quite haphazardly 'according to the governor's judgement', so that complete nonsense was made of Peter's *dolia* mathematics. The number of landraty had to be increased: in the Province of Moscow, for instance, when the number of *dolia* had been calculated, it was found that forty-four landraty were required instead of the original thirteen.

The ukaze of 1715 also abolished the governor's council of landraty which had been the central administrative body of the Province. But, having sent the landraty to administer the *dolia*, the ukaze then showed that the government was frightened of leaving the governor without supervision. It provided that two landraty at a time should do a two-month tour of duty with the governor, and that, at the end of every year, the landraty were to meet in the Provincial capital to settle their accounts and take their decisions on all the business under their jurisdiction in plenary assembly. Not unnaturally this procedure created an ambiguity in the relationship between the governor and the landraty: as administrators of

o

parts of the Province the landraty were the governor's subordinates, while as members of the council of landraty they
were his equals. As the governor was the viceroy of the Province, however, the former relationship predominated. He
treated the landraty 'as if he were their overlord, and not their
president'; he ordered them about, commanded their
presence out of town, and, despite the law, even arrested
them. These hasty institutional changes completely upset
discipline in the civil service: to the excesses of power subordinates replied with disobedience. The landraty had barely
taken over the administration of their *dolia* when, towards the
end of 1715, they were instructed to carry out a new census.
This extra task, on top of all their other administrative work,
naturally slowed down everything. The census dragged on
through 1716 and 1717, while the Senate and the Tsar did their
utmost to speed it up. The landraty were ordered to report to
St. Petersburg with the registers towards the end of 1717, but
only a few appeared in 1718. One landraty was sent fifteen
ukazes but never appeared. Then it was ordered that the recal-
citrants were to be sent to St. Petersburg in chains, and the order
sent after one of them provided not only for his arrest if he refused to go but also for the seizure of his household. He refused
to go and threatened to beat anyone who tried to take them.

   Peter's legislation for Provincial reforms showed neither
forethought nor wisdom. The aim of the reform was purely
fiscal. The Provincial institutions had a repulsive characteristic: they were presses to squeeze money out of the taxpayer,
and were concerned less and less with the well-being of the
people. Meanwhile the Treasury's requirements kept on increasing, and the governors were incapable of satisfying
them. In 1715 the fleet cost nearly twice as much as in 1711.
Ships of the line in the Baltic Fleet were afraid to put to sea
for lack of equipment. Regiments did not receive their pay
in time and turned into bands of marauders. Ambassadors

received no money and were unable to maintain themselves
or to pay the necessary bribes. Peter harassed his officials with
'cruel ukazes', said his sluggish governors were 'like crabs',
and threatened that 'he would reason with them with his
hands, and not with words'.[1] The Senate was ordered not to
'spare from fines' the governors who were unable to extract
new taxes 'without overburdening the people'. The landraty
who had not sent the taxes they had collected to the capital
were to refund their annual salary of 120 roubles. The Provincial Commissaries, who were no more than intermediaries
between the Senate and the governors, and who were inno-
cent as far as any tax deficit was concerned, were beaten twice
a week, the usual way of forcibly recovering a debt. No other
means of encouragement were found than beatings and fines!
Some governors, zealous in the Treasury's interests, tried
everything. Apraxin, governor of Kazan, and brother to the
General-Admiral, invented new taxes for his reports, and
once made Peter a present of 120,000 roubles from the imag-
inary proceeds; to cover it he then put the most incredible
pressure on the ignorant non-Russians of his Province, by
forcing them, amongst other things, to buy Treasury tobacco
at 2 roubles a pound which gave him a profit of 150,000
roubles. Unfortunately this enterprise turned out to be extremely expensive; the oppressed non-Russians left the Province *en masse* — there were more than 33,000 families —
and so deprived the Treasury of a yearly sum amounting to
more than three times the profits which Apraxin had hoped
to collect from these people. Every conceivable measure was

---

[1] This threat is contained in a letter to Menshikov dated February 1st, 1711,
and quoted by Schuyler, *Peter the Great*, London, 1884, Vol. II, p. 186: 'Up to
now God knows in what grief I am, for the governors followed the example of
crabs in transacting their business, the last term of which was fixed for Thursday
in the first week of Lent, and therefore I shall now deal with them, not with
words but with hands.' Menshikov himself was of course no different from the
other governors.

taken to make up the loss: expenditure was cut, and extra-ordinary temporary taxes were imposed, one of which, how-ever, only yielded one-third of the estimated amount, a sure sign that there was nothing left to collect.

In 1708 Peter foresaw another deficit, and, having no faith in the antiquated system of Prikazes, tried to find a solution in a decentralised administration by transferring the financial departments from Moscow to the Provinces. This was un-successful, and he then had to consider returning the de-partments to the capital, justifying the fable about musicians![1]

Under Peter the Boyar Duma had acquired certain powers which were subsequently transferred to the institution which replaced it. The Senate had originally been intended only as a provisional institution, as were the committees of the Duma which, due to Peter's long and frequent absences, began to look somewhat permanent. On February 22nd, 1711, the eve of his departure to the Turkish campaign, Peter published a short ukaze: 'We appoint the governing Senate to ad-minister in our absence.' Another ukaze was phrased in a dif-ferent way: 'Having to absent ourselves frequently during the wars, we appoint the Senate as ruler.' Thus the Senate's right to administer was only to be of a temporary nature; after all, Peter unlike Charles XII, did not intend to be always absent. The ukaze also lists the nine senators, nearly as many as the effective members of the once populous Boyar Duma. Three members of the Boyar Duma were appointed to the Senate: Count Mussin-Pushkin, Streshnev, and Plemmyannikov.[2]

[1] This is a reference to Ivan Krylov's fable, 'A Quartett,' in which a monkey, a goat, a donkey, and a bear think that if only they could sit in the right order they would be able to play. See *Russian Fables of Ivan Krylov,* translated by Bernard Pares, Penguin Books, 1942, pp. 40–1.

[2] The other senators were Prince Peter Golitsyn, Prince Michael Dolgoruky, Prince Gregory Volkonsky, the Paymaster-General Samarin, Opukhtin and Melnitsky. It is interesting that none of the nine senators were among Peter's intimate friends.

An ukaze of March 2nd, 1711, defined the Senate's duties:
it was to have complete control over the judiciary and
over government expenditure, and it was to be responsible
for the sources of revenue and a host of other commissions
dealing with the enrolment of young noblemen and boyars'
retainers into the officer reserve, the examination of government goods, trade, and bills of exchange. Its responsibilities
and powers were defined in another ukaze which proclaimed
that all persons and institutions were, under pain of death, to
obey the Senate as they would the Tsar. No complaint of
senatorial maladministration was to be made before the Tsar
returned from abroad, when the Senate would have to account to him for its actions. In 1717 Peter reproved the
Senate from abroad for its administrative irregularities 'which
I cannot supervise because I am so far away, and so occupied
with this grievous war'; he urged the senators to be more
vigilant 'for you have nothing else to do except govern, and
if you do not do this conscientiously, you will answer to God,
and will not escape justice here below'. Sometimes Peter
made the senators come to him, in Reval or St. Petersburg,
to report 'on what has been done, what has not been done,
and the reasons for it'.

None of the old Boyar Duma's legislative functions seem
to have been included in the Senate's original commission; it
was not, any more than was the Council of Ministers, the
Sovereign's Council of State. It was an executive institution
responsible for the administration of current government
business, and for special commissions entrusted to it by the
absent Tsar; in fact it was a council brought together 'to take
his Majesty's place'. Moreover the Senate had nothing to do
with either foreign affairs or the prosecution of the war. The
Senate inherited two subsidiary institutions from the Council
of Ministers: the *Rasspravnaya Palata*, or Chamber of Justice, which was a special judicial section, and the *Blizhnaya*

Kantselyariya, or Privy Chancellery, which was to help the Senate with the accounts and the control of receipts and expenditure. As the temporary headquarters on the Neva became the capital of the empire, and Alexander Menshikov, senior sergeant in the Preobrazhensky Regiment, became Duke of Izhera and 'sovereign in his own domain', as Prince Kurakin put it, so did the temporary commission with which the Senate was endowed gradually became permanent.

The formation and development of the Senate is closely associated with the Provincial Reform of 1708. Moreover it was this reform that had undermined the administration of the central departments and thrown them into confusion. Some of the central departments, such as those responsible for Siberia and Kazan, were abolished, and the Provinces of Siberia and Kazan were made responsible for their own administration. Others of the central departments were reduced to the status of offices of the Province of Moscow, like the *Ratusha* which became simply the Moscow municipal council. The organisation of the country was rather strange: there were eight vast regions, the governments of which were in no way co-ordinated in the capital. Indeed a capital did not even exist, for Moscow had stopped being one, and St. Petersburg had not yet taken its place. In the place of an established geographical centre the country had to manage with a peripatetic headquarters — the location of the Tsar. The Council of Ministers only met casually, and its composition was quite fortuitous, in spite of the ukaze which clearly provided for its composition and duties. A register for 1705 shows that there were thirty-eight councillors, boyars, *okolnichy*, and *dumnie dvoriane*. Yet when immediate and decisive action was required because Charles XII, by an unexpected forced march from Poland, had cut the communications of the army at Grodno, there were only two ministers, *dumnie lyudi*, in Moscow with the Tsar; the remainder were away travelling 'on service'.

Only departments concerned with requisitions and expenditure remained in Moscow, i.e., War, Artillery, the Admiralty, and Ambassadors. Thus control of expenditure was concentrated in the capital, and receipts were collected by the Provincial administrations, but Moscow no longer enjoyed the presence of a superior institution responsible either for the ultimate disposition of the receipts or for the supervision of the recipients — in other words, there was no government. Peter was preoccupied with military and diplomatic problems, and seemingly failed to notice that, having created eight Provinces, he had in fact only set up eight departments to recruit and maintain the army in its struggle against a dangerous enemy; he had left the state without a centralised administration, and himself without anybody to interpret and execute his sovereign will. The ministers in the Privy Chancellery could not play the part since they had neither the necessary authority nor were in permanent session; they were concerned with other business, and were obliged to sign the minutes of their meetings so that their 'stupidities' would be evident to all. At this stage Peter did not require a legislative or consultative State Council, but a simple administrative council. He needed a few intelligent men who could discover, in the laconic, cryptic, hastily written ukazes he sent them, the ideas that he wished them to embody in their ukazes, and put them into effect. In other words what was needed was a council with enough power to be feared, and with a sufficient sense of responsibility not to be without fear itself. The intention (if one admits that any intention existed at all when the Senate was created) was that, in the eyes of the people, it should be the Tsar's *alter ego*, but that it should always be sensible of the *quos ego* of the Tsar above it. Decisions in the Senate were taken on a unanimous vote, and, to avoid unanimous decisions being extorted by personal pressure, none of Peter's principal collaborators, such as Menshikov, Apraxin, Sheremetiev, or Chancellor Golovkin, were included in the Senate. These 'supreme lords', 'principals' as they are called by the ukaze, Peter's closest collaborators in military and diplomatic affairs over which the Senate had no authority, were likewise beyond the Senate's authority and could, indeed, send it 'ukazes by order of his Majesty'. At the same time, however, Peter informed Menshikov that even he, Duke of Izhera, was obliged, like other governors, to obey the Senate. Thus there were two governments acting in conflict, one sometimes subordinate to the other, and sometimes independent. The political thinkers of the period can only have accepted this situation because they either had not time to think about it or could not think out logically what was implied. Most of the Senators, such as Samarin, military Treasurer, and Prince Gregory Volkonsky, Quartermaster-General, were second-rate administrators, although they understood the Senate's main business — problems of military supply, etc. — no worse than any of the 'principals', and were certainly incapable of stealing as much as Menshikov. If Senator Prince Michael Dolgoruky could not write, then Menshikov was not much better, as he had difficulty in forming the letters of his name.

As we have seen above, two conditions, the decay of the old Boyar Duma, and the Tsar's continual absence, were responsible for the creation of the Senate, first as a temporary institution, and then as a permanent one with its authority, composition, and importance defined. The first condition, the disappearance of the central administrative body, meant that a supreme governing institution with a clearly defined commission and *permanent* members was required to concentrate exclusively on the business assigned to it. The second condition was responsible for the creation of an institution which would enforce laws and supervise other departments, but which had no consultative standing or legislative authority, and could be called on to account for the use it made of its very temporary powers.

Peter created the Senate so that it might supervise the whole administrative system, and this, at the beginning at any rate, was to be its most important function. The Privy Chancellery and the Senate were to be jointly responsible for keeping the public accounts. One of the Senate's first acts was to set up an organ of control. An ukaze of March 5th, 1711, directed the Senate to appoint an intelligent and good man, whatever his social standing, as *ober-fiscal*, to supervise secretly the administration of public affairs, and to collect information concerning inequitable judicial decisions, 'misappropriation of public funds, and other matters.' The *ober-fiscal* was to indict the offender, whatever his rank, before the Senate. If he secured a conviction he was entitled to half the fine the Senate imposed, but, if the charges were dismissed, no blame was to attach to him, and, according to the ukaze, those who 'held resentment against him' were to suffer 'cruel punishment and confiscation of property'. The *ober-fiscal* acted in conjunction with a network of fiscals spread throughout all the districts and administrative departments.[1] Since the ukaze specified that each town had to have one or two fiscals attached to it, and since there were then about three hundred and forty towns in the country, there must have been no fewer than five hundred such informers spread through the Provincial and urban administration. Later on the system became even more complicated: the fleet, for instance, had its own team of fiscals and its *ober-fiscal*. The irresponsible and arbitrary power of these officials soon led to abuse. *Ober-fiscal* Nesterov denounced all malefactors, includ-

[1] After Peter's death the post of fiscal was abolished.

ing his immediate superiors the Senators (those guardians of justice), and even accused Prince Jacob Dolgoruky, whose integrity was proverbial, and Prince Gagarin, Governor of Siberia, whom he succeeded in sending to the gallows.[1] In the end, Nesterov, champion of justice, was himself accused of accepting bribes, found guilty, and broken on the wheel.

Medieval Russian law had allowed a prosecution to be started on information received, but this was, in fact, a double-edged weapon, for, if the charges were proved false, the denunciator was put to the torture instead of the accused. Now, however, denunciation was made safe, and became part of the machinery of government. The immoral methods of the fiscals corrupted both administration and society. The episcopacy of Greater Russia, indifferent to, and incapable of giving, a moral education to their flock, remained silent; only the Ukrainian Metropolitan, Stephen Yavorsky, 'guardian of the patriarchal throne', could not contain himself, and in 1713, on the occasion of the Tsar's nameday, in the presence of the Senators, delivered a sermon openly denouncing the ukaze dealing with fiscals as immoral,[2] and even made transparent allusions to Peter's way of life. Thereafter the Senators

[1] Prince Mathew Gagarin had been connected with Siberia since 1693, first as Voevoda of Nerchinsk, then as President of the Siberian Department, a position he retained when he was Governor of Moscow. At this time trade with China was a government monopoly. Gagarin was accused of allowing private merchants to trade illegally at a great profit, as well as of selling his own goods to the Chinese, pretending that they belonged to the Government, and pocketing the proceeds. See E. Schuyler, *Peter the Great*, London, 1887, Vol. II, pp. 450–63.

[2] 'The law of God is faultless, but human laws have faults. Such a law, for example, places an inspector over judges, and gives him the power of accusing whom he pleases, and dishonouring whom he pleases. Even if he does not succeed in calumniating his neighbours, no one finds fault with him. Not so we ought to live; he has sought my head, and accused me falsely, let him lay down his own; he has spread a net for me, let him be entangled; he has dug a pit for me, let him fall into it.' Quoted by Schuyler, *Peter the Great*, London, 1884, Vol. II, note to p. 450.

forbade Yavorsky to preach, but Peter took no action against him, and it is even possible that he remembered this sermon when, in a new ukaze of 1717, he defined more carefully the duties and responsibilities of the fiscals, and charged them with the duties of procurators, to investigate 'matters of the people for which there are no rights of petition'. Another Ukrainian churchman, Theophan Prokopovich, made up for his colleague's liberal outburst by inserting in his 'Spiritual Reglament'[1] the modest injunction that lay deacons were to report disturbances in church and superstitious customs to the bishops 'as if they were ecclesiastical fiscals'. Not long after, the newly established Holy Synod dropped the shameful pretence of pseudo-fiscals, and, basing itself on the 'Spiritual Reglament', created real spiritual fiscals, borrowing the name of *inquisitor* from the familiar Catholic terminology. The Holy Synod directed that the *inquisators* were to be recruited from people with 'a clean conscience', that is, from the monastic ranks. The *hieromonakh* Pafnuty, builder of the Danilov Monastery in Moscow, was appointed *proto-inquisator*.

Far from restricting the system of informers to official relations, Peter's legislation endeavoured to widen its field of activities. The fiscals were intended to strengthen the Senate's arm, but unfortunately the fiscals informed on the Senators to the Tsar, and as a result the Senators treated them with contempt. Prince Jacob Dolgoruky, for instance, called them rascals and anti-Christs. Realising that the office of fiscal was not an easy one, and that its holder was generally despised, Peter decided to bring it under his own protection. He endeavoured to arouse popular enthusiasm for the work, and had publicly proclaimed his ukazes against embezzlement and

[1] The 'Spiritual Reglament' was a very long document which initiated the programme of church reform and set up the Holy Synod as the new governing body of the Church.

every subtle infringement of the interests of the state. He called on men of all ranks 'from the highest to the lowest' to inform the Tsar in person, without fear, of those who robbed the people and jeopardised the country's interests. Informers were to act between October and March. If the prosecution was successful, the informer was to receive the criminal's property, immovable and movable, and even his rank. According to the letter of the law, therefore, if a peasant belonging to Prince Dolgoruky informed on his master, and his case was proven, the peasant would get the Prince's estates as well as his rank of 'General-Kriegs-Plenipotentiar'. The ukazes went on to state that anyone who detected an infringement of the law, and did not report it, would himself 'be punished, or executed without mercy'. Informing became 'work' not only for the fiscals but also for the ordinary citizen who was supposed to look on it as part of his ordinary duties. As horses were commandeered for the army, so were the citizens' consciences put to work to benefit the Treasury. Thanks to the rewards some people were able to make a living from detecting and informing which, with the system of fines in general, threatened to become the state's most efficient guardians of law and order, and even decency. The medieval clergy had been able to frighten their flock with stories of punishment in the life hereafter, but had instilled into them neither respect for the clergy nor for the church as the House of God, and had not even taught the congregations to behave and keep silence at service. It was an ukaze, published in Moscow in 1719, and not a Church ordinance, that ordered congregations to stand silently in church, and provided for the appointment of good people to watch for misbehaviour, fine the culprits one rouble on the spot, and keep them in the church until they paid.

From the very beginning, the Senate, the chief custodian of justice, which was responsible for the country's prosperity, was badly served by its subordinate departments. In the capital there were vast numbers of old and new Muscovite and Petersburgian departments, chancelleries, bureaux, and commissions with overlapping jurisdictions, and undefined relationships, sometimes owing their creation only to chance. In the Provinces there were eight governors who not only disobeyed the Senate but even the Tsar. Attached to the Senate was the Chamber of Justice, inherited from the Council of Ministers, which acted as the Senate's legal department and its Privy Chancellery. One of the Senate's most important functions was 'to collect as much money as possible' and examine government expenditure in order to curtail unnecessary expenses; unfortunately accounts were not sent in, and the Senate was quite unable to keep track of the receipts, expenses, surpluses, and deficits of some years. The total absence of accounts in the middle of a war and a financial crisis must have convinced Peter that it was necessary to reconstruct the whole central administrative system. He was not capable of doing anything about this himself, and, as he had previously profited from the ingenuity of native-born projectors in his search for more revenue, so now he turned to foreign experts and foreign laws for advice on administrative organisation, and started to collect information on the organisation of the central administration of foreign countries. Foreigners sent him memoranda on the organisation of colleges, which he found existed in Sweden, Germany, and elsewhere, and he decided to introduce them in Russia.

In 1712 an attempt had already been made, with the help of foreigners, to establish a 'kollegium' of Trade, for, as Peter wrote 'their commerce is without any doubt, better than ours'. To his agents abroad he entrusted the task of collecting information on the status of colleges, finding books on jurisprudence, and above all inviting foreign officials to serve in the Russian colleges, for with no people, 'working only from books would be an impossibility, because no book ever covers every eventuality.' It was with difficulty, and slowly, that learned men of law, expert officials, secretaries, and writers, mostly Slavs, were recruited in Germany and Bohemia to organise the new institutions, and even Swedish prisoners of war who had learned the language were invited to take employment with the colleges. Having learned about the Swedish colleges, which had the highest reputation in Europe, Peter decided in 1715 to use them as models for his own central institutions. There was nothing unexpected or strange in this decision. There was no help to be found from Muscovy's past, and neither he nor his immediate companions had any ideas of their own for setting up a new type of institution. His approach to this problem was identical to the one he brought to the problem of naval construction: why design a special Russian frigate when good Dutch and English ships sail perfectly well on the White and Baltic Seas? Moreover enough Russian ships had rotted at Pereyaslav. Peter's latest scheme however, followed the usual course of Peter's reforms: the decision to introduce Swedish-type colleges was made very quickly, but its implementation was very slow. Peter sent Fick, a Holsteiner in the Russian service who admired the collegial form of government, to study the Swedish colleges at first hand. Baron von Luberas, a Silesian authority on Swedish collegial institutions, was also invited to enter the Russian service. Both Fick and von Luberas produced hundreds of regulations and a mass of information on the Swedish colleges, together with their own ideas on how to adapt them to Russian conditions. Von Luberas also engaged about one hundred and fifty experienced men from Germany, Bohemia, and Silesia to serve in the Russian colleges, and both von Luberas and Fick, especially the latter, took an active part in their foundation. At last, in 1718, a plan for the new institutions was ready, their composition established, presidents and vice-presidents appointed, and all of them ordered to draw up their own regulations on the Swedish model. Swedish rules which were irrelevant or 'which are not acceptable in our country are to be replaced by other, more suitable ones'. The presidents were expected to organise their colleges in 1718, and to be ready by 1719. But there were numerous delays and alterations, so that, while some were ready by the end of 1719, others were not till 1720. The ukaze of December 12th, 1718, set up the first nine colleges of Foreign Relations, State Revenue, Justice, Revision, 'control of all receipts and expenditure', i.e., a Department of Financial Control, Army, Admiralty, Commerce, Mines and Manufactures, and State Expenditure. This list shows plainly with what matters the government was most concerned, and what most required attention. Of the nine colleges, five were concerned with economic development, finance, and industry.

The colleges differed from the Prikazes in two ways: there was a more systematic division of responsibilities, and business was transacted in the colleges on a consultative basis. Only two resembled the old Prikazes: the college of Foreign Relations the Prikaz of Ambassadors, and the college of Revision the Prikaz of Accounts; the remainder were completely new departments of state. The authority of each Prikaz had extended only over a specified area but, when they were replaced by the colleges, the authority of each college covered the whole country. The Provincial reform had done away with many of the Prikazes, and the remainder disappeared with the introduction of the college system. The unnecessary Prikazes were either engulfed by the colleges, or subordinated to them — the college of Justice, for instance absorbed seven Prikazes. An attempt was thus made to simplify and rationalise the central administration. There still remained, however, a number of new offices and chancelleries (post-

prikaz creations) which were now either subordinated to the
colleges, or turned into independent administrative departments. For example, the Chief Commissariat Office, the
Artillery Office, and the Chief Quartermaster's office, which
was responsible for recruiting and clothing the army, all continued alongside the Military college.

The collegial reform had failed to produce that simplification and rationalisation of the administrative system suggested
by the ukaze of December 12th, 1718. Peter was unable to
overcome the Muscovite habit of excessive subdivision in
administration which he had inherited from previous generations of statesmen who apparently cultivated a system in
imitation of contemporary architectural practice. Moreover
it was in the interest of a systematic and reasonable division of
duties that the original college plan had undergone so many
changes. The Prikaz of Pomestie Estates, for instance, was originally subordinated to the college of Justice, but, because of
pressure of business, it was converted into an independent
college of Votchina Estates. The college of Mines and
Manufactures was divided into two, and the college of
Revision, a general department of financial control, was
merged with the Senate, which had the final responsibility for
financial control. In the ukaze authorising this merger it was
freely admitted that the creation of the college of Revision
had been 'an injudicious and thoughtless act'. At the end of
Peter's reign there were ten colleges in all. In the college
system, business was conducted on a consultative basis, although this had been known to happen in the Prikaz system.
The *Ulozhenie*, for instance, stated that judges, and directors of
Prikazes, were to consult with one another, and with their
chief clerks and colleagues, before arriving at a decision. But
this method of procedure was never properly formulated, and
fell into desuetude under the pressure exerted by powerful
directors. Peter, in extending the consultative system to the

Council of Ministers, the Provincial and district administration, and later on to the Senate, wanted it to apply to all central institutions, for an autocratic monarch needs advice more than law: 'the best organisation comes from good counsel' stated Peter in his Military Regulations. One man, of course, can conceal an irregularity more easily than a group, one of which will always be indiscreet. Each college had a board of eleven members, president, vice-president, four councillors, four assessors, and one foreign councillor or assessor, and two secretaries, of whom one was foreign. The assessors and councillors, themselves in charge of departments within the college, reported to the board, which took its decisions by majority vote. Experienced foreigners were brought into the college organisation to work with, and help, the inexperienced Russians, and to this end Peter usually appointed a foreign vice-president and a Russian president. Thus Menshikov was president of the Military college with General Weide as his vice-president; and Prince Golitsyn was president of the college of State Revenue, with the landraty from Reval, Baron Nirot, as his vice-president. An exception was the appointment of the artillery expert, General Bruce, as president of the college of Mines and Manufactures, with von Luberas as his vice-president. An ukaze of 1717 provided that 'in organising their colleges', i.e., setting up the boards, presidents were to choose two or three candidates for the positions of councillor and assessor who were 'neither to be relations', nor 'creatures of their own making'. The members of all the colleges were to fill the vacant places by election from this list.

To sum up, then, the differences between the college and the Prikaz systems were that each college was responsible for a different branch of government, that it exercised its powers over the whole country, and that it introduced new methods into existing administrative practice.

P

Chapter Nine

★

THE COLLEGE REFORM effected great changes in the administrative system, and particularly in the position of the Senate. For nine years the Senate had been the government, and indeed had been responsible for nearly all the central administration of the country. The chief secretary to the Senate remarked that all the prikazes were dependent on 'messieurs the Senators', and were, in some measure, the Senate's administrative departments. The Senate received ukazes from the Tsar on finance, economics, logistics, recruiting, bills of exchange, and taxfarming; it communicated them in turn to its subordinate central and regional institutions, and gave instructions for their implementation. The Senate also examined, and decided upon the many administrative and judicial problems sent up by subordinate institutions and individuals. Above all the Senate was called on to exercise its supervisory and executive powers. 'Now everything devolves on them' . . . 'so it all depends on you,' wrote Peter, bidding everybody to address themselves to the Senate, and not to him. The colleges relieved the Senate of much of its daily business, and were granted some independent powers, so that the Senate was able to give more attention to controlling other institutions and departments. The colleges, however, were directly responsible to the Senate, to which they were obliged to send any unresolved business, and complaints about their dilatory methods were taken to the Senate.

As Peter's own thinking on the fundamentals and problems of creating an apparatus of government became more thorough, so did his ordinances take on a more specialised administrative character, so that officials were required to look at them carefully before drafting the new ukazes. Directives to the Senate became enquiries or suggestions 'for its consideration'. The Senate was still responsible for the country's economic well-being, and remained the supreme judicial body, but abandoned executive for advisory functions. It was Peter himself who saw to it that the Senate's main business should be to draft laws, and furnish him with advice. His directives to the administration lost their dictatorial tone; he now demanded not that they should be put into immediate effect, but that there should be a preliminary draft of the law. In 1720 he gave it as his opinion that the children of runaway peasants should not be surrendered with their fathers, but 'were to remain in the place where they had been born', and added 'the Senate must state in writing whether it agrees or not, lest confusion arise thereafter'. Again, in 1722, he insisted that when the Senate found itself unable to come to a decision without a memorandum from him, it was to hold preliminary discussions and send him, together with the report, notes of the arguments used by the Senators, 'otherwise his Majesty will have great difficulty in deciding on his own.' Sometimes Peter joined the Senators, and put forward his own ideas for discussion. When it was, for instance, urgently necessary to cut the Ladoga Canal in 1718, Peter, not knowing quite how this was to be done, wrote to the Senate, 'I send you my ideas on this subject, and ask you to discuss them; whether it be done in this, or some other way, it has to be done.' The problem was solved by the Senate 'in some other way', and not quite in accordance with Peter's ideas, as is seen from the ukaze that appeared soon after. Thus the Senate, in theory the highest of the legal and administrative bodies subject to the Tsar's authority, in practice participated in that authority in a consultative capacity.

It also became necessary to devise a formula distinguishing a legislative from an administrative ukaze. Peter renounced, for himself and the Senate, the right to issue verbal ukazes. According to the *General Reglament* of February 28th, 1720, the colleges were to confine themselves to the law as expressed in the written ukazes of the Tsar and Senate. The commentary to the *General Reglament* established a distinction between ukazes for instant execution and ukazes commanding a method of execution. In the latter case, it seems, 'a verbal command may be issued' and be discussed, but the decision reached after the discussion may only be put into effect by written ukaze. In an emergency, the Senate together with the Synod could proceed without 'ratification'. During the Persian campaign in 1722, Peter wrote to the Synod saying that he refused to commit himself in certain matters without first consulting the Senate and the Synod; that other problems could wait, and 'if God wills we will decide on our return'; that urgent business was to be communicated to him only 'as a matter of information; and together with the Senate, you must take a decision without waiting for my approval, for how can I issue ukazes from such a distance?' This letter is obviously more like an ukaze 'for instant execution' than one commanding a method of execution', for Peter promised in advance not only to approve the decision, but also its execution, since otherwise either urgent business would not be treated urgently or decisions would be put into effect provisionally, with the danger that they might be rescinded.

The Senate's dual function of legislature and executive was reflected in its structural evolution. Peter was unable to make up his mind about the Senate's exact composition, and he blamed himself for the many changes that it underwent. When the colleges were first set up the presidents were raised to the Senate, which then resembled a committee of Ministers. It is difficult to guess Peter's motive here, although this was the Swedish method, recommended by one of the foreign advisers. The Boyar Duma had customarily included the heads of the Prikazes, and the Council of Ministers which replaced it was often composed of them alone. Once again relationships were confused, only this time Peter noticed. Presidents of colleges sitting in the Senate tended to become superior to those of their colleagues who were only Senators, but as heads of departments they were responsible to the Senate, and were thus actually subordinated to themselves. Moreover the president-Senators were unable to contend with both Senate and college business, so in 1722 they were ordered to keep their seats in the Senate but give up the presidencies of the colleges, and choose others to take their place. 'At the beginning this matter was badly organised, and now must be put right;' the ukaze went on to explain that the Senators had to work unceasingly to maintain order and justice in the Senate, and supervise the colleges 'while remaining independent of them, for if they are also of the colleges, how can they judge themselves?' Only on certain occasions were the Presidents of the three most important colleges, those of Foreign Relations, Army, and Naval affairs, called to attend the Senate. This modification in the composition of the Senate produced yet another change, for Peter found a shortage of experienced men fit for the Senate, so that four months later college presidents were ordered to resume their seats in the Senate 'because of the scarcity of men', and to attend three times a week.

The Senate exercised enormous power. An ukaze called on it to work unceasingly 'to bring order into the State', and to organise the 'hitherto disorganised' administration. It played a leading part in the general reconstruction of the government undertaken by Peter in the last years of his reign, and enjoyed as much authority as any institution could under such a monarch as Peter. It dispensed justice, laid down legal principles, and, by virtue of the order 'to collect as much money as possible', imposed new taxes; it also clarified the Tsar's vaguely worded ukazes, and guessed at his still embryonic legislative ideas. Nothing could be started without the Senate's consent, and nothing decided; it took the Tsar's place in his absence; the law put it on an equal footing with the highest terrestrial authorities, God, the Tsar, and 'the whole honest world'. Unfortunately, even when deprived of this rhetoric, it was difficult to raise the Senate and its members to such heights. For the Senate was a body for transmitting the autocrat's will, and had no independent will of its own; its powers were those of an agent, and not of a principal; it had no sovereign powers, and was merely responsible for carrying out instructions; it was an administrative instrument, and not a political force. Errors and failures produced no threats of ministerial dismissals, but threats of a master's punishment: 'You have acted in a contemptible manner accepting bribes according to ancient and stupid customs, and when you come before me, you will be called to account in a different way.'

The administrators, however, were used to being treated in this way. The officials themselves were second-rate, and standards of behaviour were not improved when the colleges were set up and staffed by such aristocrats as Prince Menshikov and Prince Golitsyn. It now became necessary to supervise the Senate, although the creation of an organisation competent to supervise the chief administrative body was a difficult matter, especially since it would have to conform to a pattern of behaviour that included the Tsar rebuking the Senate, and imposing fines on individual Senators as well as on departmental officials. In 1719, for instance, five Senators were fined for having made a wrong decision. Methods such as these tended to discredit the institution and its authority with its subordinate institutions and the masses. Peter had, therefore, not only to discipline the Senators, but also to maintain their authority if his reforms were to be successful. In the interests of discipline Peter used paternal methods on the dignitaries who had displeased him; he would take a cudgel to Menshikov, or some other offender, in the privacy of his workshop, and then invite him to dinner as if nothing had happened. In order to avoid scandal Peter replaced punishments with preventive methods, and different methods of surveillance were introduced to this end. The insubordination of officials who disobeyed not only their immediate superiors, but also the Tsar's ukazes, became in Peter's time a real administrative problem, and surpassed even the indiscipline of the old Muscovite secretaries who once stubbornly noted on the fifteenth ukaze demanding the dismissal of a clerk: 'as a result of the mighty sovereign's ukaze, no clerk was dismissed'. Neither fines, nor threats of 'complete dismissal', nor even forced labour, had any effect.

In 1715 the post of Inspector-General or Inspector of Ukazes was created, and given first to Basil Zotov, an educated man who had studied abroad, and whose father Nikita was President-General of the Privy Chancellery and Peter's Chief Jester. The ukaze ordered the Inspector-General to sit 'in the same place as the Senate', to take note of the Senate's ukazes, to see that they were enforced, to denounce and fine negligent Senators, and to 'complete' any unfinished business. The Inspector-General's influence over the Senate was not, at this stage, intended to stretch beyond the terms of reference laid down by the ukaze. His principal duty was 'to see that everything got done'. But Zotov's reports show that he did in fact exceed his terms of reference: the Senators, themselves obliged to punish negligence, were in fact the worst offenders, failed to attend the Senate for the required three

days a week, and in three years only concluded three affairs
of any importance; they imposed no fines, and ignored the
reports and recommendations of the projectors. In 1720 a new
rule was introduced to the Senate which prescribed that
'meetings are to be properly conducted, without shouting and
"other manifestations" ', and that the following standing
order was to be adopted: 'the business is to be stated, and is to
be thought about and discussed for half an hour; if, however,
it be complicated and more time is asked for, then it is to be
postponed until the following day; if the business is urgent.
extra time up to three hours will be granted for further
deliberations, but as soon as the hour-glass shows that time
has run out, paper and ink are to be handed out, and every
Senator is to note down his opinion and sign it; if a Senator
fails to do this, business is to be stopped, while somebody runs
to tell the Tsar, wherever he may be.' But who was to maintain order in the Senate, and see that these rules were enforced? The doyen of the Senators? No, the man chosen was
the Senate's chief secretary, Shchukin, director of the Senate's
Chancellery and its rapporteur. One year later duties of the
Inspector-General and the chief secretary were delegated to
the military, and staff officers of the guard were attached to
the Senate for a month each to keep order. If a Senator mis-
behaved, the officer was to arrest him, put him in the fortress,
and report to the Tsar. An officer who neglected this duty
was threatened with death or degradation, and the loss of all
rights.

Finally, in the following year, a new mentor was found for
the young Senate, a Procurator-General appointed by an
ukaze of January 12th, 1722. Peter gave a great deal of
thought to this post. Contrary to his usual habit of improvis-
ing a law and leaving its elaboration to the Senate, he worked
on this innovation himself. He also read projects, and examined the other ukazes designed to control the Senate — in

other words he studied this problem with very great attention. Yet even after his instructions to the Procurator-General
had been ratified, he introduced further modifications, and
the results of his efforts appeared in the ukaze of April 27th,
1722, on the functions of a Procurator-General, which repeated part of the other ukazes, but also contained new ideas.
He first of all defined the new post: 'he who fills this post is
our eye and our mandatory in affairs of state,' which meant
that he would be the Tsar's representative in the Senate.
Moreover the Procurator-General was put at the head of the
Senate's secretariat, and the Senate became like a limbless
body, possessing only an hour-glass and the right to ask for
delay 'in order to think'. Any business which the colleges
found particularly perplexing, or which lay outside their
jurisdiction, was sent to the Procurator-General to put before
the Senate, and so were reports from governors and *voevodas*
on business outside the colleges' jurisdictions. The fiscals,
who were the Senate's principal agents, were now subordinated to the Procurator-General who acted as intermediary between the Senate and its subordinate departments.
In fact, the responsibility for supervising the whole administrative machinery passed from the Senate to the Procurator-
General, who also supervised the Senate itself. Indeed, he was
was not only to preserve order and decency at its meetings,
but was also to sit in judgement on its activities, pointing out
any injustice or bias in discussion and opinion. If the Senators
disagreed with the Procurator-General, the latter had the
power to stop the discussion, but had then to report to the
Tsar immediately. Alternately, the Procurator-General was
to consult 'with whom he deems best', but the consultation
was to last for no longer than one week. The ukaze reduced
the risk of the Senate and the Procurator-General coming
into conflict by the insertion of a clause to the effect that 'the
Tsar would not blame the Senate' for an unintentional breach

of duty, 'because it is better to speak and make a mistake, than to remain silent and make one,' although frequent mistakes 'would not be overlooked'. Peter, after all, was loth to admit that his 'eye' in the Senate could be wrong.

The Procurator-General also had it in his power to initiate legislation. In the old Boyar Duma, legislation could be initiated by the Tsar himself, or by the Directors of Prikazes, who were generally *dumnye lyudi*, for in this matter, there was no separation of powers between the Tsar and his Duma who together represented one indivisible supreme power. As we have seen, however, some parts of the Duma lost the right of legislative initiative. Under Peter the antiquated Council of Boyars lost its power, and the Senate which took its place, although endowed with great authority, had only executive power, since Peter kept in his own hands the right, which circumstances prevented him from exercising personally, of initiating legislation. He was completely absorbed with military and foreign policy, and did not have time to direct domestic affairs. He could formulate military and financial policies, but not legislation. In this he needed help, in exactly the same way as he had needed help from the projectors in his search for new sources of taxation. Peter realised that the Senate was, in fact, the place to initiate legislation. He tried, therefore, to force it to act independently, by refusing to issue ukazes while he was away, and by making it discuss different proposals and adopt the best one.

Unfortunately the rows, futile quarrels, and careless management which in 1722 resulted in the accumulation of 16,000 unresolved problems, all rendered the Senate powerless to take domestic policy into its own hands, and when Peter had more leisure, he decided to confer the power to initiate legislation on his personal representative in the Senate. The difficult task of drafting the ukazes was, however, left to the Senate, for the Procurator-General only brought forward problems which seemed not to be clarified by the law, and invited the Senate to frame a clear and precise ukaze. This in effect is what was done with the ukaze of April 17th, 1722, dealing with the maintenance of civil rights, which was to be laid before all tribunals, from the Senate down to 'the last place of law', 'to act as a mirror for those who sit in judgement'; the ukaze warned judges against playing with laws as if they were packs of cards, and against undermining 'the fortress of justice'.[1] This ukaze also laid down the procedure to be adopted by the Senate. The Procurator-General brought a problem to the notice of the Senate, which would then arrange for joint sessions, to be held between itself and the colleges, at which the problem 'would be thought over and discussed under oath'. The opinion of the Senate was then communicated to the Tsar by the Procurator-General, and the resolution of the Tsar became law. In this way the Procurator-General replaced the Senate as the mainspring of the administrative machinery. It is important to realise that, although the Procurator-General was not a member of the Senate, and had no voting rights, he was in fact its president, and was responsible for the maintenance of order during sessions, for tabling legislative questions, ruling on the correctness of the Senate's actions, and finally, for timing the Senate's discussions by means of the hour-glass. The Senate's other powers were similarly restricted, and it was transformed into a political institution with very little authority.

In 1722 the positions of Requetmeister and Heraldmeister were created. The first was responsible for 'looking after the affairs of petitioners', received and examined their complaints

---

[1] 'Nothing is so necessary to a government as the exact observance of the laws, since it is of no use to write laws if they are not kept, or if they are played with like cards, putting one suit against the other, which has never been anywhere in the world so common as with us, where people try in every way to undermine the fortress of right.' Quoted by Eugene Schuyler, *Peter the Great*, London, 1884, Vol. II, pp. 443–4.

against the dilatoriness or injustice of decisions by the colleges, saw that decisions were made within the prescribed time limit, and personally investigated judicial injustices and interceded on behalf of the victims. Although the Senate was the highest judicial body in the country, appeals against decisions of the colleges were taken out of its jurisdiction and were addressed directly to the Tsar by the Requetmeister, and only when the appeals had been endorsed were they referred back to the Senate. The Heraldmeister was the successor to the Razriadny Prikaz, which had become part of the Senate's Chancellery. He was responsible for administrative relations with the nobility, and for selecting noblemen for particular missions or posts 'when asked to do so'. Although the Senate retained the right to nominate a candidate to a post, even an important one, it was bound to choose from a list of two or three proposed by the Heraldmeister. Thus departments, which had been created in the first instance ostensibly to help the Senate, achieved the reverse, isolated it from the people, and, hemming in 'this fortress of right', were responsible for limiting its development.

The changes in the central administration meant that the Provincial institutions had also to be reorganised if a unified administrative system was to be achieved. The central administration had been organised on a Swedish basis, and now the Provincial institutions had to be recast in a similar fashion. The Provincial Reform of 1708 did not bring with it the hoped-for financial improvements, partly because the governors were as dishonest as the Prikazes (indeed, the Governor of Siberia, Prince Gagarin, had been hanged for dishonesty), and partly because tax-collection was still in arrears, and peculation continued as before. In 1718 Peter ordered extracts from the regulations governing Swedish local institutions to be sent to the Senate 'so that it might enquire how best to make them compatible with Russian customs'. The Senate decided to adopt the Swedish system, and on November 26th, 1718, Peter confirmed this decision in an ukaze which provided for 'instructions on the entire Swedish procedural practice, with amendments if necessary' to be sent to the new institutions, which were to come into operation in 1720. Fick, the organiser and interpreter of the Swedish system, actively participated in the Senate's work on the new territorial division of Russia. He insisted that, as in Sweden, the administrative divisions, and the amount of work they had to transact, must correspond with the working capacity of their administrators. This point of view, however, was not shared by the Russian bureaucrats who, thinking of their perquisites, were afraid rather that there would be too little business than that there would be too much, and wanted an equal amount of business in all divisions, whether large or small. The difference in sheer size between the two countries made it impossible to reproduce exactly the Swedish system in Russia. Yet somehow the Swedish administrative uniform was stretched over the Russian giant. The Senate decided to retain the Province (which had no place in the Swedish system) as the biggest territorial unit. It increased the number of Provinces to eleven by dividing Kazan into Nizhni Novgorod and Astrakhan, and making part of the Province of St. Petersburg into the Province of Reval. Thus the character of a Province changed.

The Provincial sub-divisions were responsible to the Provincial central administration only in judicial and military matters, and, indeed, it was only over these two that the central administration had any authority at all. The Province was divided into counties, which themselves were subdivided into districts. The counties replaced the *dolia* of the landraty, but were somewhat larger. There were about fifty counties, instead of $146\frac{3}{5}$ *dolia*. Counties, as we have seen, had already begun to appear after the Provincial Reform of 1708; they now became the normal subdivision everywhere. Moreover the *ober-kommendant*, who had been in charge of the county created by the reform of 1708, was now completely subordinated to the Provincial governor. According to the documents showing the division of the Provinces into counties (May 29th, 1719), it is clear that, with some exceptions, they were to be 'self-contained'; this meant that the counties, although subordinated to the Provincial governors in military and judicial matters, were in all else to be self-governing.

The chief administrator of the county was the *voevoda* who dealt with financial, police, and economic affairs, about which he communicated directly to the central authorities and not through the Provincial governor. The governor himself, however, became a county *voevoda* within his Province in his capacity of head of the Provincial capital. Expressing the duality of his position, one governor wrote that the *voevodas*, himself among them, 'became independent within their own counties, being no longer within the jurisdiction of the Provincial governor,' i.e., that he himself as a county *voevoda* was outside his own control as Provincial governor. The *voevoda* worked through a local government office (*zemskaya kantselarya*), had under him a local superintendent (*zemskii kamerer*) whose particular job it was to collect taxes, and who worked though a sub-office (*zemskii kontor*) with a local cashier (*rentmeister*) who kept all tax-receipts in his own safe in the county treasury, and a *proviant-meister* who took charge of the grain collected for the treasury stores. The smallest unit in a Province was the district which the Senate tried unsuccessfully to turn into a standard unit of not more than 2,000 households. Some districts had in fact the same boundaries as the old *uezdy*, while others included several *uezdy*, and a very few were formed by subdividing the *uezdy*. The administrator of the district was the *zemskii commissar* whose duties included the supervision of financial, police, economic, educational, and even moral affairs. His most important duty, however, was the collection of taxes, which in fact turned him into a district agent of the county administration. At the bottom of the organisation came the old village police who were elected at village meetings of the *sotskie* (hundreds) and *desyatskie* (tens). They were sworn in by the *voevoda* and served as agents of the *zemskii commissar* but remained outside the hierarchy of officials. The Senate would not make up its mind to impose on Russia the smallest Swedish rural unit, the parish council, with its *focht* and elected peasants who sat to hear preliminary judicial investigations, because, it said, 'there are no intelligent peasants in the *uezdy*.' The Senators decided that the peasants did not have an official mentality; yet projectors of peasant origin understood this official type of mind, and Pososhkov characterised it by writing that the Russian administrators 'do not consider a Russian worth a groat, and would themselves be ready to die for a groat', but were at the same time undisturbed by the loss of thousands of roubles. On the landed estates the smallest unit was the manor house, as it had become in the seventeenth century, and as it remained for nearly a hundred and fifty years after Peter.

It might have been supposed that the Russians had suffered sufficiently from all the administrative changes and upheavals consequent upon the introduction of Provinces, *dolias,* counties, and districts. They had now, however, to contend with a fifth innovation. We have already pointed out that, when the poll-tax was introduced in 1724, the new billeting arrangements which were made simultaneously led to the creation of a number of new institutions which cut across the existing Provincial system. The revisional souls who were to provide for the maintenance of the regiments quartered in their midst were grouped into 'regimental districts' (*polkovoi distrikt*). Since the cost of maintaining a regiment varied, depending on whether it was in the field or in garrison, from 16,000 roubles to 45,000 roubles a year, the burden of taxation would have been unequal had the regimental districts not been of unequal sizes with different numbers of taxpayers. The result, however, was that the regimental districts cut across the borders of counties, rural districts, and *uezdy,* sometimes containing several districts belonging to different counties. The billeting arrangements thus led to confusion in the system of local government and territorial subdivision. Towards the end of 1723 the collection of the poll-tax and the recruitment tax was transferred from the Provincial and county authorities to special commissars elected by the nobility of the regimental districts, or, in the Northern regions of Russia where there was no nobility, by the representatives of the taxpayers of the district.

In his book on *The Local Reforms of Peter the Great,* M. Bogoslovsky has established from the documents that there was a difference between the elected *komisar ot zemli* — the special commissar mentioned above — and the *zemski* — the official placed in charge of a district created by the Provincial Reform of 1719, and appointed by the college of State Revenue; both officials acted at the same time, but only in certain areas did the elected official take the place of the official nominated by the college. Local councils, called *zemstvo,* were called on to co-operate with the government in the special and important task of maintaining the regiments; no mention is made of these councils in the earlier reform of 1719, although the word *zemski* had appeared there as an admirable translation of the Baltic provinces administrative terminology (land-commissar, Landrentmeister, etc.), and was used for Provincial posts and functions. Nevertheless their participation in the administration did not rejuvenate the old district associations of nobles which had been quite overwhelmed by the pressure of Peter's military reforms. These associations were held together neither by self-interest nor by class solidarity, mutual responsibility, nor any feelings of military comradeship. Indeed no good work was to be got out of men just because they were obliged to meet once a year, under the orders of a colonel, to take cognizance of the outgoing commissar's activities and elect a new one to collect money and stores for the benefit of the armed masses who had been imposed on local society. Regimental headquarters became grasping and authoritative, harassing and hampering the local administration by the exercise of their police and financial powers. As for the rural population, it viewed the quartering of an army of more than one hundred regiments in its midst as an invasion.

At this stage it is worth mentioning one other institution created by the Provincial Reform of 1719, although it is more important as a guide to Peter's ideas on reform than as a part of the actual reorganisation. New types of judicial institutions were created in the Provinces. An ukaze of January 8th, 1719, provided for the creation of nine new courts,[1] which [because they were responsible to the college of Justice rather than the Provincial Governments[2]] were known as *hof-gerichte*, or, in some documents, *nadvornye sudy*, that is, aulic courts. Aulic courts already existed in Enissei and Riga, which brought the total for the whole country to eleven. These new courts, were, however, unequally distributed, and there were, for instance, two in each of the Provinces of St. Petersburg, Riga, and Siberia, and none in the Provinces of Archangel and Astrakan. The ukaze of January 8th, 1719, also instituted two different sorts of courts of the first instance which were part of the structure of the college of Justice. There were the

[1] For a short sketch of the courts and their functions see S. Kucherov, *Courts, Lawyers and Trials under the last three Tsars*, Praeger, New York, 1953, pp. 1, 26-31.

[2] Cf. B. H. Sumner, *Peter the Great and the Emergence of Russia*, English Universities Press Ltd., 1950, p. 129

Q

county courts, which were to be found in the larger towns,[1] and were presided over by an *ober-landrichter* with assessors, and there were the town or local courts which were to be found in the smaller towns and districts, and were presided over by an official sitting alone. In fact, the Russian court system was very similar to the Swedish.

Did Peter intend a separation of the judicial from the administrative power?[2] It is always dangerous to attribute modern ideas to the past, but it is possible that the notion of the separation of powers was known to the drafters of the projects and instructions. It is doubtful, however, if Peter had in mind an independent department of state, completely free of outside influence. It is more probable that he shared the medieval Russian view of a court as part of the administration. There had, under the old system, been some special judicial Prikazes, but under Peter these were absorbed into the college of Justice, whose jurisdiction ran throughout the country. The Provincial Reform of 1719 did not provide for the separation of the judiciary from the rest of the administration. Peter had, none the less, intended that the responsibility of each college for its own work should extend throughout the country. Thus he considered that the colleges which were responsible for internal affairs, such as the college of State Revenue and the college of Justice, should be represented in the Provinces by branch offices. The judiciary was only separated from the administration in the same way as the business of collecting money taxes, the responsibility of the local superintendent, was separated from the business of collecting grain taxes which came within the jurisdiction of the *proviant-meister*. To copy an institution is

[1] Moscow, St. Petersburg, Smolensk, Kazan, Nizhni-Novgorod, Simbirsk, Novgorod, Yaroslav, and Voronezh.

[2] S. Kucherov is of the opinion that Peter recognised the necessity for separation of powers but did not achieve it in his reform. See S. Kucherov, *Courts Lawyers and Trials under the last three Tsars*, Praeger, New York, 1953, pp. 26–32.

always easier than to understand the idea on which it was based, and this was reflected in the ultimate fate of the Provincial judicial institutions. When the aulic courts were set up in 1719, seven out of the eleven presidents were heads of the local administrative system, governors, vice-governors, and *voevodas;* in 1721, all presidents were also local administrators, and in 1722 the courts of first instance were abolished, and their powers transferred to the chief administrators, sitting either alone or with assessors. Once again foreign ideas clashed with Russian custom, and the separation between the courts and the administration only led to trouble between the two: governors and *voevodas* interfered with the affairs of the college of Justice, which in turn, as in 1720, complained of the governors and *voevodas* that 'they stirred up trouble, disobeyed, and interfered with business'. The Reform had started by putting the *voevoda* in charge of an *uezd,* but everybody admitted that this was an unsuitable appointment; an attempt was then made to replace him by introducing the foreign system, but this failed, and a return to the system of *voevodas* took place, with the difference that the *voevoda* was transferred from the *uezd* to the larger territorial unit of a county.

Finally the college and Provincial Reforms were followed by a reform of the municipal administration also based on a foreign model adapted to Russian conditions. The Provincial Reform of 1708 transformed the *Ratusha*[1] of Moscow into a Board of the city, and suppressed the elected offices, such as *burmister,* which had united the commercial and industrial classes of the towns. It was now decided to replace them 'so that the scattered company of Russian merchants be once more brought together'. As usual, Peter thought at first that this would be an easy matter to arrange. Fick had urged the appointment of town councils, and had pointed out that it

[1] See Florinsky, *Russia,* Macmillan, New York, 1953, Vol. I, pp. 366-7.

was important to provide them with sensible regulations. Peter acted on this suggestion, and in 1718 somewhat light-heartedly resolved 'that magistracies [town councils] be created, modelled on those of Riga and Reval'. Eighteen months went by, and nothing was done. Then, at the beginning of 1720, Prince Trubetskoi was instructed to start by setting up a town council in St. Petersburg, and then to take this as a model for similar collegial institutions in other towns. But 1720 passed, and still nothing was done. At the beginning of 1721 the town council of St. Petersburg was renamed the *Glavny Magistrat,* or Chief Town Council, and subordinated to the Senate. A *reglament* ordered the Chief Town Council and its *ober-president,* Prince Trubetskoi, to establish councils in other towns, draw up rules for their guidance, and supervise them. But 1721 went by, and again nothing was done. Then at the beginning of 1722 the dilatory *ober-president* was stimulated by the threat of hard labour, and Peter ordered him to settle the matter in six months. It was another two and a half years before the rules were finally drawn up.

At the same time as town councils were being established, a new division of the urban tax-paying population was effected. The upper class was divided into two guilds. Bankers, wealthy 'eminent' merchants, physicians, apothecaries, and master-craftsmen in highly skilled trades constituted the first guild; small merchants and artisans formed the second, and were required to form themselves into trade associations with their guild. The rest of the labouring population, the manual workers, were formed into a third class of 'common people', *podlye lyudi,* and recognised as citizens by the rules, but distinguished from the 'eminent and regular citizens'. It is worth mentioning in passing that *podlye lyudi* in Petrine Russia meant no more than the lower class, lying *pod,* i.e., under, the upper class, and had not the unpleasant moral connotation which it later acquired. The reforms which brought in town councils, and a more cohesive organisation of urban society, also altered the character of municipal administration. The ukaze of 1699 had provided for the election of *burmisters* to serve for one year, whereas members of the town councils were elected for an indefinite, and even permanent, term of office; evidently it was admitted that greater stability in municipal administration was required. Previously *burmisters* had been chosen from the whole body of the townspeople by the urban population gathered together at town meetings, but now the *reglament* stated that candidates for town councils were to be chosen only by the *burmisters* and 'eminent men in society' from 'those who belonged to the first category', i.e., from the first guild. In the more important towns a council consisted of a president and a number of *burmisters* and councillors.

The town councils enjoyed greater power than had the old local offices; in the large towns the councils enjoyed judicial authority, similar in fact, to the authority of the aulic courts, and were able to judge not only civil cases but criminal cases as well. Death sentences, however, had to be confirmed by the *Glavny Magistrat*, which was the appellate court for all urban town councils. The town councils were responsible for the economic development of the towns, the police, the encouragement of manufacture and trade, and the establishment of municipal primary schools, hospitals, etc. The town councils were also empowered to sit in open session, and transacted a great deal of business with the citizens or representatives of the citizens, who were called *starshins* if they were elected by the guilds, and *starosts* if they were elected by the *starshins*. In matters of importance the town councils were obliged to convene a 'municipal council' to be attended by the guild representatives and even the citizens; the town councils were also to listen to suggestions for town improvements put forward by the guild *starosts*, and were to allow the *starosts* and *starshins* to reassess the taxes, and 'with the consent of the citizens' were to choose the tax-collectors. Only the guild delegates were, in fact, allowed to attend the municipal council convened to discuss 'matters touching all the citizens', and even then they only had the right to speak; the common people, who were something apart from the 'regular' citizens, and enjoyed only limited rights, could only make representations through their elected *starosts* and 'tenth men'. The special provisions of the Municipal Government Reform, by turning the members of the guilds into an urban ruling class, started the growth of an urban aristocracy. None the less, this only legalised the position of the upper merchant class which had already been created by financial legislation effected prior to Peter. The merchants were the most heavily taxed of all the classes, and were the most heavily burdened in the matter of state services. But it was the merchants' capitalist strength which was responsible for alleviating the burden on the rest of the citizens, and for the large part played by the merchants in municipal affairs.

The Municipal Government Reform, however, introduced an ambiguous relationship between the *magistrat* and the urban community. The *magistrat* did not replace the town's elected representatives, the *starshins* and *starosts*, but was placed over them, and endowed with new judicial and administrative powers. The *magistrat* was elected by the guilds (of which he was a member) which also elected the *starshins* and *starosts* with whom the *magistrat* was obliged to consult; at the same time the *magistrat* was placed in a position of authority over the *starshins* and *starosts*; and over the citizens who had elected him, but, because of the permanency of his tenure, he became not the town's elected representative, but its official head. The *reglament* of 1721 and the *instruction* of 1724 both describe the *magistrats* as 'the actual heads'[1] of the citizens. The members of the town councils, the elected presidents, *burmisters*, and councillors tended in these circumstances to become mere officials; they were encouraged in this by the law, which promised them, as a reward for their work, a place in the official hierarchy as laid down by the Table of Ranks, and presidents were even promised elevation to the nobility for their services. Not unnaturally these conditions tended to alienate the *magistrats* from the citizens, and particularly from the labouring masses.

Thus it was that Peter, who had originally organised municipal government as a system of oligarchic corporations, ended the reform by establishing the *magistrats* as members of the central government's bureaucracy. This was due to a change in Peter's point of view on the problems of municipal autonomy. In 1699 his only interest had been in creating the most profitable system of tax-collection, and that the first thing to do was to free the urban taxpayers from the rapacity and oppression of the *voevodas*. By 1720, which was the year in which the Municipal Government Reform was first undertaken, he had turned from his original narrow view of taxation to a broader view of the economy as a whole, for he had realised that it was more important to increase the state's sources of revenue than to exploit too far those it already had. To widen his sources of revenue it was necessary to employ foreign techniques and to ensure that they were generally accepted. He either found, or was told, that the solution lay in creating in his towns the system of *magistrats* which was so efficient in the towns of Western Europe. Convinced that only a well-organised people could assure the state a sufficient and steady income, Peter entrusted the town councils with

---

[1] As Florinsky points out, the Russian word *nachalnik* used in the *instruction* of 1724 means literally 'superior' or 'chief', and connotes the idea of an officer of the Crown whose orders it is wise to obey. See Florinsky, *Russia,* Macmillan, New York, 1953, Vol. I, p. 300.

the responsibility, not only for collecting taxes, but also for other important economic duties, including the advancement of industry and commerce, the propagation of learning, and social welfare. Since these tasks were beyond most of the citizens and their *burmisters*, who were only elected for a year at a time, Peter transferred the running of municipal affairs to 'honest and intelligent men' chosen from 'eminent' merchants who were to be helped by permanent elected men, capable of making themselves heard and respected. The *magistrats* were ordered 'to conduct themselves decently and honestly, so that they might be as respected and honoured as *magistrats* in other countries'. Evidently Peter was dreaming of a rich and influential bourgeoisie like that of Western Europe. Unfortunately he was disappointed, since the *burmisters* of the town council were no better than the local *burmisters* — but this was not Peter's fault.

So much for the review of Peter's administrative reforms, it could have been shorter, though our main consideration was not one of length. Peter met with many failures in his administrative reforms, and was himself responsible for many mistakes. These mistakes were due neither to accidental nor to temporary causes. After Peter, unsuccessful attempts at reform became a constant nuisance, and successive governments fell into something like a habit of repeating the same mistakes; and yet these were regarded as a sacred inheritance from the Great Reformer, although he had sometimes realised his failures and had even admitted his errors. It is imperative to understand the causes of the maladministration which continued for nearly two centuries after Peter, and which cannot be dismissed merely by reference to conditions which existed in Petrine Russia.

Let us recall the conversation between Peter and his collaborators at a banquet in 1717, when Prince Jacob Dolgoruky pointed out that Peter had enjoyed military and diplomatic successes, but had failed to do anything about the country's internal development. Peter's intensive legislative work dates from this year. He achieved more in five or six years than was accomplished in the preceding and subsequent five or six decades. The organisation of the colleges, the transformation, or more precisely the re-creation, of the Senate, and the second Provincial Reform, were all accomplished by Peter in the last years of his reign. Among the hesitations, experiments, advances, and retreats, certain coherent principles and systems began to emerge. These were: (1) a more precise delineation, which in the old Muscovite system had been very vague, between central and Provincial administration; (2) an attempt to affect a systematic division of duties both in the central and in the Provincial administrations, and a resolute attempt at insulating judicial affairs from the administration; (3) an inclination to return to the old Muscovite collegiate administrative system, which was fairly successful at the centre, but a failure in the Provinces; (4) the idea, partially successful, of giving the central colleges executive bodies in the Provinces; and (5) three regional subdivisions.

Not only did Peter separate the central from the Provincial administration, but he also tried to place them on different foundations. He was induced to do this by the peculiar social composition of the governing institutions of Muscovy. There were two different systems of administration: the aristocratic type which obtained when the preponderant social class, or classes, ruled through its elected representatives, and the bureaucratic type of administration, which obtained when the right of administration was conferred by the supreme power on persons familiar with the business, or on specialists, irrespective of their origins. The main concern of the first type is naturally to protect the interests of the governing classes, while the second type has for a long time been considered more suitable for defending the interests of

both country and people. The old Muscovite administration
was a mixture of both in its composition and character. It resembled a bureaucracy in its structure and scope, and in its
attitude to the ruler and the society it administered. Moreover
the chief officials were nominated by the Crown, and performed their duties in a bureaucratic fashion, without any
participation, other than a very passive one, on the part of
society. In the seventeenth century the autonomous activities of popular institutions, from the regional *starosta* to the
Zemsky Sobor, gradually diminished. Yet in spite of all this the
administration was an aristocratic one: the high officials were
members of the privileged class of 'men of service' who had
inherited their privileges. The secretaries and under-secretaries, and the officials of other classes, played only a subordinate role in the administrative system as departmental
employees, while the elected or nominated *Zemstvo* representatives were only passive instruments responsible for fulfilling the government's financial commissions. It follows,
therefore, that the old Muscovite administrative system was a
mixture of types, and could be called 'a bureaucratic class
system'. Peter set out to achieve two things: first, to organise
the state's military strength and financial resources, and,
second, to organise the economy, and increase productivity,
as a necessary pre-requisite to achieving his military and
financial aims. It is clear that the two objects differ in essence;
the first was a matter of administration, while the second
touched society more closely. Peter took these factors into
consideration when he reconstructed the old Muscovite administration, which he called 'disorderly'. He did not divide
the administrative system into two systems on different
foundations, but he wanted to keep it in two distinct parts,
and give each a different responsibility — one part was to be
of a purely bureaucratic nature, the other was to be aristocratic. The most important matters, such as the organisation

of military and financial affairs, were entrusted to the central administration, which therefore required reasonably well-educated men with some practical knowledge and technical training, whatever the social position they might have inherited. The central administration, therefore became a bureaucracy staffed from all classes and somewhat apart from society. Thus, under Peter, the highest administrative positions were filled indifferently by an aristocratic boyar, his one-time major-domo, noblemen of all ranks, 'a favourite without a fortune,' an ex-clerk, and many foreigners.

Peter considered that economic affairs were the immediate responsibility of the regional authorities under the general supervision of the central government. Two classes were of particular importance in this connection: the land-owning nobility, and the merchants of the first guild, in whose hands were concentrated the two main forms of capital, land and industry, on which the whole economy depended. The central government with its officials was entrusted with the main business of State, but Peter also wished to see to those matters on which the development of the country depended. He therefore tried to persuade the landed nobility and the merchants of the first guild to participate actively in local administrative affairs by endowing them with the characteristics of a privileged class. The noblemen of the villages and Provinces, and the guild merchants of the towns, were the two classes which, standing at the head of local associations, were together with the regional offices of the central government to administer industry and agriculture. The administrative reform was therefore more of a technical than a political reform as no new principles were introduced into the machinery of government. The new arrangements suggested by the foreign advisers, who divided administrative affairs into several parts, consisted of new combinations of old methods. In this way the new administration was built with old materials, a procedure which Peter had employed in his other reforms.

The last of Peter's administrative reforms were very carefully elaborated. The responsibilities of each institution, from the Senate down to the local commissars and *waldmeisters,* were carefully defined by instructions and regulations. These regulations, which were mostly translations or adaptations from the statutes of Sweden and other Baltic states, were based on the assumption that people had liberal ideas on the nature and problems of administration; and they defined the composition, competence, duties, and procedure of these institutions in very great detail. Notwithstanding their foreign origin, the regulations reflect Peter's political outlook in the last years of his reign, and are therefore of particular interest. It is doubtful whether Peter had the time to read the many memoranda submitted by Fick and von Luberas on the statutes and regulations of the Swedish colleges, but he took an active part in composing the regulations, and attentively followed the progress of the administrative reforms. His participation in this work familiarised him with a number of problems which he had previously had no time to think about. He began to feel that he was falling behind the times, realised his own mistakes, and began to show more respect for the opinions of others. His thinking about what had happened made him alter his political outlook. Though previously he had put his trust only in individuals, he ended by grasping the purpose of governmental institutions, and their importance in the political education of the people. Earlier in his reign he had guessed that such an education might in fact be important: in 1713 he had suggested in an ukaze that to stop harm being done out of ignorance 'it is necessary to explain just what are the interests of state, and make them comprehensible to the people'. It was only now, however, that he realised that the popular understanding of his objects depended on the way in which his laws were framed and his institutions were conducted. He saw that by reducing the arbitrary powers of his officials he would inspire greater respect for the law and for public welfare. He thought that this could be achieved through his new tribunals and colleges, and he frequently assured people that they would get justice from these institutions, and would not need to appeal to him for it.

Peter's assurance was premature. The regulations and instructions 'with their ambitious solutions' failed to influence anybody as much as they had influenced Peter. They had the effect rather of political dissertations than of practical instructions. The improvements in the administrative system did not immediately improve the quality of the administrators. The new institutions did not fit the times; they demanded trained and disciplined executives who were not to be found among the available officials. Peter created his institutions in the same way that a thrifty mother makes clothes that are far too big, and will only fit her children when they grow up! Unfortunately Peter's officials, his privy councillors, *magistrats,* and assessors, all tore their clothes to pieces before they had time to grow into them. Minutes found in the archives show how the new institutions failed to justify Peter's hopes. It was not easy to fill all the new positions, and Peter had unwillingly to send for foreigners. When Fick suggested this in 1718, Peter disagreed, saying that foreigners were not needed, and 'men must be found near at hand'. Russia was in fact searched for capable men. They were chosen at inspections of the nobility, and appointed to serve in the aulic courts and elsewhere. The Heraldmeister had to send the colleges lists of nobles who might be suitable for certain positions. A source of recruitment was a necessity, and Fick wrote to Peter 'on the not too difficult task of teaching young Russian children' and preparing them for service: it was only necessary to set up suitable schools. Peter replied: 'let academies be set up', ordered a search for educated Russians, and directed that books on jurisprudence be translated. He tried everything in his search for suitable officials. Now flouting class prejudice, now submitting to it, he ordered officers to be recruited from the literate serfs, and departmental secretaries from the petty nobility. Minor sons of the nobility were sent to colleges as 'junkers' to serve an apprenticeship. The complexity of service status was made worse by the rivalry between the military and the civil branches of service. Most of the civil posts were filled, as before, by the nobility, but the most capable noblemen were sent to the regiments so that the departments and the legal tribunals were staffed by officers on permanent leave, retired officers, or men who had evaded military duty. The new institutions created many new posts, and Kirilov, the Senate's *ober-secretary* at the end of Peter's reign, calculated in his statistical work, *The Flourishing State of the Empire of all the Russias* (1727), that there were 905 departments and offices employing 5,112 administrators, officials, and fiscals, and it is probable that this figure is an underestimate. The increase in personnel was not accompanied by a proportionate increase in expenditure, and the officials were allowed perquisites which cannot be distinguished from bribes. Moreover, when there was a shortage of money, as many as a quarter of the officials salaries was unpaid.

No adequate legal code existed: the *Ulozhenie* of 1649 was obsolete, and had been buried under new laws. A commission of high officials appointed in 1700 to bring the *Ulozhenie* up to date worked hard, but achieved nothing. The Senate at its foundation was entrusted with the work of codification, but it also failed to achieve anything. Towards the end of 1719, during the period of Swedomania, Peter instructed the Senate to draw up a code by selecting suitable articles from the Swedish Codex and the *Ulozhenie,* or 'to draft new clauses' where necessary. Peter made it clear that he expected the Senate to finish this work by the end of October, 1720. In other words he expected the Senate to do in ten months what had not been done in the preceding twenty years, and what in fact took more than a century to accomplish. The Senate, by its lack of preparation or discipline, and its haphazard conduct of business, set all too clear an example to its subordinate departments and institutions. When the country was divided into Provinces in 1719 the Senate sent the relevant official papers from St. Petersburg to Vologda via Archangel![1] Moreover the Senate was often the scene of violent quarrels and indecent behaviour.

The *ober-procurator,* Skornyakov-Pisarev, and the Procurator-General, Yaguzhinsky, hated each other; the under-chancellor, Baron Shafirov, hated the chancellor, Count Golovkin; the well-born Senators, Princes Galitsyn and Dolgoruky, hated the highly favoured but low-born Prince Menshikov; and all of them brought their personal and party grievances to the Tsar. Meetings of the Senate often degenerated into brawls, with the Senators accusing each other of being thieves. Once, at a gathering in the house of the Procurator-General to celebrate the fall of Derbent in 1722, the Senate's *ober-procurator,* who had already had two passages of arms with the procurator of the college of Justice, barely avoided a fight with the under-chancellor; each subsequently denounced the other to the Tsar and Tsaritsa, and excused himself by saying that if he was drunk, the other was drunker.

With such behaviour, the Senate was unlikely to become an impartial judge. Indeed Prince Menshikov once told the assembled Senators that they spent their time on trifles, and were not in the least concerned with the well-being of the

[1] i.e., round two sides of a triangle.

country. But worse still, few Senators, and not even Prince Dolgoruky, could escape being arraigned for, or at least suspected of, corruption. That scourge of the Senate, Senator Prince Menshikov, was the worst peculator of all. Endowed with enormous wealth by Peter, this man of common birth showed real cunning. Peter remonstrated with him, beat him with a cudgel, threatened him, but all to no purpose. Menshikov surrounded himself with a band of pillaging officials who enriched themselves, and their patron, at the Treasury's expense. These officials included Kursakov, the vice-governor of St. Petersburg, and two Senators, Princes Volkonsky and Opukhtin, who were publicly knouted. Menshikov himself avoided drastic punishment only because of Peter's friendship and the intervention of the Tsaritsa Catherine. The Tsaritsa was Menshikov's faithful protectress, and indeed owed him her career. Once Peter, particularly outraged by his favourite's exploits, said to Catherine as she interceded on his behalf 'Menshikov was conceived in inquity, brought into the world in sin, and will end his life in deceit; unless he reforms he will surely lose his head.' Menshikov's fortune amounted to tens of millions of roubles (in the currency of 1900). With such a powerful protector sitting in the Senate, there was more bribery and embezzlement than ever before. Peter's concern was to recover the Treasury's money 'which flowed from everybody's sleeves', and once, in a rage after listening to a Senate report, he ordered the immediate publication of an ukaze that whoever robbed the state of so much as the value of a piece of rope would hang for it. The Procurator-General, Yaguzhinsky, the sovereign's 'eye in the Senate', exclaimed: 'Would your Majesty like to be a ruler without any subjects? We all steal, only some do it on a bigger scale, and in a more conspicuous way, than others.' Peter laughed, and did not publish the ukaze.

He did, however, devote a great deal of attention in the

last year of his reign to the laws concerning embezzlement of public money, and appointed a commission to investigate the problem. It was said that *ober-fiscal* Myakinin,
secretary to this commission, once asked Peter, 'Are only the
branches to be cut off, or are the roots to be cut out?' 'Destroy everything,' replied Peter, 'roots and branches alike.'
Vokerodt, who tells this story, and was then living in St.
Petersburg, goes on to say that had Peter lived a few months
longer, the world would have heard tell of many executions.
Peter published a number of ukazes in the last years of his
reign which showed a change in emphasis. His ukazes were no
longer short and trenchant documents, but lengthy dissertations in which he complained of the general lowering of
standards, and of the lack of respect for the law, which, he
said, threatened the state with a decline similar to that of the
Byzantine Empire. He also complained that petitioners gave
him no peace, and added that, in the middle of conducting a
war, he was unable to look into everything himself; he remarked that he was not an angel, and that not even angels
were omniscient, because each had his appointed place —'he
is here — not there.' The resentful and sorrowful tone of
these ukazes is reminiscent of the despondent look so noticeable in Peter's later portraits.

The new institutions, borrowed from countries with
different backgrounds and customs, were unable to find root
in a system of autocracy and violence. The instruction to
magistrats expressed the hope that they would be as respected
in Russia as they were in other countries. The town council
of Kolomna, which consisted of a councillor, three *burmisters,* and an urban elder, experienced something other than
respect. One of the *burmisters* was ridden down by General
Saltykov, and left for dead; the councillor, the second *burmister,* and the elder were beaten by an *ober-officer* called
Volkov, who had been sent to escort the Persian Ambassa-

dor; the last *burmister* reported that he was the only unin-
jured member of the council, and was incapable of dealing
with everything alone. The public had only two ways of
protecting itself from inefficient and arbitrary officials: fraud
and violence. When the census lists were revised, it was found
that no less than one and a half million souls, or nearly 27 per
cent of the taxpaying population, had been deliberately
omitted. Ukazes ordered a search to be made for the runaway
serfs, although they were living openly in colonies on the
large estates of powerful noblemen round Moscow, at
Piatnista, Ordynka, and outside the gates of Arbat, or had
found refuge in the forests. Contemporary writings mention
an incredible increase in brigandage: bands of pillagers, commanded by deserters, joined together in well-organised and
well-armed cavalry groups, and attacked 'in regular formation', destroying well-populated villages, impeding the collection of taxes, and even penetrating into the towns. One
Provincial governor was afraid to travel through his own
territory, and even Prince Menshikov, Governor-General of
St. Petersburg, who considered himself capable of building
the Ladoga Canal, was not ashamed to inform the Senate that
he was incapable of dealing with the brigands in his Province.
This was the answer given by the brigands of the lower classes
to those of the upper classes: on one side there existed a tacit
solidarity in iniquity and incapacity, on the other, an infinite
despair. The civil servant in the capital, the general on a
mission, the nobleman on his distant estates, all ignored the
Tsar's terrible ukazes; neither they, nor the brigands in the
forests, cared what the semi-autocratic Senate, and the nine,
or later ten, Swedish-type colleges, with their carefully defined jurisdictions, achieved in the capital. An imposing
legislative façade merely concealed the general disorder which
prevailed throughout the country.

Chapter Ten

★

OUR SURVEY of Peter's reforming activities is not yet complete, for we have discussed neither their effects on education and welfare nor the changes they caused in the ideas and customs of the people. Some of his measures were not directly connected with his more urgent reforms; some had effects which were not obvious in his lifetime; and some affected only certain classes. We have already pointed out that the purpose of all Peter's reforms was originally either financial or military, and, in our discussion so far, we have concentrated on the way in which the reforms, aimed at these particular objects, affected society as a whole. It should now be possible to form an appreciation of the significance and character of Peter's reforming activities, or at any rate of some of their aspects.

The question of the significance of Peter's reforms is largely a question of the development of Russian historical understanding. For over two hundred years Russians have written a great deal, and talked even more, about Peter's activities. Whenever a discussion of isolated facts in Russian history has turned to consideration of their general significance, it has been found necessary to refer to Peter's activities; and anyone discussing Russia's past philosophically has found it necessary to establish his academic respectability by commenting on Peter's activities. Very often, indeed, Russian philosophies of history have been in the form of judgements of the Petrine reforms; and, by a remarkable feat of condensation, the meaning of all Russian history was looked for in the significance of those reforms, and in the relationship between the old and the new Russia. The Petrine reforms became the focus of all Russian history: they were taken as a starting point for the study of the past, and used by historians in an attempt to elucidate the future. Thus Russian history was divided into two periods, pre-Petrine and post-Petrine. Naturally opinions differed, but for a long time these opinions were not based on a detailed study of the reforms. During the one hundred and forty years between Peter's death and the appearance of the fourteenth volume of Soloviev's *History*, hardly any proper historical investigation of the reforms was made. What was done was done by Golikov, a merchant of Kursk, who, towards the end of the eighteenth century, published a vast collection of material for a biography of Peter, called *The Acts of Peter the Great, with a series of additions* (1788–98). But this work had little influence on historians, for, to quote Soloviev, it was a thirty-tomed hymn in praise of the reformer, an over-long and clumsy panegyric, which was unlikely to stimulate historians into studying the reforms, and was in any case too prejudiced. So, except for this superficial and biased work, no serious study was made in all these years. The transient impressions the reforms had made on people whose mood was, in any case, influenced by many other things, formed the only evidence on which historians based their judgement. For a long time after Peter's death, society remained under the influence of his masterful personality, and almost made a cult of reverence for his work. Nartov, a working cabinet maker, who was twenty years old when Peter died, said of him in later years 'Though Peter the Great is no longer with us, his spirit lives in our souls, and we who have had the honour to be near the monarch, will die true to him, and our warm love for him will be buried with us.' Lomonosov called Peter a 'God-like man', and Derzhavin asked:

'Was it not God
Who in his person came down to earth?'

Nevertheless, Derzhavin's contemporaries, influenced by the
French philosophers, had already begun to look at Peter's
reforms in a different way. They were, after all, used to abstract speculation on society, and the examination of subtle
questions of academic morality, and were not to be impressed
by a policy concerned with concrete details of military and
financial administration, which seemed to them too materi-
alist, and quite unworthy of Peter's intellect and position.
This, at any rate, was the point of view of those who compared Peter's reforms with the activities of Catherine II.
Kheraskov wrote:

'Peter gave Russians a body,
Catherine gave them a soul.'

The brilliant society of Catherine's reign, which delighted in
acclaiming so many philosopher-rulers, did not approve of
Tsars who worked with their hands. The discussion was
further complicated when the reforms were studied from a
nationalist and moralist point of view. In his notes on *The
Decadence of Custom in Russia,* Prince Shcherbatov admits that
Peter's reforms 'were useful, but perhaps superfluous',
meeting the needs of the people, but too radical, and too
varied. Peter was not content with necessary legislative,
military, economic, and educational innovations, but tried to
ameliorate private life by humanising and refining the gross
habits of his people. Unfortunately, Peter's attempts resulted
in licence, and subsequently in moral decadence. In 1788, at a
dinner given by Prince Kaunitz in Vienna, Princess Dashkov
criticised Peter's passion for shipbuilding and other artisan
pursuits. The Princess went on to say that such trifles were
unworthy of a monarch, and declared that, had Peter possessed
the mind of a great legislator, he would have left the passage

of time to bring about the improvements he tried to introduce by force. 'If,' she continued, 'he had appreciated the good
qualities of our ancestors, he would have refrained from insulting them by introducing foreign customs.' This intelligent
and subtle lady, who was the director of the Academy of
Science, was as incapable of appreciating Peter's labouring
activities as were the labourers themselves.

New ideas were introduced into Russia in the nineteenth
century, and consequently new judgements of Peter. Events
in France had filled people with the fear of revolutions and a
senile love of the past. Karamzin was a representative of this
school of thought, and believed he saw a revolution in Peter's
brusque and nervous changes. But in his youth Karamzin,
basing himself on the cosmopolitan view that, compared with
the interests of humanity as a whole, the interests of a small
part of it were of little account, had gloried in Peter's civil-
ising reforms, and had thought the complaint that Peter had
altered the Russian character was a deplorable jeremiad.
Twenty years later, however, in his *Notes on Ancient and
Modern Russia,* Karamzin became a Jeremiah himself. Since
the time of Tsar Michael, customs and institutions had been
gradually and imperceptibly changing; Karamzin's regret
was that this development had been ended by the effect on the
spirit of the people of Peter's methods, which were lawless
even for an autocrat. 'We began,' said Karamzin, 'to be citizens of the world; but we ceased in some measure to be
citizens of Russia — and the fault was Peter's!' The Restoration in Europe, and the excesses of the French during the
Revolution and Empire, provoked a nationalist movement
among the defeated or disunited peoples of Europe, who
demanded their political unity and independence. This
renaissance of nationalism tended to discredit Peter's reforms
even further. Debates on the old and the new Russia began
afresh in the 1830's and 40's. The Westerners maintained that

Russia's future lay in following Western Europe, as Peter had started to do; the Slavophiles, and especially Khomyakov, revived Karamzin's criticism that Peter had interrupted Russia's natural development by alienating educated people from their own customs and traditions. Khomyakov compared these people to a colony of Europeans thrown among savages. The Slavophiles maintained, indeed, that the proper way for Russians to conduct themselves was not to be learnt in Western Europe, or even from the Russia immediately preceding the Petrine era, as Prince Shcherbatov and other 'lovers of Russia' had said, but in the old Russia still untouched by reforms with Westernising tendencies.

Thus the Petrine reforms were a rock on which, for more than a century, Russian historical thought was divided. As one criticism follows another there emerge two schools of thought, one which idealises the pre-Petrine Russia, and the other which develops as a cult the search for the mysterious soul of the people. These ideas were developed in an unscholarly atmosphere; witty conjectures were taken for historical facts, and leisured dreams were represented as popular ideas. No scientific examination of the actual course and consequence of the reforms was undertaken; discussions in salons and in journals were confined to a comparison of the old Russia with the new; historical truth was replaced by a semi-historical, semi-philosophical construction, the idea of two worlds in opposition, Russia and Europe.

It was in this atmosphere that Soloviev's scientific study first appeared. Soloviev was the first Russian historian of Peter's reforms to use the documentary sources, and was also the first historian to put the reforms in their historical perspective. His definitive opinion is to be found at the end of Chapter III of the eighteenth volume of his *History,* published in 1868. His broad outlook, in conjunction with a lofty tone and intellectual self-discipline, is astonishing; his account of the reforms is not merely the result of scientific inquiry, it is also a polemic against Peter's detractors, and a vindication of his historical position. Soloviev takes the view that no nation in the history of the world had achieved so much as Russia under Peter, and that no people had experienced so great, so varied, and so profound a reformation, followed by so many important consequences, affecting not only their own lives, but also the history of the rest of the world. New political principles were introduced, and new arrangements were made in civic affairs. The introduction of the colleges into the administrative system, the adoption of the electoral principle, and the development of town autonomy, all had the effect of arousing society's interest in political affairs. The significance of the oath taken to Empire as well as to Emperor was understood by both sovereign and people. The position of the individual might be radically altered by his own efforts: Peter's concern to reward meritorious service might result in the individual being absolved from family obligations, from paying the souls tax, or from marriage contracts dictated by parents or masters. Even women were rewarded, and began to emerge from their isolation in the *terem*.[1] The consequences of the reforms to the rest of the world were: (1) the transformation of a weak, impoverished, and almost unknown nation, into a potentially formidable power; and (2) the union of the two halves of Europe, the West and the East, by the integration into the European system of the Slavic race, which, represented by the Russian nation, finally began to share in the general life of Europe.

Soloviev's judgement contains a well-developed formulation of opinions which have been expressed in Russian literature, and which in the past had been shared by the adversaries of the reforms. It was maintained that the Petrine

---

[1] The *terem* was an apartment at the top of the house traditionally reserved for the women. Generally the rooms were small and dark.

reforms effected a profound change in Russian national life which completely transformed the whole of society — a terrible and awe-inspiring revolution, as Soloviev calls it. Some considered that this revolution was a great service to humanity, while others took the view that it was a great misfortune for Russia. But the whole position is derived from the thoughts of Peter's collaborators and contemporaries, for, whether or not they were in sympathy with Peter's work, they were convinced that they were witnessing an upheaval and dislocation without parallel in Russian life, which was being reconstructed on new principles and according to new forms. It is, of course, perfectly natural that Peter's contemporaries should have held this opinion; men who find themselves living in a turbulent age are commonly disposed to exaggerate the extent and importance of events. Nepluev, who was one of Peter's youngest and most gifted collaborators, and was Resident at Constantinople, wrote in his memoirs on hearing of Peter's death: 'This monarch had brought our country to a level with others; he taught us to recognise that we are a people. In brief, everything that we look upon in Russia has its origin in him, and everything which is done in the future will be derived from this source.' The same idea was expressed by Count Golovkin, the Chancellor, in a solemn oration addressed to Peter on October 22nd, 1721, at the celebrations of the Treaty signed with Sweden at Nystadt: 'By your tireless labours, and under your guidance, we have been led from the shades of ignorance to the stage of glory before the world. We have been, so to speak, led from nothing to life, and we have rejoined the company of political nations.' Thus Soloviev's opinion in the 1860's coincides with an opinion formed a century and a half before his time, and reflects the impression made by the reforms on Peter's contemporaries. Do we find the views expressed wholly satisfactory? It seems to us that there are still a few points that must be clarified.

First of all, how did Peter become a reformer? The name of Peter makes us think of his reforms, and indeed 'Peter the Great and his reforms' has become a cliché. 'Reformer' has become his sobriquet, and the name by which he is known to history. We tend to believe that Peter I was born with the intention of reforming his country, and that he believed that this was his predestined historical mission. Nevertheless it was a long time before Peter took this view of himself. He was certainly not brought up to believe that he would reign over a state which was good for nothing, and which he would have to rebuild from top to bottom. On the contrary, he grew up knowing that he was Tsar, though a persecuted one, and that, as long as his sister and the Miloslavskys were in power, he was in danger of losing his life, and was unlikely to occupy the throne. His games of soldiers and with boats were the sports of his childhood, suggested to him by the conversations of his entourage. He realised very early that when he grew up and began to rule, he would need an army and navy, but he was, it seems, in no hurry to ask why he would need them. He only gradually realised, when he had discovered Sophia's intrigues, that he would need soldiers to control the Streltsy who supported his sister. Peter acted on the spur of the moment, and was not concerned with making plans for the future; he regarded everything he did as an immediate necessity rather than a reform, and did not notice how his actions changed both people and established systems. Even from his first foreign tour he brought back, not plans for reform, but impressions of a civilisation which he imagined he would like to introduce into Russia; and he brought back, too, a taste for the sea, that is to say, a desire to wage war against the country which had won access to the sea away from his grandfather. Indeed it was only during the last decade of his life, when the effect of his reforms was already fairly obvious, that he realised that he had done something new and spectacular. His better understanding of what he had done, however, did not help him to understand how he might act in the future. Peter thus became a reformer by accident, as it were, and even unwillingly. The war led him on and, to the end of his life, pushed him into reforming.

In the history of a country, war generally impedes reform, since foreign war and domestic reform are mutually exclusive and reform prospers best in times of peace. But in the history of Russia the correlation is different. Since a successful war has always served to secure the *status quo,* and an unsuccessful war, by provoking internal discontent, has always forced the government to review its domestic policy and introduce reforms, the government has always tried to avoid war, often to the detriment of its international position. Reforms at home were commonly achieved at the price of disaster abroad. In Peter's time the relationship between war and domestic change was different. Reforms were stimulated by the requirements of war, which indeed dictated the nature of the reforms that were undertaken. In other times the effect of war has been to force change on an unwilling government, but Peter, as he said himself, was able to learn from war what changes were needed. Unfortunately the attempt to carry on both war and reform simultaneously was unsuccessful: war slowed up reform, and reform prolonged the war because there was opposition and frequent revolt, and the forces of the nation could not be united to finish the war.

There were also interminable controversies about whether the reforms had been sufficiently elaborated, and whether they were introduced to meet the needs of the people, or had been forced on them as an unexpected act of Peter's autocratic will. In these discussions the preparations for reform were examined. It was asked whether they were deliberately calculated to bring about improvement, or were simply

forced upon Peter by urgent difficulties, and were therefore
only by accident measures which led to new possibilities and
a new way of life. Soloviev's view was that the reforms had
been prepared by Russia's past history, and even that 'they
had been demanded by the people'. Some changes had been
borrowed from the West and introduced in Russia as far
back as Peter's grandfather, and after him by Peter's father,
elder brother, and sister. Long before Peter's reign, indeed, a
fairly extensive plan for reforms had been drawn up, which
in many ways anticipated his own, and in some issues went
further. It is true that this programme was not fully understood by medieval Russians, for it had been prepared by a
few men with new ideas who had in many ways overcome
the limitations of contemporary thought. Thus although
changes had long been in preparation they were by no means
identical with Peter's reforms. Indeed the reorganisation of
Russia could have gone in one of several directions, and, given
peace, could have been spread over many generations, just as,
at a later period, the emancipation of the serfs was in preparation for over a century. Under Theodore and Sophia, for
instance, 'politesse à la polonaise,' to use a contemporary
expression, had been introduced in carriage styles and costume, and people had begun to study the Latin and Polish
languages; at Court the long, wide, and ungainly medieval
Russian cloak had been abolished, and, had the educational
programme been taken further, the kaftan might well have
been replaced by the kuntush, and the Russian dance by the
polka mazurka. For the matter of that, during the century and
a half after Peter's time, the medieval Russian beard was made
legal again.

Peter's first reforms were adapted from the Dutch and then
from the Swedish systems. Moscow was replaced by St.
Petersburg, a city built on the swamps, and Peter forced the
nobility and merchants to build their houses in his new capi-

tal; to achieve his purpose he transported thousands of labourers from central Russia. The reform as carried out by Peter was his personal enterprise, and though it was an enterprise of unexampled ruthlessness, it was not arbitrary and was, indeed, necessary, otherwise Russia could not have developed fast enough to deal successfully with the dangers that threatened her. Even under Catherine the Great men realised that it would have been impossible to avoid violence by leaving the modernisation of Russia to the process of time. As we have already seen, Prince Shcherbatov disapproved of Peter's reforms, and thought that their effect would be to ruin the Russian people; on the other hand, the Prince was not a defender of autocracy, and considered such a system positively harmful to a nation. Yet this part-historian, part-publicist attempted a chronological calculation in the following terms: 'In how many years, in the most favourable conditions, could Russia by herself, without the autocracy of Peter the Great, have attained her present level of eduction and glory?' According to his calculations, Russia would not have reached even the imperfect situation it was in at the end of the eighteenth century until, say, 1892 (i.e., one hundred years later). He assumes, of course, that Russia would be at peace, that there would be no internal troubles, and that no monarch would appear to impede the country's progress by nullifying his predecessor's efforts. And who could guarantee that there would not be in all this time a Charles XII, or Frederick II, ready to annex part of Russia and interrupt its natural development? Thus Shcherbatov, although he idealised the life of medieval Russia, was not hopeful about a successful regeneration of the country if it was 'left to the natural awakening of the people'.

It is even more difficult to estimate the influence and effect of the reforms, and this, after all, is the main problem. In order to attempt a solution it will be necessary to dissect minutely its complex component parts. So many clashes of interest, influence, and motive were involved in the Petrine reforms that we must try to distinguish between indigenous and imported ideas, between that which was foreseen and that which was arrived at haphazardly. Indeed we shall not arrive at much understanding of these reforms by looking at some simple point in isolation. We should look at three parts of this problem, first, Peter's relations with the West, second, his attitude to medieval Russia, and third, his influence on the future. In fact this last point should not be surprising, since the work of a great man commonly survives him and is even carried on by others. We must therefore include in our judgement of Peter's reforms effects which only appeared after his death. The three parts of the problem we must look into are, then, how much Peter inherited from unreformed Russia, how much he borrowed from Western Europe, and what he left Russia, or more accurately, what happened to his work after his death.

Peter inherited from medieval Russia sovereign power of a peculiar sort, and an even stranger organisation of society. At the time of the accession of the new dynasty, the sovereign power was recognised as hereditary because of its proprietorial character. As soon as it lost this proprietorial character, it was left with neither definite juridical definition nor defined scope, and began to expand or contract according to the situation and character of the monarch. Peter inherited almost complete authority, and managed to extend it even further. He created the Senate, and by so doing rid himself of the pretensions which were associated with the Boyar Duma; by abolishing the Patriarchate he also eliminated both the risk of further Nikonian scandals and of the cramping effect of the exaggerated and unctuous respect which was accorded to the Patriarch of All the Russias.

At the same time, however, it is important to remember

that Peter was the first monarch to give his unlimited power a moral and political definition. Before his reign the notion of the state was identified with the person of the Tsar, in the same way as in law the owner of a house is identified with the house. Peter made a distinction between the two ideas by insisting on two oaths, one to the State, and one to the Monarch. In his ukazes he repeatedly insisted that the interests of the state were supreme, and, by so doing, made the Monarch subordinate to the state. Thus the Emperor became the chief representative of the law and the guardian of general prosperity. Peter considered himself a servant of state and country, and wrote as an official would about his victory over the Swedes at Doberau: 'From the time I *began to serve*, I have never seen such firing and such discipline among our soldiers.' Indeed the expressions *interest of the state*, *public good*, and *useful to the whole nation*, appear in Russian legislation for the first time I think, in Peter's time.

None the less Peter was influenced unconsciously by historical traditions in the same way that he had been unconsciously influenced by instincts. Because he thought that his reforms were in the interest of state, and for the public good, he sacrificed his son to this supreme law. The tragic death of the Tsarevitch led to the Statute of February 5th, 1722, on the law of succession. This was the first law in the history of Russian legislation to have a constitutional character. It stated: 'We issue this Statute in order to empower the ruling sovereign to specify the person to whom he wishes the heritage to pass, and to charge that person according to his judgment.' The Statute, by way of justification recalls the example of the Grand Prince Ivan III who arbitrarily disposed of the succession, appointing first his grandson and then his son to succeed him. Before Peter there had been no law of succession, and its order had been decided by custom and circumstance alone. Under the old dynasty, which looked on the state as its patrimony (*votchina*) it was customary for the father to pass on the throne to his son 'by testament'. A new system of succession, election by the Sobor (the National Assembly) was introduced in 1598. By the seventeenth century the new dynasty did not look on the state as its patrimony, but, while the hereditary system fell into disuse, the elective system was not yet established; the new dynasty was recognised as hereditary for one generation only, and in 1613 the oath was taken to Michael Romanov and his children, but no farther. In the absence of an established system, the throne was occupied sometimes after an election by the Sobor, and sometimes by presenting the heir to the people in the Square at Moscow, as was done by Tsar Alexis with the Tsarevitch Theodore, or as happened when the rebellious Streltsy and an irregular Sobor established the Dual Monarchy of Tsars Peter and Ivan.

Peter replaced the hereditary and elective systems of succession with a system of 'personal nomination' coupled with the right to revoke; that is to say, he re-established succession by testament, legalised a situation for which no law existed, and retarded constitutional law by returning to the *votchina* system of succession. The Statute of February 5th, 1722, merely reiterated the words of Ivan III who said 'To whom I wish to him shall I give the rule.' Not only did Peter irresponsibly reproduce the past in his innovations, but he also let it influence his social legislation.

Peter did nothing to change the organisation of society which had been set up by the *Ulozhenie*, nor did he alter a division of classes which was based on obligations to the state, nor did he attack serfdom. On the contrary, the old system of class obligation was complicated by the imposition of further burdens. Peter made education compulsory for the nobility; he divided the civil service from the military; he organised the urban taxpayers into a compact group first under the administration of the *zemskie izby*, and then under the town councils; and he made the merchants of the guilds, the upper urban class not only pay their ordinary taxes but form companies to lease and run factories and workshops belonging to the state. In Petrine Russia factories and workshops were not privately owned, but were state enterprises administered by a merchant of the guild who was compelled to do so. Nevertheless there were compensations, for the merchants, manufacturers, and workshop superintendents were granted one of the privileges of the nobility, that of buying villages with serfs to work in the factory or workshop. Peter did not alter the nature of serfdom but did modify its structure: the many types of serfdom, each with a different legal and economic position, were combined, and one class of taxable serfs was the result. Some of the 'free idlers' were registered as inferior urban citizens, so that 'idlers shall take themselves to trade in order that nobody shall be without an occupation'; others were conscripted, or forced into bondage. Thus Peter, by abolishing the intermediate classes, continued the work of simplification started by the *Ulozhenie*; and his legislation forced the members of the intermediate classes into one or other of the main classes. It was in Peter's time that Russian society was organised in the fashion planned in seventeenth-century legislation; after Peter's reforms Russian society was divided into clearly defined classes, and every class was burdened with complicated and weighty duties. Peter's attitude to the political and social régime of old Russia, which we have discussed in other connections, has now been made clear. He neither disturbed old foundations, nor built new ones, but altered existing arrangements by separating classes previously combined, or combining classes hitherto divided. Both society and the institutions of government were made more vigorous by these changes, and the state benefited from their greater activity.

s

What was Peter's attitude to Western Europe? He had inherited the precept 'Do everything after the example of foreign countries', that is to say Western European countries. This precept combines large doses of despondency, a lack of confidence in Russia's strength, and self-denial. How did Peter interpret this precept? What did he think of Russian relations with Western Europe? Did he see in Western Europe a model to imitate or a master who could be dismissed at the end of the lesson? Peter thought that the biggest loss suffered by Muscovy in the seventeenth century had been the Baltic littoral, by which Russia was deprived of contact with the civilised nations of the West. Yet why did he want this contact? Peter has often been accused of being a blind and inveterate Westerner who admired everything foreign, not because it was better than the Russian, but because it was unlike anything Russian; and it was believed that he wanted rather to assimilate Russia to Western Europe than to make Russia resemble Western Europe. It is difficult to believe that as sensible a man as Peter was troubled by such fantasies.

We have already seen how, in 1697, he had travelled incognito with the Great Embassy, with the intention of acquiring general technical knowledge and recruiting West European naval technicians. Indeed it was for technical reasons that the West was necessary to Peter. He was not a blind admirer of the West; on the contrary, he mistrusted it, and was not deluded into thinking that he could establish cordial relations with the West, for he knew that the West mistrusted his country, and was hostile to it. On the anniversary in 1724 of the Peace of Nystadt, Peter wrote that all countries had tried hard to exclude the Russians from knowledge in many subjects, and particularly military affairs, but somehow the countries had let information on military affairs escape them, as if their sight had been obscured, 'as if everything was veiled in front of their eyes.' Peter found this a miracle from God, and ordered the miracle to be forcefully expressed in the forthcoming celebrations 'and boldly set out, for there is a lot of meaning here', by which he meant that the subject was very suggestive of ideas. Indeed we would gladly believe the legend which has come down to us, that Peter once said, as Osterman records it: 'We need Europe for a few decades; later on we must turn our back on it.' Thus for Peter association with Europe was only a means to an end, and not an end in itself.

What did Peter hope to gain from a rapprochement? Before answering this question, we must remember why Peter sent scores of young Russians to study abroad, and ask what type of foreigner he attracted to Russia. The young Russian was sent to study mathematics, the natural sciences, naval architecture, and navigation; the foreigners who came to Russia were officers, naval architects, sailors, artisans, mining engineers, and later on jurists and specialists in administration and finance. With their help Peter introduced into Russia useful technical knowledge and skills lacked by the Russians. Russia had no regular army: he created one. It had no fleet: he built one. It had no convenient maritime commercial outlet: with his army and navy he took the eastern littoral of the Baltic. Mining was barely developed, and manufacturing hardly existed, yet by Peter's death there were more than two hundred factories and workshops in the country. The establishment of industry depended on technical knowledge, so Peter founded a naval academy, and many schools of navigation, medicine, artillery and engineering, including some where Latin and mathematics were taught, as well as nearly fifty elementary schools in provincial and sub-provincial main towns. He even provided nearly fifty garrison schools for soldiers' children. There was insufficient revenue, so Peter more than trebled it. There was no rationally organised administration capable of managing this new and complicated business, so foreign experts were called on to help to create a new central administration.

The above is, of course, an incomplete account of Peter's achievements, but it does show what he hoped to do with the help of Western Europe. Peter called on Western Europe to work and train Russians in financial and administrative affairs, and in the technical sciences. He did not want to borrow the results of Western technique, but wanted to appropriate the skill and knowledge, and build industries on the Western European model. The intelligent Russian of the seventeenth century realised that it was essential to increase Russia's productive capacity, by exploiting the country's natural and virgin riches, in order that the increased requirements of the state might be more easily met. Peter shared this point of view, and gave effect to it as did nobody before or after him, and he is therefore unique in the history of Russia. In foreign policy he concentrated on solving the Baltic problem.

It would be difficult to assess the value of the many industries he introduced. The evidence of the increased wealth was not a higher standard of living, but increased revenue. All increased earnings were, in fact, used to pay for the war. Peter's intention had been general economic reform, but the only evidence of success was the improved financial position. When Pososhkov wrote to Peter in 1724 that 'it was a great and difficult business to enrich all the people', he was not explaining a theory but sadly stating what he, and many others, had observed to be fact. In Peter's time men worked not for themselves but for the state, and after working better and harder than their fathers, probably died a great deal poorer. Peter did not leave the state in debt for one kopeck, nor did he waste a working day at the expense of future generations. On the contrary, he left his descendants rich reserves to draw on. His superiority lies in the fact that he was a creditor of the future, not a debtor. We will pursue this point later when we discuss the results of his reform. Were we to draw up a balance sheet of Peter's activities, excluding those affecting Russia's security and international position, but including those affecting the people's welfare, we would find that his great economic ambitions (which were the basis for his reforms) failed in their purpose, and, in fact, their only success was financial.

Thus Peter took from the old Russia the absolute power, the law, and the class structure; from the West he borrowed the technical knowledge required to organise the army, the navy, the economy, and the government. Where then was the revolution which renewed or transformed the Russian way of life, which introduced not only new institutions, but new principles (whether they were good or bad, is for the moment, immaterial). Peter's contemporaries, however, thought that the reforms were revolutionary, and they communicated their opinion to their descendants. But the reforms did not stop the Russians from doing things in their own way, and it was not the innovations that agitated them so much as the methods Peter used. Some of the results of the reforms were only felt in the future, and their significance was certainly not understood by everyone, and contemporaries anyhow only knew the effect the reforms had on them. Some reactions, however, were immediate, and these Peter had to account for.

The reforms were influenced not only by Peter's personality, but by wars and internecine struggles. Although the war had caused Peter to introduce reforms, it had an adverse influence on their development and success, because they were effected in an atmosphere of confusion usually consequent on war. The difficulties and demands of war forced Peter do to everything hastily. The requirements of war imposed a nervous and feverish tempo on the reforms, and an unhealthily fast pace. Peter's military preoccupations did not leave him time for critical analysis of a situation or careful consideration of his orders and the conditions in which they would be carried out. He could not wait patiently for natural improvement; he required rapid action and immediate results; at every delay or difficulty he would goad the officials with the threats which he used so often that they lost their power. Indeed for any offence against the law, such as petitioning the Tsar without going through the proper authorities, or felling an oak, or even a spruce, or failing to appear at a nobleman's review, or buying or selling clothes of the old Russian pattern, Peter ordered confiscation of property, loss of civil rights, the knout, forced labour, the gallows, or physical and civil death. This extravaganza of punishments produced an increase in wrongdoing, or a general feeling of oppression and perplexity that resulted in neurasthenia. General-Admiral Apraxin, one of Peter's most eager collaborators, has vividly described this state of mind in a letter written in 1716 to Makarov, the Tsar's personal secretary: 'Verily, in all affairs we wander like blind men, not knowing what to do; everywhere there is great agitation, we do not know to whom to turn, or what to do about it for the future; there is no money anywhere, and everything will come to a stop.'

Moreover the reforms were evolved in the middle of bitter internal struggles, which often burst into violence; four terrible uprisings and three or four conspiracies were directed against Peter's innovations, and all appealed to people's feeling for antiquity, to the old prejudices and ideas. These troubles reinforced Peter's hostility to the old customs and habits which to him symbolised the prejudices and ideas of the past. The political education he had received was primarily responsible for this hostility. From his childhood he had witnessed the struggle which had divided Russian society from the beginning of the seventeenth century. On one side were the advocates of change who turned to the West for help, and on the other were the political and religious Old Believers. The beards and clothes of the Old Believers were symbols adopted expressly to distinguish them from the Western Europeans. In themselves these trivialities of dress were no obstacle to reform, but the sentiments and convictions of their wearers were certainly an obstacle. Peter took the side of the innovators, and hotly opposed these trifling practices, as well as the ancient traditions that the Russian insisted on observing. The memories of childhood were responsible for the Tsar's excessive attention to these details. He associated these symbols with the risings of the Streltsy and the Old Believers. To him, the beard worn by an Old Believer was not a detail of masculine appearance, but, like the long-skirted coat, the mark of a political attitude, the spirit of opposition. He wanted to have clean-shaven subjects wearing foreign clothes, in the belief that this would help them to behave like Western Europeans.

When he returned to Moscow in 1698, on hearing of the rising of the Streltsy, one of the first things he did was to shave beards, cut the long coats of his entourage, and introduce wigs. It is hard to imagine the difficulties of legislation, and the uproar that was produced by this forcible transformation of costume and fashion. The clergy and the peasants, however, were not affected by these measures; they retained their class privilege of remaining orthodox and conservative. In January 1700, the order that, by next Shrovetide, everyone else was to appear in a Hungarian kaftan, was proclaimed with rolling drums in streets and squares. In 1701 a new ukaze was issued: men were to wear a jacket in the French or Saxon style, a waistcoat, breeches, gaiters, boots, and caps, in the German style; women were to wear bonnets, petticoats, skirts

and shoes, in the German style. Censors of dress and beards
were posted at the gates of towns, with instructions to fine the
wearers of beards and illegal dress, which was to be torn to
pieces. Noblemen who appeared at reviews with beards and
moustaches were unmercifully beaten. The bearded Old
Believers were compelled to wear special clothes, while their
wives, though spared by nature from paying a fine on beards,
had, because of their husbands' beards, to wear long robes and
peaked bonnets. Merchants who sold old-fashioned clothes
were knouted, had their property confiscated, and were sent
to forced labour.

All this might be amusing if it were not so contempible!
It was the first time that Russian legislation abandoned its
serious tone and concerned itself with trifles better left to
hairdressers and tailors. These caprices aroused much hostility
among the people. These petty annoyances explain the dis-
proportion, which is so striking, between the sacrifices
involved in Peter's internal reforms, and their actual achievements. Indeed it is astonishing to find the number of difficulties that had to be overcome to achieve even modest
results. Even Peter's fervent admirer, Pososhkov, vigorously
and appropriately described the difficulties Peter had to overcome, Peter who alone pulled the chariot of state up the hill,
while millions pulled in the opposite direction. Another of
Peter's admirers, one Nartov, a turner, wrote in his memoirs
of everything 'that has been conceived against this monarch,
what he underwent, and the hurt he suffered'. Peter went
against the wind, and by his rapid motion increased the resistance he encountered. There were contradictions in his
actions which he was unable to resolve, discordances which
could not be harmonised.

As he grew older, and left his unruly youth behind him, he
became more anxious than any other Tsar had been for the
welfare of his people, and he directed the whole of his forceful

energy to its improvement. His devotion attracted such intelligent men as Bishop Mitrophan, Nepluev, Pososhkov, and
Nartov, who understood what it was that was driving Peter
on, and who became his fervent admirers. Nartov, for
instance, in calling Peter a god, added 'without fear we call
him father; he has taught us truth and a noble fearlessness'.

Unfortunately Peter's methods alienated those indifferent
to his reforms, and turned them into stubborn opponents.
Peter used force, not example, and relied on mens' instincts,
and not on their moral impulses. Governing his country from
the post-chaise and stagehouse, he thought always of business,
never of people, and, sure of his own power, he neglected to
pay sufficient attention to the passive resistance of the masses.
A reforming zeal and a faith in autocracy were Peter's two
hands; unfortunately one hand paralysed the energy of the
other. Peter thought that he could supplement the lack of
proper resources by using power to urge people on, and
aimed at the impossible. As a result the officials became so
intimidated and inefficient that they lost their ability to do
what they were normally quite capable of doing. As Peter,
for all his zeal, was unable to use people's strength, so the
people, in their state of inert and passive resistance, were unable to appreciate Peter's efforts.

Thus without exaggerating or belittling the work of Peter
the Great, we can summarise it as follows: the reforms were
brought on by the essential requirements of state and people;
the need for reform was understood by an authoritative, intelligent, energetic, and talented individual, one of those who,
for no apparent reason, appear from time to time. Further, he
was gifted, and, animated by a sense of duty, was resolved 'not
to spare his life in the service of his country'. When Peter
came to the throne, Russia was not in an advantageous position compared with other European countries. Towards the
end of the sixteenth century the Russians had created a great

state, which was one of the largest in Europe; in the seventeenth century, however, it began to fail in moral and material strength. Peter's reforms did not aim directly at changing the political, social, or moral order, nor did they aim at forcing Russian life into an alien Western European pattern. The reforms only aimed at providing the Russian State and people with Western European intellectual and material resources, so that Russia might take its just position in Europe, and its people increase their productive capacity. But Peter had to do all this in a hurry, in the middle of a dangerous and bitter war, by using constraint at home; he had to struggle with the rapacity of his rascally officials, a gross landed nobility, and the prejudices and fears instilled by an ignorant clergy. The first reforms had been modest and limited, aimed only at reconstructing the army and developing the financial resources of the state; later, however, the reforms were the occasion for an obstinate battle which disturbed the existing pattern of living, and upset society. Started and carried through by the sovereign, the people's usual leader, the reforms were undertaken in conditions of upheaval, almost of revolution, not because of their objects but because of their methods, and by the impressions they made on the nerves and imaginations of the people. Perhaps it was more of a shock than a revolution, but the shock was the unforeseen and unintended consequence of the reforms.

Let us end by giving our opinion of Peter's reforms. The contradiction in his work, his errors, his hesitations, his obstinacy, his lack of judgement in civil affairs, his uncontrollable cruelty, and, on the other hand, his wholehearted love of his country, his stubborn devotion to his work, the broad, enlightened outlook he brought to bear on it, his daring plans conceived with creative genius and concluded with incomparable energy, and finally the success he achieved by the incredible sacrifices of his people and himself, all these different characteristics make it difficult to paint one painting. Moreover they explain the diverse impression he made on people; he sometimes provoked unqualified admiration, sometimes unqualified hostility. Generally the criticism prevailed because even his good actions were accompanied by disgusting methods.

Peter's reforms were the occasion for a struggle between the despot and the people's inertia. The Tsar hoped to arouse the energies and initiative of a society subdued by serfdom with the menace of his power, and strove, with the help of the noblemen, the oppressors of serfs, to introduce into Russia the European sciences and education which were essential to social progress. He also wanted the serf, while remaining a serf, to act responsibly and freely. The conjunction of despotism and liberty, of civilisation and serfdom, was a paradox which was not resolved in the two centuries after Peter. It is true that Russians of the eighteenth century tried to reconcile the Petrine reforms with humanitarian instincts, and Prince Shcherbatov, who was opposed to autocracy, devoted a treatise to explaining and even justifying Peter's vices and arbitrary conduct. Shcherbatov recognised that the enlightment introduced into Russia by Peter benefited the country, and attacked Peter's critics on the grounds that they themselves had been the recipients of a culture, bestowed on them by the autocracy, which permitted them to distinguish the evils inherent in the autocratic system. Peter's faith in the miraculous power of education, and his respect for scientific knowledge, inspired the servile with little understanding of the meaning of civilisation; this understanding grew slowly, and was eventually transformed into a desire for truth and liberty.

Autocracy as a political principle is in itself odious. Yet we can reconcile ourselves to the individual who exercises this unnatural power when he adds self-sacrifice to it, and, although an autocrat, devotes himself unsparingly to the public good, risking destruction even on difficulties caused by his own work. We reconcile ourselves in the same way to the impetuous showers of spring, which strip branches from the trees, but none the less refresh the air, and by their downpour bring on the growth of the new seed.

GLOSSARY

Artel: An association of artisans formed to carry out specified units of work, or to carry on certain industries, or to render personal services on the joint responsibility of the members of the artel, and for their joint account.

Cherespolosno: Strip ploughing.

Chernososhnye krestiane: Black-ploughing peasants.

Denshchik(s), denshchiki (pl.)*:* Young courtiers who were the Tsar's personal attendants, and who combined the duties of orderlies with those of aides-de-camp.

Dolia: literally a 'fraction'; an accounting unit invented by Peter the Great.

Dvoryanin: A nobleman.

Dvoryanstvo: The nobility.

Glavny Magistrat: Chief Town Council.

Gubernator: A governor of a Province.

Guberniya: A Province.

Kholopy kabal'nye: Serfs bound by contract.

Kholopy polnye: Serfs whose bondage was permanent.

Kholopy zhilye: Serfs whose bondage was temporary.

Komisar ot zemli: A special commissar elected by the nobility of the regimental districts.

Krepostnye lyudi: Bonded people.

Landraty: Members of boards or councils.

Magistrats: Town councillors.

Obrok: Annual payments made by serfs, either in money or in kind, to their masters for the use of land they farmed on their account, or annual payments by state serfs to the Treasury for the use of allotments of land; also taxes consolidated into one payment.

Odnodvortsy: Freeholders.

Oprichnina: An entailed domain created by Ivan IV. A special household, whose members were called 'oprichniks', was created to administer this domain, which was exempt from the jurisdiction of the general administration.

Pashennye sluzhilye lyudi: Agricultural labourers.

Podlye lyudi: The common people.

Polkovoi distrikt: A regimental district.

Pomeshchik: The possessor of a pomestie.

Pomestie: An estate held in service tenure. The enjoyment of an estate of this type was conditional on the tenant and his heirs performing military service and other duties.

Poteshnie: The name given to Peter's regiment of boy soldiers.

Prikaz: A government department.

Sovmestnoi: A mutual system of possessing land.

Starosts: Representatives elected by the *starshins.*

Starshins: Representatives of urban citizens elected by the guilds.

Stol'niki: Courtiers who served food and drink at the Tsar's ceremonial banquets.

Stryapchie: Courtiers who carried the Tsar's sceptre, head-dress, and mantle in processions or at Church, and who in war time looked after the Tsar's armour and sword.

Tsaredvortsy: Courtiers of the Tsar.

Tserkovniki: The children of the clergy.

Vol'nitsy: Free people.

Votchina: An hereditary estate originally unencumbered by service obligations.

Zhil'tsy: Courtiers who slept at court.

INDEX

Adrian, Patriarch, 48

A History of the Swedish War, 73–4; its content, 76

Alexandrovsk, expedition to, 22

Alexis, Tsar, dates, xii; marriages, children, death, 1–2; education, 5; establishment, retinue, 10, 33; comparison with Peter, 51–3; court and family, 53; his government's views on foreign policy, 58; effect of his wars on provincial nobility, 89; founds *Monastyrskii Prikaz* (1649), 165, 260

Alexis, Tsarevitch, 41 n. 1, 56, and Statute of February 5th 1722, 259

Altranstaedt Agreement (1706), 191, 191 n. 2

Andrusovo, Truce of (1667), 59, 59 n. 1

Anne, Empress; married to Duke of Courland, 68; her Turkish war, 69; the Supreme Council, 86 n. 2

Apraxin, Peter; Governor of Kazan, 199–200

Apraxin, Count Theodore (1671–1728), 20; rebuked by Peter, 21; drives piles, 97; joins a company, 144; 'supreme lord', 204; on neurasthenia, 266

Archangel, 14; expeditions to, 22; as a port, 153–4

Army; organisation, 77–8; recruitment, 78–82; administration, 82–3; budget, 83; the nobility, 89–99; recruits, 114; maintenance in peace time, 115; census and poll tax, 116–120; cost 176–7; district associations of noblemen, 187–8, 198, 263

Association, industrial, 140–2

Astrakhan; rising of 1705, 65, 191

Augustus II, King of Poland, 61, 62, 64, 68; abandoned by Peter, 71, 191

Austria, 60, and Treaty of Karlovitz, 60–1

Avvakum, Archpriest; leader of dissenters, 3, and n. 3

Azov; campaigns of 1695 and 1696, 23; acquired by Muscovy, 61; lost to Russia, 69, 82

Baltic Sea, 58, 59, 60, 61, 68, 82, 150, 153, 155

Bashkirs, revolt of, 66 n. 1, 149

Batachev, ironmaster, 148

Bazhenin, 141

Black Sea, 59, 60, 61, 69, 151

Boerhaave, Dr.; his anatomical theatre, 27

Boyar Duma, 17, 86, 90, 101; activities, 182–4, 193, 200–1; decay, 204–5, 217, 222, 258

Boyars; see also nobility, noblemen and Streltsy revolt, 7, 16, 85–6, 91, 138, 143, 184

Bruce, Major-General, 72, 72 n. 1; president of college of Mines and Manufactures, 213

Bulavin, rising of, 66

burmisters, 186; the *Ratusha*, 188–90,

PRINTED IN GREAT BRITAIN BY ROBERT MACLEHOSE AND CO. LTD
THE UNIVERSITY PRESS, GLASGOW